# Data Stewardship

# Data Stewardship

## An Actionable Guide to Effective Data Management and Data Governance

### SECOND EDITION

**David Plotkin**

*Enterprise Information Management*

Academic Press is an imprint of Elsevier
125 London Wall, London EC2Y 5AS, United Kingdom
525 B Street, Suite 1650, San Diego, CA 92101, United States
50 Hampshire Street, 5th Floor, Cambridge, MA 02139, United States
The Boulevard, Langford Lane, Kidlington, Oxford OX5 1GB, United Kingdom

**Notices**
Knowledge and best practice in this field are constantly changing. As new research and experience broaden our understanding, changes in research methods, professional practices, or medical treatment may become necessary.

Practitioners and researchers must always rely on their own experience and knowledge in evaluating and using any information, methods, compounds, or experiments described herein. In using such information or methods they should be mindful of their own safety and the safety of others, including parties for whom they have a professional responsibility.

To the fullest extent of the law, neither the Publisher nor the authors, contributors, or editors, assume any liability for any injury and/or damage to persons or property as a matter of products liability, negligence or otherwise, or from any use or operation of any methods, products, instructions, or ideas contained in the material herein.

**British Library Cataloguing-in-Publication Data**
A catalogue record for this book is available from the British Library

**Library of Congress Cataloging-in-Publication Data**
A catalog record for this book is available from the Library of Congress

ISBN: 978-0-12-822132-7

For Information on all Academic Press publications
visit our website at https://www.elsevier.com/books-and-journals

*Publisher:* Mara Conner
*Editorial Project Manager:* Joshua Mearns
*Production Project Manager:* Swapna Srinivasan
*Cover Designer:* Matthew Limbert

Typeset by MPS Limited, Chennai, India

Working together
to grow libraries in
developing countries

www.elsevier.com • www.bookaid.org

*As this book is written, we are in the middle of the coronavirus pandemic, protests in the streets, and a contentious US presidential election. Sitting down to focus on creating a major update to my book was very difficult.*
*The fact that I was able to do it is largely due to the love and support I got from my wife Cynthia (Cyd). She encouraged me and took over many of my chores while I wrote in the evenings and weekends in addition to my regular "day job." And while it may seem clichéd for me to dedicate my book to my spouse, it is nonetheless the truth. Those of you out there who have ever been grateful for spousal support in achieving a cherished goal know from whence I speak.*
*I thank God every day that after being a widower for 7 years, I crossed paths once again with an old friend from high school, and she decided to take a chance on me.*

# Contents

# About the Author

**David Plotkin** made the jump from Chemical Engineering to Data Management more than 30 years ago and after 15 years working for a big oil company. Since then, he has worked in data modeling, metadata, data administration, data quality, and data governance. Much of his career has been in financial services and insurance, but he also spent 3 years as a consultant in enterprise information management, leading efforts at client companies to plan and implement Data Governance, both as standalone efforts and as part of other initiatives such as data-quality improvement and Master Data Management. He was responsible for implementing Data Governance at an insurance company, leading worldwide Data Stewardship at another insurance companies, running the Data Governance Competency Center at a large bank, and managing data-quality improvement at two large banks. He has extensive experience in managing the use of commercial Data Governance and data-quality tools to drive and support these efforts and has been the business owner of the Collibra tools at four different large companies.

In addition to this book, he has built and delivers a multiday tutorial on "The Complete Guide to Data Stewardship" that offers extensive and detailed training with the goal of making the Data Stewardship effort successful in a variety of different types of enterprises.

He is a popular speaker at DAMA chapters and conferences and serves as a subject-matter expert on many topics related to metadata, Data Governance, and data quality.

# Acknowledgments

A book is the labor of many people. I want to thank my acquisitions editor, Mara Conner, and Executive Project Manager, Joshua Mearns, for helping me lay out what the book would cover and then hounding me until I agreed to write it. I also want to thank the project manager, Swapna Srinivasan, who made sure everything got done and answered all my questions promptly and respectfully. And, of course, there were the hard-working copyeditor Elspeth Mendes and tech editor Indumathi Viswanathan who made sure the writing was accurate, coherent, and flowed properly.

I want to make special mention of my friend Danette McGilvray of Granite Falls Consulting and author of *Executing Data Quality Projects − Ten Steps to Quality Data and Trusted Information*. She and I have been friends and collaborators for many years, and it was Danette who not only was supportive of this second edition of my book but also reached out to me to ensure that where our books used the same terms, we defined them the same way. Imagine!

I want to also make special mention of my friend Sunil Soares, founder of Information Asset, LLC. Sunil's help and counsel was invaluable in pulling together some of the more complex topics.

There are a group of people who never seem to get acknowledged but should be. Down through the years, I have held a string of really good jobs, each one building on the last. I have gained experience as a practitioner and have been able to share that experience with others. So, I want to thank the people who hired me into those jobs, believed that I knew enough to perform them, and that I could learn what was needed to be successful. These folks include Lee Klein (InPower and Longs Drugstores), Brian Kilcourse (Longs Drugstores), David Harberson (Wells Fargo), Ralph Blore (CSAA, which became AAA NCNU), George Acosta (Bank of America), Martha Dember and Joe Dossantos (EMC Consulting), Jim Chipouras (Wells Fargo), and Tim Swan (MUFG).

Finally, I especially want to thank and acknowledge Tony Shaw of Dataversity, who has had me back again and again to attend and speak at his conferences. Over the years, Tony has asked me to develop new material he thought would be of interest or expand existing material into longer presentations. Time and again, he has provided me with a forum to share information and learn from the experiences of others. Thank you, Tony!

# Introduction

## INTRODUCTION

Companies are getting serious about managing their data, including improving Data Quality, understanding the meaning of the data, leveraging the data for competitive advantage, and treating data as the enterprise asset it should be. But doing a proper job of managing data requires accountability—that is, business functions must take responsibility for the data they own and use. The formal recognition of the need to have a structure, organization, and resources in place to manage data—and the actual implementation of that need—has come to be known as Data Governance. Within the umbrella of Data Governance is Data Stewardship. Various kinds of Data Stewards (detailed later in the book) work closely with the data as well as other subject-matter experts and stakeholders to achieve the goals and deliverables laid out by the Data Governance effort. The Data Stewardship efforts are managed and coordinated by the Data Governance Program Office and supported by high-ranking officers of the company. This book provides usable and actionable information and instructions on how to set up and run a Data Stewardship effort within Data Governance. The book is designed to provide everything a new Data Steward or Data Governance Manager needs to be effective and efficient when it comes to Data Stewardship. It also provides the details needed by those taking on the responsibilities of a Data Steward.

## PROBLEM STATEMENT

There are many challenges that must be faced when working with data, including:

- *Data doesn't explain itself.* Someone must provide an interpretation of the data, including what it means, how to use it properly, and how to evaluate whether the data is of good quality or not.
- *Data is shared and used by many, for many different purposes.* So, who owns it? Who makes decisions about it and is responsible when the data goes "wrong"?
- *Many processes that use data depend on people upstream of the process to "get it right."* But who says what "right" is? And who determines when it goes "wrong"?
- *The software development life cycles require many handoffs between requirements, analysis, design, construction, and data use.* There are lots of places where the handoffs can corrupt the data and endanger the data quality.
- *Technical people tasked with data implementation are not familiar with the data's meaning or how it is used.*
- *Those of us in the data community have a long history and habits around tolerance of ambiguity, both in data meaning and data content.*

All of these factors lead to poor understanding of the data and a perception of poor quality, with little ability to know the difference. It also leads to mismanagement of data in ways that run afoul of new regulations that establish stringent rules for privacy protections and consumer rights.

The answer to these challenges is that data needs to be actively and efficiently managed. Keep in mind too that the rather haphazard "methodology" used by many companies to collect metadata does not represent true or effective data management. Some of the failures include:

- *Data definitions*: These are often written in haste by project staff (if they are written at all) and the definitions are not rationalized across the enterprise, leading to multiple definitions of the same term, often under different business data element names.
- *Data quality*: The data quality rules are often not defined and the quality itself is rarely measured. Even when the rules are defined, the context for the rule (the data usage for which the rules applies) is often ignored. All of this leads to confusion about what data quality is required, as well as what data quality is achieved.
- *Documentation*: Documents containing metadata are rarely officially published, and are often lost, tucked away on shelves or in archived files. The documentation is not widely and easily available, nor is there a robust search engine so that interested users can find what they need.
- *Creation and usage business rules*: There is often a lack of understanding about the conditions under which an entity (such as customer or product) can or should be created, as well as how data should be used. This lack of understanding leads to incomplete or inaccurate information being collected about the entity, as well as data being used for purposes for which it was never intended. The end result is that business decisions based on the data may lead to suboptimal results.

Formal enterprise-wide Data Stewardship, as part of a Data Governance effort, is crucial in managing data and achieving solutions to these challenges. With Data Stewardship, the organization can begin treating data as an asset. Like other assets, the data needs to be inventoried, owned, used wisely, managed, and understood. This requires different techniques with data than with physical assets, but the need is the same. With the data asset, inventorying and understanding the data takes the form of a formally published business glossary, often in conjunction with a metadata repository.

Establishing ownership requires understanding how the data is collected and who uses it, then determining who can best be responsible for the content and quality of the data elements. Finally, ensuring that data is used wisely means understanding and managing how the data is created, for what purpose the data was created, and whether it is suitable for use in new situations that may arise—or even in the situations for which the data is being used currently.

# ROLES OF THE DATA STEWARD IN MANAGED DATA

Properly managed data enables major enterprise efforts (such as those listed next) to be successful with fewer missteps and less wasted effort. The Business Data Stewards play important roles in each of these (and many other) efforts. They determine the following.

- *In data warehousing*:
  - What dimensions are needed and what they mean.
  - What facts are needed and what dimensions they depend on.
  - How to define the facts and the derivation and aggregation rules.
  - Where different terms proposed for dimensions or facts are really the same thing.
  - Who must take responsibility for the data elements that make up the dimensions and the facts.
  - How data will be transformed to use it in the data warehouse.
- *In master data management*:
  - What master data entities (customer, product, vendor, etc.) should be handled, in what order, and what the entities mean (e.g., What is a customer?).
  - What identifying attributes are needed (with good quality) to implement identity resolution.
  - What is the sensitivity for determining uniqueness of identity (sensitivity to false positives and false negatives).
  - What are the appropriate reference data values for enumerated attributes, and how to derive the values from the available data.
- *In Data quality improvement*:
  - What level of data quality is needed for a given purpose.
  - What data should be profiled to rigorously examine the values.
  - What constitutes "expected" values for the data. These expectations can include range, specific values, data type, data distribution, patterns, and relationships.
  - What possibilities exist for the root causes of poor-quality data.
  - What requirements must be given to IT to fix root causes and/or cleanse the data.
- *In system development*: The Data Stewards play a pivotal role in ensuring:
  - That data used by a system is well-defined and that the definition and business rules meet enterprise standards. If the definitions or rules are missing or of low quality, the Business Data Stewards are instrumental in providing high-quality definitions and rules.
  - That data models meet enterprise standards as well as project requirements.
  - That the requirements for managing data as an asset don't get ignored because of project schedule.
- *Managing "big data" in a data lake*:
  - What the data means.
  - The priority and order in which the data should be ingested and the business needs that must be satisfied by the data.
  - The appropriate level of Data Governance and Data Stewardship for each zone.
  - The transformations needed to address business needs.

These topics and the roles that Data Stewards play are discussed in detail in this book.

## WHAT THIS BOOK COVERS

This book is divided into 11 chapters, with each chapter focused on an aspect of Data Stewardship. The chapters are:

- Chapter 1: *Data Stewardship and Data Governance: How They Fit Together.* This opening chapter discusses Data Governance program deliverables, the roles and responsibilities of program participants (including Data Stewards), and how Data Stewardship fits into a Data Governance program.
- Chapter 2: *Understanding the Types of Data Stewardship.* This chapter describes each type of Data Steward. It also discusses the type of person needed for the role, and how the various types of Data Stewards are chosen and assigned.
- Chapter 3: *Stewardship Roles and Responsibilities.* This chapter provides a detailed list of the responsibilities for each type of Data Steward. It also describes how the stewards work together in a Data Stewardship Council, as well as the role of the Enterprise Data Steward, who manages the stewardship efforts on behalf of Data Governance.
- Chapter 4: *Implementing Data Stewardship.* This chapter describes how to kick off the Data Stewardship effort. It describes how you gain support, ascertain the structure of the organization, identify the types of Data Stewards who will be needed, figure out how information flows through the organization, determine what documentation you have already, and decide what tools you'll need and what you already have. It also describes how to determine what metadata is already available, such as valid value lists and data quality rules.
- Chapter 5: *Training the Business Data Stewards.* This chapter discusses how to train Business Data Stewards since most of those selected for the role will not know how to perform their duties. It discusses the lesson plan, the various categories of training, and which tools the Data Stewards will need to learn about. It also provides guidelines on how to get the most out of the training efforts.
- Chapter 6: *Practical Data Stewardship.* This chapter describes the practical aspects of the main tasks and responsibilities of Data Stewardship. These include the identification of key business data elements and the collection of metadata about those elements, determining ownership, and working through the day-to-day issues with an issue log and repeatable processes. Also discussed is how the different types of stewards cooperate, and logistics like meeting schedules and working groups. The basic tools are also described.
- Chapter 7: *The Important Roles of Data Stewards.* Data Stewards have an extremely important role in all the data management activities, but they play an especially key role in certain areas. This chapter describes how Data Stewards contribute to improving data quality, improving metadata quality, managing reference data, ascertaining identifying attributes (for identity resolution) and other aspects of Master Data Management, managing information security, managing metadata, supporting quality assurance, compiling lineage, managing process risk, and supporting the management of data consistent with the new privacy regulations that are becoming more common.

- Chapter 8: *Measuring Data Stewardship Progress: The Metrics*. A Data Stewardship program requires resources and effort. This chapter shows you how to identify and measure the results you are getting from those efforts in two main areas: business results metrics (measures the effectiveness in supporting the data program) and operational metrics (measures the acceptance of the program and how well the Data Stewards are performing).
- Chapter 9: *Rating Your Data Stewardship Maturity*. The Data Stewardship effort can increase in maturity as you develop it. This chapter describes a maturity model with multiple levels and dimensions. The model helps you rate your maturity, as well as identify what a well-developed Data Stewardship program should look like. It also discusses how to use the results of measuring maturity to remediate gaps in your efforts.
- Chapter 10: *Big Data Stewardship and Data Lakes*. "Big Data" (often stored in "data lakes") requires some differences in the approach to Data Stewardship, though those differences are not as large as many may think. This chapter explains how Data Stewards interact with the ever-increasing volume and speed of data, and how the importance of Data Stewardship has increased with the multitude of complex transformations within the data lake. It also discusses managing the level of Data Governance that is an appropriate balance against the flexibility of the data lake.
- Chapter 11: *Governing and Stewarding Your Data Using Data Domains*. More companies are migrating from business function–based Data Stewardship (where data owners come from a business function that produces or is critically affected by key business data elements) to data domain–based Data Stewardship (where data is grouped into "data domains" managed by groups of Business Data Stewards). This chapter details how to identify the right data domain for data, govern that data using a group of Business Data Stewards in conjunction with other roles, and the challenges that are faced as your company makes the transition.
- Appendix A: *Example Definition and Derivation*. This appendix provides an example of a robust definition and derivation for a business data element.
- Appendix B: *Sample Training Plan Outline*. This appendix provides training plans for Technical Data Stewards and Project Managers. Other training plans are covered in Chapter 5, Training the Business Data Stewards.
- Appendix C: *Class Words for Naming Business Data Elements*. This appendix provides a list of "class words" that are used at the end of business data element names to indicate what kind of data the business data element represents.

## WHAT IS NOT IN THIS BOOK

Although this book talks about how Data Stewardship fits into Data Governance, it does not provide all the information needed to set up and run the wider Data Governance effort. For that, references are provided in the text.

## WHO NEEDS THIS BOOK?

This book is designed for anyone with an interest in Data Stewardship. It will be especially useful to someone charged with organizing and running a Data Stewardship effort because it is based on the actual experience of someone who has done it multiple times, and not just talked about it. Thus, the information reflects real life, not just theory. But this book will also be useful to those who will be Business Data Stewards, because it explains what is expected of you, provides tips and tricks, and details how your role adds value to the company and the business function you represent. Finally, this book will be useful to those (including executives) charged with supporting Data Stewardship and Data Governance because it describes what is supposed to be going on and how progress and maturity are measured.

# Data Stewardship and Data Governance: How They Fit Together

## INTRODUCTION

Data has become so vital to the success of almost all organizations (both large and small) that many are attempting to implement a Data Governance program. When done properly, a Data Governance program provides the means to manage the overall collection of data (the "data asset"), including the structure, processes, people, and organization needed to manage key data elements. A vital component of a Data Governance program is Data Stewardship. But to understand the role that Data Stewardship plays in Data Governance, one would need to understand the overall Data Governance program itself, including the purpose, deliverables, roles and responsibilities, and value that Data Governance adds to the company. One would also need to understand how Data Stewardship interacts with other aspects of the Data Governance program, and what part Data Stewardship plays in the success of the program.

This chapter defines Data Governance and Data Stewardship, and explains the structure and inner workings of the organization needed to support the effort. It details the responsibilities of each type of participant, including Executives, Data Governors, Data Stewards, members of the Data Governance Program Office (DGPO), and IT support staff. It also provides a "target"—the end result of what a good Data Stewardship effort can and should achieve.

## WHAT IS DATA GOVERNANCE?

Ask a room full of Data Governance practitioners what *Data Governance* means, and you'll probably get as many definitions as there are people. One of the best ones I have ever run across comes from my friend, Gwen Thomas of the Data Governance Institute:

> *Data Governance is the exercise of decision-making and authority for data-related matters.*

**Data Stewardship. DOI: https://doi.org/10.1016/B978-0-12-822132-7.00001-2**

*It's a system of decision rights and accountabilities for information-related processes, executed according to agreed-upon models which describe who can take what actions with what information, and when, under what circumstances, using what methods.*

The key thing to take away from this definition is that the practice of Data Governance has more to do with establishing the roles and responsibilities about how *people* manage and make decisions about data than about the data itself. That is, Data Governance—and Data Stewardship—is all about making sure that people are properly organized and do the right things to make their data understood, trusted, of high quality, and ultimately, suitable and usable for the enterprise's purposes.

> **NOTE**
>
> It is not the purpose of this book to fully define and discuss Data Governance. Instead, this book focuses on the practical details of Data Stewardship, which is a necessary component of Data Governance. For an excellent reference on Data Governance, please see *Data Governance: How to Design, Deploy, and Sustain an Effective Data Governance Program* by John Ladley, published by Elsevier.

## SOME BEST PRACTICES TO DRIVE DATA GOVERNANCE

Some basic principles are inherent for Data Governance in driving Data Stewardship. Without these principles, data cannot be managed properly:

- Data is a strategic asset and must be managed. If data is not managed, it often ends up duplicated, of poor quality, and doesn't support the insights that are valuable products of good data.
- Data requires stewardship and accountability. This principle requires that individuals be assigned as stewards and caretakers of the data. Information about Data Stewardship is valuable metadata and must be maintained.
- Data Quality preserves and enhances the value of data. The insights provided by data are at serious risk if the data quality is poor or unknown. There is also a risk of making incorrect business decisions, and other issues detailed in Chapter 7, The Important Roles of Data Stewards.
- Data must be made secure and follow privacy regulations. The horrors of data breaches and the risks and expenses to both an enterprise and the customers of the enterprise are well-known. These include damage to reputation, stolen identities, and monetary punishment. Improper privacy classification can lead to inappropriate sharing of data, violation of regulations with resulting penalties, and failure to protect data.
- Metadata must be easy to find and of high quality. Data Stewards play a key role in evaluating and improving the quality of metadata. If the metadata is hidden or of poor quality, the data it describes will be misunderstood and potentially misused. Keeping metadata clean and accurate is described in Chapter 7, The Important Roles of Data Stewards.

## WHAT IS DATA STEWARDSHIP?

Data Stewardship is the operational aspect of Data Governance—where most of the day to day work of Data Governance gets done. According to Danette McGilvray:

> *Data Stewardship is an approach to Data Governance that formalizes accountability for managing information resources on behalf of others and for the best interests of the organization.*

As Danette also notes in her book, *Executing Data Quality Projects*, a steward is someone who manages something on behalf of someone else. In the case of Data Stewardship, the "someone else" is the business that owns and uses the data, represented by the business function's representative on the Data Governance Board (Data Governor).

Put another way, Data Stewardship consists of the people, organization, and processes needed to ensure that the appropriately designated stewards are responsible for the governed data.

Data Stewardship is crucial to the success of Data Governance (which, in turn, is crucial to the success of Data Management). This is because it is through Data Stewardship (and Data Stewards) that all of the metadata (definitions, business rules, and more) is collected and documented. In addition, having stewards who are responsible for the data as well as having a set of procedures that require these stewards to be consulted on decisions about the data they steward helps to ensure that any decisions taken are based on knowledge and are made in the best interests of all who use the data. The combination of designated stewards, processes, and a mission to manage data in the best interests of all leads to the data asset being improved in quality and enables the data to be used to drive competitive advantage and regulatory compliance for the business.

## THE OVERALL GOALS OF DATA STEWARDSHIP

So, what does "good" Data Stewardship look like? That is, what goals should a Data Stewardship program be striving toward—what are we trying to achieve? The goals should align with the highest level of maturity that the enterprise decides to achieve (discussed in Chapter 9: Rating Your Data Stewardship Maturity) and should include:

- A smoothly functioning Data Stewardship Council.
- Policies and procedures that are in place, and have become part of the corporate culture.

- Designated Business Data Stewards participating from every business function that owns data and *no* participation from business functions that do *not* own data. Data Governance and Data Stewardship include outside business partners.

- Designated Technical Data Stewards from all enterprise applications, data stores, data warehouses, data marts, and extract, transform, and load (ETL) processes.

- Data Stewardship involvement integrated into enterprise processes such as Project Management and System Development Methodology. Data Stewards are viewed as an integral and necessary part of data management.

- Clearly defined roles and responsibilities for all Data Stewards and ratings for how effectively those roles and responsibilities are performed built into each steward's compensation objectives.

- The responsibility of all employees for the management of data is accepted as part of the corporate culture.

- Executive support and endorsement for Data Stewardship. Executives must publicly support the policies and actively promote adherence to them as well as the creation of procedures to implement the policies.

- A clearly defined and recognized value being added by Data Stewardship.

- Key business elements (KBEs) identified and defined, and business rules determined and linked to physical instances of the data. Where appropriate, lineage has been determined and the data profiled to understand and correct data quality.

- Data Stewardship decisions have been clearly documented and published to interested parties using sanctioned communication methods.

- Training for all involved parties (including stewards, project managers, and developers) has been written and is being given on regular schedule.

- Supporting tools (such as a metadata repository, business glossary, central issue log, and data profiling tool) are installed, supported, and in regular use.

- Innovation in maintaining the vision of data quality and remediating data issues is being encouraged as well as creativity and competitive advantage in using high-quality data.

- Management and Data Governance staff is keeping abreast of important emerging trends in Data Management and adapt accordingly.

**NOTE**

"Key Business Elements" (KBEs) are often also referred to as "Key Business Terms." This book will use business elements phraseology, but both are common and correct.

- Processes and procedures are written, approved, and in use in order to:
  - Identify KBEs.
  - Collect, review, and approve business metadata for the KBEs.
  - Log, analyze, prioritize, and remediate data and data quality issues.
  - Support projects.
- When business data elements are arranged and governed by *data domains* (see Chapter 11: Governing and Stewarding Your Data Using Data Domains), there are well-defined domains of data with KBEs aligned to these domains. Each data domain is governed by a team of Business Data Stewards representing business functions that produce or depend on the data to run their business.
- Data Stewards are being quickly replaced as necessary.
- Data quality improvement opportunities are regularly reviewed and analyzed.
- Data Stewardship work being done is documented and published through appropriate channels to the enterprise.

## MOVING DATA TO A GOVERNED STATE

At its simplest level, the purpose of executing Data Governance is to move data from an ungoverned state to a governed state. Ungoverned data refers to most of the data that an enterprise has, at least at the beginning of a Data Stewardship effort. It is rarely defined, its quality is unknown, its business rules are non-existent or conflict with one another, and no one is accountable for the data. Governed data is data that is *trusted* and *understood* and for which someone is *accountable* for both the data itself and for addressing issues about the data.

In addition, in fully governed data, all of the factors listed here are known:

- *The standardized business name of the business data element.* This is the standard business name by which a term is referred to (ideally) everywhere in the company. Where a business unit has a need to call it something else, that alias is documented.
- *The standardized business definition of the business data element.* Just as there should be one standard business name, there should also only be one standard business definition for a business data element. Where there is disagreement on the definition, these differences must be resolved. If they cannot be resolved, it usually indicates that there are multiple business data elements embodied in the definition, as described in Chapter 6, Practical Data Stewardship. In that case, a

new business data element (or multiple new business data elements) must be defined and given new names.

- *For calculated or derived business data elements, the calculation or derivation rule.* The rule needs to be highly specific so that there is no confusion about how a quantity or value is derived. As with the standard business definition, if there is disagreement, either the derivation rule must be changed or a new business data element (with a different derivation) must be defined.
- *The physical location of the business data element in one or more databases/systems.* A physical data element is essentially a mapping of a business data element to (for example) a column in a table in a database in a system, or something equivalent. This mapping is sometimes done directly (business data element to physical data element). It may also be done through a logical layer (sometimes called a "data attribute") that represents a more business-friendly name of the physical data element. This data attribute might be the screen name or field name of the physical data element.
- *The data quality rules, in context.* This includes the rules(s) that specify good quality (e.g., format, range, valid values, pattern, and so on) as well as the level of quality needed for each intended use of the data.
- *Rules for creating the business/physical data element.* These are rules that must be followed before an instance of the data element can be created. When applied at the entity level (e.g., Customer, Product, Policy, etc.), having *and following* the creation rules can ensure that all the needed data is present and of appropriate quality before the new entity (Customer, etc.) is created. These rules are critical when implementing Master Data Management (MDM) to ensure that "half-baked" data is not created.
- *The usage rules for the business/physical data element.* Usage rules specify what purposes the data can be used for as well as what it cannot be used for. For example, a patient's name in a pharmacy might be fine to use for filling a prescription, but *not* for generating mailing labels for refill reminders.
- *The individuals responsible for the business data element.* These are the individuals who serve as authorities and decision-makers about the data—the people who are accountable for the data. It is important to understand that a proposed change to any of the items on this list *must* be authorized by these individuals. When Data Stewardship is organized by business function, the responsible individual is the Business Data Steward for the owning business function. In the case where Data Stewardship is organized by data domain, it is the group of Data Stewards assigned to make decisions for that data domain

**NOTE**

Business data elements are often physically represented in many physical locations that are not important to the overall business. Attempting to map them all can be overwhelming and not terribly valuable. Instead, the mapping should be done to critical locations such as where the data is produced and to a known high-quality source where cleansed data is used for important purposes. These sources are often referred to as "golden sources" or "certified provisioning points." These types of sources usually have stringent controls in place to catch (and correct) errors, providing a guarantee of high quality. In many companies, mapping the data to the producer and golden source or certified provisioning point is sufficient for data to be considered "governed."

(run by the Lead Data Steward). Failing to consult the responsible individuals can lead to unforeseen ramifications (see the sidebar).

In addition to determining and documenting the bulleted items at the business or physical data element level, governed data is data to which the approved procedures and processes for change management and issue resolution are rigorously applied. That is, even if all the metadata for the data elements are known, if the governing processes and procedures are not used to manage the data, then the data is not "governed."

### USING DATA INCORRECTLY

This story about incorrect data usage comes from the early days of my career. A pharmacy at a major chain drug store recorded patient names and used that data to fill prescriptions. However, having no place to put certain pieces of key data in the aging system, the pharmacists took to adding various characters to the end of patients' names to indicate certain conditions they needed to keep track of. For example, if a patient had no insurance, the pharmacist might append a "$" to the last name. Or, if the prescription was related to a Worker Compensation claim (the individual needed the medication because they had been injured on the job), the pharmacist might append "(WC)" to the last name.

All was well until someone decided to use that data to generate mailing labels for refill reminders, a use for the data that had never been anticipated. The problem, of course, was that when the mailing labels were generated and the letters sent out, all those character strings were printed on the labels, causing confusion and some angry responses from the customers. While there wasn't a formal Business Data Steward for that data, there was a well-known expert in the company who was the unofficial steward. Had anyone checked with her *first*, she would have pointed out the issue and a plan could have been made to improve the data quality to the point where it could be used.

### NOTE

The terms *Data Governor and Data Owner* are used interchangeably in many organizations, and are defined later in this chapter. From here on this book will refer to the middle layer in the Data Governance organization as Data Governors. *Business Data Steward* is defined in Chapter 2, Understanding the Types of Data Stewardship.

Looking at Fig. 1.1, at the beginning of a Data Stewardship effort, the bulk of the data is ungoverned, as shown by the outside rectangle. There are many drivers for getting data into the governed state, represented by the inner circle. Among these drivers are building a data warehouse, instituting MDM, improving data quality, implementing Information Security, Privacy and Compliance, and migrating data into a new system. The role of Data Stewardship in some of these activities is discussed more fully in Chapter 7, The Important Roles of Data Stewards.

While all of these efforts can be (and have been) attempted without Data Governance and Data Stewardship, they are much more prone to delay, poor quality results, and failure. That is because without a clear decision-maker about the data, a lot of guessing goes on, often by IT personnel doing their

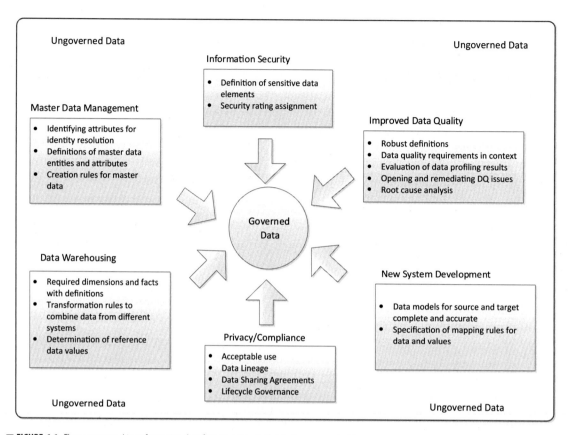

■ **FIGURE 1.1** There are many drivers for moving data from an ungoverned state to a governed state.

best to figure things out and deliver on a deadline. For example, think about how many times a fruitful discussion has disintegrated into an argument about what a piece of data means, or how it is calculated. With an assigned Business Data Steward or team of data stewards as the documented authority on that data, all you have to do is *ask*. The data authority can either provide the answer or take responsibility for finding the answer, thus, relieving other people of a responsibility they shouldn't have had in the first place.

## THE THREE P'S: POLICIES, PROCESSES, AND PROCEDURES

In order to have effective Data Governance and Data Stewardship, it is necessary to have the three P's, that is, Policies, Processes, and Procedures. Generating these items is one of the key early deliverables from a Data Governance effort. Policies establish a set of goals and state "this is what needs to be done" at the enterprise level. Processes (which can be represented by a process flow diagram such as a swimlane) state what is required to comply with the policy. A process specifies a high-level set of tasks, the flow of the tasks, decision points, and who is responsible for completing each task. Finally, procedures describe in detail how exactly to perform the tasks.

An example might help to illustrate the three P's. The enterprise might have a policy that states that redundant business data elements are not permitted and define what is meant by a "duplicate." The process would then lay out the tasks and flow (query the Business Data Steward/Lead Data Steward, initiate a search through the Business Glossary by name, do a definition comparison, resolve potential duplicates, create new business data element). The procedures would then state exactly how to perform a search, what amount of overlap in the definition should signal a potential duplicate, how to specifically resolve duplicates, and exactly how a new business data element is created.

Common policies established by a Data Governance effort might include policies for Data Governance itself, Data Quality, Data Remediation, Communication, and Change Management. And because policies require a high level of authority to give them "teeth," they tend to be approved at the executive levels of the company.

Business Data Stewards don't write the policies, but they must be aware of what policies have been written. In many ways, the policies drive what the Business Data Stewards are responsible for achieving and formalize the goals of Data Stewardship. The processes and procedures are intended to carry out the goals established by the policies.

Business Data Stewards have a considerable amount to say about processes and procedures. Processes and procedures state *how* the work actually gets done, including what steps have to be taken and who needs to approve decisions. For example, when a data issue is raised, there is a process (or should be) to analyze the issue, assign the responsible individuals, remediate (or choose to ignore) the issue, and get approvals for the decisions made from the Data Governors. It is the Business Data Stewards who do the work, going through the processes and procedures to reach an end result. Thus it should come as no surprise that to meet the goals of the policy, the processes and procedures need to be designed, tested, and modified as necessary with extensive input from the Business Data Stewards.

> **NOTE**
>
> It is rare that executives actually write the policies. Data Governance policies are typically drafted by someone in the Data Governance Program Office, often with input from Data Governors and Business Data Stewards. Executives are then responsible for approving the policies, and taking the necessary action when policies are violated.

## HOW DATA STEWARDSHIP FITS INTO DATA GOVERNANCE

In a nutshell, Data Stewardship is the operational aspect of an overall Data Governance program—where the actual day to day work of governing an enterprise's data gets done. Business Data Stewards, working together in the Data Stewardship Council, perform a multitude of tasks, which are detailed in Chapter 2, Understanding the Types of Data Stewardship. Quite frankly, without Data Stewardship, Data Governance is just a framework of good intentions that never get implemented.

By now it is probably apparent that an overall Data Governance effort involves several levels as well some support from the organization. There are a number of ways to organize a Data Governance Program, but Fig. 1.2 shows a fairly simple structure that works well in many

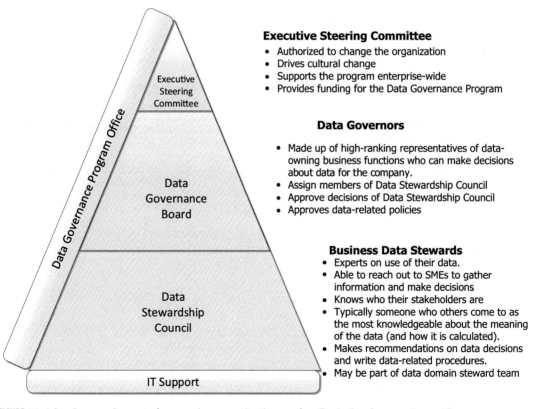

**Executive Steering Committee**
- Authorized to change the organization
- Drives cultural change
- Supports the program enterprise-wide
- Provides funding for the Data Governance Program

**Data Governors**

- Made up of high-ranking representatives of data-owning business functions who can make decisions about data for the company.
- Assign members of Data Stewardship Council
- Approve decisions of Data Stewardship Council
- Approves data-related policies

**Business Data Stewards**
- Experts on use of their data.
- Able to reach out to SMEs to gather information and make decisions
- Knows who their stakeholders are
- Typically someone who others come to as the most knowledgeable about the meaning of the data (and how it is calculated).
- Makes recommendations on data decisions and write data-related procedures.
- May be part of data domain steward team

■ **FIGURE 1.2** A Data Governance Program is often arranged as a pyramid, with support from IT and a Data Governance Program Office.

organizations. It also illustrates the relationship between various parts of the program.

The pyramid structure illustrates both the level of data responsibilities and the typical number of participants at each level. Relatively few executives are needed to provide the support, any necessary culture change, and impetus to drive the program. They may, on occasion, also make far-ranging decisions such as changing how people are incentivized to drive data quality. The Data Governors represent their business function, appoint Business Data Stewards, and make decisions based on the recommendations of the Business Data Stewards. The largest number of participants are the Business Data Stewards, who understand the use of the data, the impacts of changes to the data, and what rules must apply to the data. The Business Data Stewards create the metadata (definitions, etc.) and make recommendations for the Data Governors to act on.

## The Executive Steering Committee

Not surprisingly, the tip of the Data Governance pyramid is occupied by the Executive Steering Committee. Its "not surprising" because any program of the scale and potential impact of Data Governance needs executive support and a well-defined escalation path. The Executive Steering Committee:

- *Drives cultural changes needed to treat data as an asset and manage it effectively across business area boundaries.* Treating data as an asset and making decisions that benefit the enterprise as a whole takes executive support and a careful balancing of priorities. In addition, the culture of the organization may not be immediately conducive to Data Governance. In many organizations, the concept of a "data owner" is foreign, and all decisions are made by consensus. But Data Governance requires that someone be ultimately responsible and accountable (two different things) for the decisions made about the data, and that may well mean that consensus is *not* reached. Sometimes it gets to the point where one has to make some group unhappy in order to move forward for the greater good. Executives need to communicate that this is acceptable and expected as part of Data Governance.
- *Makes necessary changes to the organization and tools as required for effective Data Governance.* Organizational changes are necessary to implement Data Governance. New headcount is usually required, at least for the Data Governance Manager, and other support personnel may be needed as the program matures. In addition, IT tools may

need to be added such as a metadata repository, a business glossary, data quality profiling tools, and web-based collaboration software. Adding tools not only requires funding (for licenses and hardware), but the expenditure of efforts to specify requirements, evaluate vendor proposals, install, and maintain the new tools. Typically, organizational changes and early funding require executive support.

- *Creates and promotes the vision for the Data Governance Program.* With the changes needed to manage the implementation of a successful Data Governance program, employees will be looking to the executives to state what they want to happen (a vision) and throw their support solidly behind that vision.

- *Authorizes the Data Governance Board budget.* While not always possible, providing a budget for the Data Governance Board to manage enables that governing body to not only make decisions about important issues, but to fund the decisions that have a high enough priority to warrant remediation. But in most companies, establishing a budget requires executive approval.

- *Balances business priorities with operational needs across the enterprise.* There can be conflicts between priorities established by a Data Governance effort and keeping normal operations running. For example, something as "simple" as standardizing a calculation for a derived business data element may have wide-ranging impacts to operational systems. And while analyzing those impacts falls to the Business Data Stewards, balancing the benefit of the standardization against the modifications that may be needed to key operational systems is a decision that has to be made at the Data Governance Board level— or, if of sufficient impact—by the Executive Steering Committee.

- *Approves Data Governance Policies.* Policies establish a set of rules (and possibly penalties) for the enterprise. Data Governance generates a set of policies, and in order for these policies to have credibility and impact to the organization, they must be approved by the executives.

- *Reviews, evaluates, and reports to executive sponsorship on the Data Governance performance and effectiveness.* Ideally, the executive sponsor for Data Governance is a member of the Executive Steering Committee, but if that is not the case, the Steering Committee needs to review and evaluate progress reports (typically created by the Data Governance Manager and Data Governors) and provide a summary to the executive sponsor.

- *Provides advice, direction, counsel, and feedback to the Data Governors (members of the Data Governance Board).* There needs to be an open line of communication between the Data Governors and the executives, especially since the Data Governors may need executive support to drive the Data Governance program forward. The form of the feedback can vary, but frequently results from discussions on agenda items from Executive Steering Committee meetings, which are then relayed back to the Data Governance Board via the chairperson and meeting notes.

- *Ensures that decisions regarding the data support the strategic direction of the organization.* The executives are in the best position to gauge the long-range needs of the organization, and evaluate decisions based on those needs. It may well be that the Data Governors are not even aware of upcoming initiatives, and, thus, their decisions could have a negative impact that they aren't even aware of.

- *Ensures active participation by the business and IT.* The Data Governance Manager (who often chairs Executive Steering Committee meetings) is in a good position to know whether business and IT participation are sufficient for Data Governance to be effective. For example, terminations or reorganizations may leave a business function without adequate representation or a new business area may need to be added to the program. In either case, the executives will need to ensure that the appropriate people are designated to have the necessary duties. Further, if the designated participants are not participating at the level needed, this situation will also need to be dealt with.

- *Represents their business function's direction and views in regard to the adoption and deployment of enterprise policies and practices.* The executives represent different areas of the business, and must evaluate proposed policies and practices to ascertain how they affect the business direction. Where there is a conflict, decisions have to be made at the executive level to either change a policy or practice or adjust a direction.

- *Appoints Data Governors from their business function(s).* The executive representing a business function has the authority—and the responsibility—to appoint the Data Governor(s) who represent them on the Data Governance Board.

- *Resolves issues escalated by the Data Governance Board.* It is reasonable to expect that most issues related to data usage and management will be made at the level of the Data Governance Board. On occasion, however, it may be necessary to escalate a decision up to the executive level. This can happen when one or more of the Data Governors refuse to budge on an issue, perhaps advocating a "solution" that safeguards the data usage by their own business area to the detriment of the enterprise as a whole. As an example, a front-line application (e.g., for writing policies in an insurance company) owned by one business area may be used to capture only the data needed by that area even though it is capable of recording other data needed by other business areas. If the owning Data Governor refuses to have the users take the extra time to record the additional data, then this issue may need to be escalated.

---

**WHERE DO DATA GOVERNANCE PARTICIPANTS COME FROM?**

The participants at each level of a Data Governance effort are assigned by the level above, as illustrated in Fig. 1.3. This starts with the business sponsor who provides the authority to request cooperation from line-of-business (e.g., Sales, Marketing, Finance, and so on) executives who need to assign Data Governors that will represent their portion of the business. These Data Governors then assign the Business Data Stewards to represent them in the day to day operations of Data Governance. If Project Data Stewards are needed, these are assigned (and potentially hired or contracted) by the Data Governance Manager or Enterprise Data Steward.

On the IT side, there is an IT sponsor who provides the authority to request cooperation from IT application owners to assign Technical Data Stewards.

---

## The Data Governance Board

At the middle level in the Data Governance Pyramid is the Data Governance Board. The board members (referred to as Data Governors or Data Owners) tend to be the primary decision-makers, acting on recommendations from the Data Stewardship Council. If a line of business has its own Chief Data Officer (CDO) (as many lines of business do), these individuals may represent the line of business on the Data Governance Board.

The Data Governance Board makes decisions about changing data usage, making data quality improvements, and (especially) making decisions that require resources (both funding and personnel) to be expended to make a change or remediate an issue or impact. To be more specific, Data Governors prioritize issues to be remediated (or approve the priorities assigned by the Business Data Stewards) and assign resources to work on remediating high-priority issues.

However, it is rare indeed that *all* the "recommendations" made by the Business Data Stewards get escalated to the Data Governors for a decision as that would simply not be practical. In the case of business function—based Data Stewardship, metadata decisions such as definitions,

| Business Sponsor | ⟹ | COO (or equivalent) |
| IT Sponsor | ⟹ | CIO (or equivalent) |

| Roles and Relationships | | |
| --- | --- | --- |
| Organization Executive (e.g., Sales) | Works with the | Data Governance Manager |
| Data Governor | Is assigned by | Organization Executive |
| Business Data Steward | Is selected by | Data Governor |
| Enterprise Data Steward | Is hired or assigned by | Data Governance Manager |
| Project Data Stewards | Are assigned by | Enterprise Data Steward |
| Enterprise IT Application Owner | Is assigned by | IT Sponsor |
| Technical Data Stewards | Are assigned by | Enterprise IT Application Owner |

■ **FIGURE 1.3** Responsibilities for assigning Data Governance Program participants.

derivation rules, and data quality requirements are determined by the Business Data Steward (representing the business function that owns the business term in question) with input from stakeholders as needed. For example, though the Sales business function may own a specific business data element and set the data quality requirements, Finance may need to have a say in the required quality because the element is used in a report. Only if the stakeholder Business Data Stewards can't agree on the quality requirements would this get escalated to the Data Governors.

In the case of data domain—based Data Stewardship (see Chapter 11: Governing and Stewarding Your Data Using Data Domains), the group of Business Data Stewards assigned to the data domain to which the business term belongs should already include the producers of the data as well as the consumers/users of the data, so an agreement on changes would be made by this group.

In either case, if the agreement on quality required that funds be spent to upgrade the system to prevent data quality degradation, that decision would need to go the Data Governance Board.

The Data Governance Board:

- *Has funding authority to spend budget on data management improvements.* The ideal situation is for the Data Governors to have the ability to spend budget money to correct high-priority data management issues. This enables them to correct issues without going through the normally onerous task of getting projects approved and funded. It also makes sense for the Data Governors to have expenditure authority because they are responsible for prioritizing issues and deciding what is important enough to be remediated.
- *Prioritizes decisions regarding data to address the most relevant needs of the organization.* There will undoubtedly be many issues that get raised about data, and it is up to the Data Governors to prioritize their decisions so that the most important issues are addressed by the limited resources available. Ideally, Data Governors are in a position to know most of what is going on in the company and act accordingly.
- *Review, evaluate, and report to the Executive Steering Committee on Data Governance performance and effectiveness.* The Data Governance Board needs to work with the Data Governance Manager to create progress reports for the Executive Steering Committee.
- *Ensure that annual performance measures align with Data Governance and business objectives.* When a Data Governance program first starts up, participants are chosen from the ranks of business and IT to drive it forward. Initially, these participants will have objectives (often tied to variable compensation) that do not include Data Governance deliverables. Unfortunately, if that state of affairs is left unchanged, there is a likelihood that duties leading to additional compensation will get prioritized ahead of Data Governance participation. To take care of this, people who are assigned to participate in Data Governance should have their objectives adjusted to reflect the importance of that participation. Data Governors would make these decisions, typically in conjunction with the executives and the Human Resources department.
- *Reviews and approves Data Governance policies and goals.* Data Governors review the policies and goals laid out by the Data Governance Program Office (DGPO), and typically play an active role in adjusting the policies and goals to match enterprise priorities. The Data Governors then provide approval, after which the policies are sent to the Executive Steering Committee for final approval.
- *Are ultimately accountable for business data use, data quality, and prioritization of issues.* As will be discussed, Business Data Stewards are responsible for making a lot of recommendations about how data will be used, the required data quality, and what issues are important

enough to be addressed. However, the ultimate accountability for the proper use of data rests with the Data Governors as they have (or should have) the authority to ensure that business data use and data quality are properly determined and documented, and that issues are properly prioritized and acted upon. This is especially true when the Data Governors are acting in the role of Chief Data Officer (CDO) for their line of business.

- *Makes strategic and tactical decisions.* In a nutshell, the Data Governors are responsible for making decisions about the data. Some of these decisions are strategic—should an aging system that is corrupting data quality and causing regulatory problems be replaced? Other decisions are tactical—is it necessary for the front-line customer service people to record email addresses and mobile phone numbers, even though they don't need it for their own purposes? Keep in mind, however, that the input for decision-making will come largely from the recommendations of the Business Data Stewards.

- *Reviews, and where appropriate, approves the recommendations made by members of the Data Stewardship Council.* Business Data Stewards are typically people who directly feel the pain of poor data usage, quality, or confusion about the meaning and the rules about data. They are also the people who know the data best (which is one of the criteria for choosing the right Business Data Steward, as discussed in Chapter 2: Understanding the Types of Data Stewardship). However, Business Data Stewards are rarely placed highly enough in organizations to be able to make decisions that others will pay attention to and execute. Thus Business Data Stewards need to make recommendations to the Data Governors, who *are* placed high enough to make these decisions. However, not all "recommendations" need to be referred upward to take effect. For example, if a Business Data Steward is designated as the steward for certain business terms, that Business Data Steward can usually define and assign the business rules without having to have a "decision" made by a Data Governor.

- *Assigns Business Data Steward(s) to the Data Stewardship Council.* Data Governors represent a business function, as do Business Data Stewards, so it makes sense for the Data Governor to assign the Business Data Steward (s) for that function. There may be multiple Business Data Stewards for a given Data Governor because the Business Data Stewards require more detailed knowledge of the data as well as direct responsibility for managing the metadata. For example, a Data Governor may be assigned to handle the insurance portion of a business, but will likely require

**NOTE**

There are exceptions to the rule that the Data Governor and the Business Data Steward have to be different people. This can occur when a highly placed manager also directly uses the data, and, thus, fills the role of both Data Governor and Business Data Steward. This can be seen in small organizations with flat structures.

separate Business Data Stewards to handle Claims, Underwriting Operations, and Actuarial because no one individual knows and uses the data in each of these areas. One of the more interesting aspects of this responsibility is that Business Data Stewards do *not* have to report organizationally to the Data Governor—they can pick pretty much anyone in the organization. That may not sit well with the designated steward's supervisor, but in a proper Data Governance program, the Data Governor has the right to pick the best person for the job. Of course, a balance must be maintained between Data Governance and the other functions of the business.

- *Represents all data stakeholders in the Data Governance process.* Ensures appropriate representation and participation in Data Governance across the enterprise. It is key for the Data Governors to take the "enterprise view" of managing data properly, and protect the interests of everyone who has a stake in the data. In fact, one of the few causes for escalating an issue to the next level (Executive Steering Committee) is when a Data Governor does not represent all the data stakeholders. In addition, ensuring that there is appropriate representation and participation in Data Governance includes dealing with:
  - *A lack of representation from a business area.* As a Data Governance effort matures, a time will come when the data being discussed will not have a Data Governor. This can happen as the Data Governance effort expands into a new area of the company. It can also occur when a Data Governor realizes that data that they are assumed to own is actually part of a different business function. For example, a Finance Data Governor on one engagement realized that the data being discussed was accounting data, which he did not work with or know much about. He suggested that a Data Governor be added along with a Business Data Steward from Accounting, which was accomplished and filled the gap.
  - *Understaffing of Business Data Stewards.* It is important that the Business Data Stewardship effort be fully staffed and that there be continuity when the stewards change. It may become necessary to replace a Business Data Steward due to normal organizational changes such as when someone changes assignments or leaves the company. Just as the Data Governor was originally tasked with appointing the Business Data Steward, the Data Governor must also appoint a successor.
  - *Governing the Business Processes that produce data.* Data Governors have to take responsibility for knowing and getting

input from the business process owners of the processes that produce the data in their business function. This coordination activity is important because bad data is typically a symptom of a broken or poorly defined process. Business Process Owners themselves have a crucial role in Data Governance, despite the word "process" in their title! They know what part of the business their process supports, and the link between business data elements and the data used in their process.

- *Identify and provide data requirements that meet both enterprise business objectives and the objectives of their business function.* Balancing the needs of the enterprise (or other business functions) against the needs of the producing business function can be tricky, and requires that the Data Governors work closely together to reach solutions that benefit all the data stakeholders.
- *Define data strategy based on business strategy and requirements.* The data strategy must satisfy more than just the needs of the producing organization, it must drive forward the overall enterprise business strategy.
- *Communicate concerns and issues about data to the Data Stewardship function.* Since the Data Governors are in contact with each other on a regular basis, issues may be brought to them from peers or other concerned parties. In such cases, the concerns and issues must be communicated to the Business Data Stewards to research, validate, and make recommendations on the advisability of a fix or proposed solution.

## The Data Stewardship Council

The bottom of the Data Governance pyramid is the Data Stewardship Council, comprised of the Business Data Stewards. Who these people are, their qualifications, what makes a good steward, and their day to day tasks will be discussed in much more detail throughout the rest of this book. But make no mistake; although they sit at the bottom of the pyramid, they are extremely important—much like the bottom of a real pyramid, they are the foundation of Data Governance. I have seen relatively successful Data Governance efforts occur without the Executive Steering Committee or the Data Governance Board—but I have never witnessed any success without the Business Data Stewards. Stewardship—in the sense of "taking care of something on behalf of others"—can and does take place in the absence of a formal Data Governance structure when the employees understand that the quality of their data has an impact on organizational success. It is also imperative that employees are the kind of people who want things to work right!

**NOTE**

The make-up of the Data Stewardship Council can be somewhat dependent on how many Business Data Stewards there are. In small organizations with a relatively small number of Business Data Stewards (say, less than 50) it is typical for all the Business Data Stewards to participate. In larger organizations, including those that have a highly diverse business model, many international subsidiaries, or a large number of data domains, it is more typical for a "lead data steward" representing their group to participate instead.

## IT Support Through the Technical Data Stewards

The primary role of IT Technical Data Stewards is to provide technical expertise in support of the Data Governance efforts with respect to systems and application impact analysis for proposed changes and data quality issues. IT resources are assigned to this role officially by IT management and are expected to respond to requests for assistance from Data Governance in a timely manner as part of their regular duties. The Technical Data Stewards are often lead programmers, database administrators, and application owners, and their detailed responsibilities will be discussed in much more detail in Chapter 2, Understanding the Types of Data Stewardship.

## The Data Governance Program Office

A Data Governance effort—including documentation, communication, and enforcement—is run by the Data Governance Program Office (DGPO). The DGPO must be staffed with ample resources to do the work, including at least a full-time Data Governance Manager. Failing to create the DGPO and staff it adequately or depending on part-time resources with other responsibilities is a sure recipe for failure. *So don't do it.*

The coordination of the Data Governance program is the responsibility of the DGPO, and that includes chairing the three committees already discussed, namely the Executive Steering Committee, the Data Governance Board, and the Data Stewardship Council. The DGPO is also responsible for making sure everything that the Data Governance effort does is fully documented and made available to all interested parties. Table 1.1 summarizes the responsibilities of the DGPO, and many of these items will be discussed further in the book.

## THE OVERALL DATA GOVERNANCE ORGANIZATION

The pyramid is a useful way of conceptually showing the various levels of the Data Governance organization, but it does not show the relationships between all the participants. Fig. 1.4 shows how the various individuals come together to participate in Data Governance.

There are some things to note about this figure. First of all, there is both a business sponsor and an IT sponsor for the Data Governance program. These positions are crucial to a successful program because they provide the key executive sponsorship. The Business Sponsor is often the CDO or equivalent, whereas the IT Sponsor is usually either the Chief Information Officer (CIO) or directly reports to the CIO. However, these are not hard and fast rules. In the absence of a CDO,

> **NOTE**
>
> The person who runs the Data Governance Program Office is referred to as the Data Governance Manager or Chief Data Steward. In this book, Data Governance Manager is used, but either title is common.

> **NOTE**
>
> Although the Data Governance Manager is ultimately accountable for everything that goes on in the Data Governance Program Office, it is common to have an additional role (often called the *Enterprise Data Steward*) that is more closely aligned to the Data Stewards. The responsibilities of the Enterprise Data Steward are covered in detail in Chapter 3, Stewardship Roles and Responsibilities.

**Table 1.1** Responsibilities of the Data Governance Program Office

| Role | Responsibility |
|---|---|
| Data Governance Program Office | • Supports, documents, and publishes the activities of the Executive Steering Committee, Data Governance Board, and Data Stewardship Council.<br>• Defines and documents best practices in Data Governance.<br>• Creates and makes available education curricula and training delivery programs to support Data Governance. These include training for Data Governance Board members, Data Stewards, Project Managers, and development and IT support staff.<br>• Enforces data-related policies and procedures, and escalates where necessary.<br>• Manages the logs to document risks and issues.<br>• Gets the "Data Governance message" out to the enterprise, including the vision, strategy, processes, and value of the program.<br>• Documents, publishes, and maintains Data Governance–related policies, procedures, and standards.<br>• Recommends Data Governance metrics and measures the progress of the Data Governance program. |
| Data Governance Manager | • Tracks membership of the Executive Steering Committee, Data Governance Board, and Data Stewardship Council. Ensures that all appropriate business areas are fully represented.<br>• Builds consensus for the Data Governance strategy with the Data Governors.<br>• Obtains appropriate involvement from support organizations for Data Governance, escalating to the Data Governance Board or Executive Steering Committee as necessary.<br>• Collaborates with leadership across the organization to identify business needs and implement Data Governance capabilities and processes.<br>• Works with the Executive Steering Committee and Data Governance Board to ensure that annual performance measures align with Data Governance and business objectives.<br>• Ensures that Data Governance processes are integrated into the appropriate Enterprise processes (e.g., Project Management and Software Development Life Cycle or SDLC). Monitors the implementation of processes.<br>• Reports to the Executive Steering Committee on Data Governance performance.<br>• Responsible for getting escalated issues and conflicts resolved.<br>• Defines and implements the Data Governance program metrics (see Chapter 8: Measuring Data Stewardship Progress: The Metrics); tracks and publishes results.<br>• Ensures that Data Governance deliverables (such as policies, procedures, and the communications plan) are properly documented in the appropriate tools and available to the enterprise.<br>• Manages the issue resolution process (see Chapter 6: Practical Data Stewardship), including reviewing issues and meeting with the Business Data Stewards and stakeholders to understand their needs and the feasibility of proposed options.<br>• Has ultimate responsibility for getting the Data Governance message and vision out to the entire enterprise.<br>• Manages the community of Data Stewards from a Data Governance standpoint. This responsibility is often taken on by an *Enterprise Data Steward* (see note), who coordinates and manages the activities of the Data Stewards as they perform their Stewardship duties. |

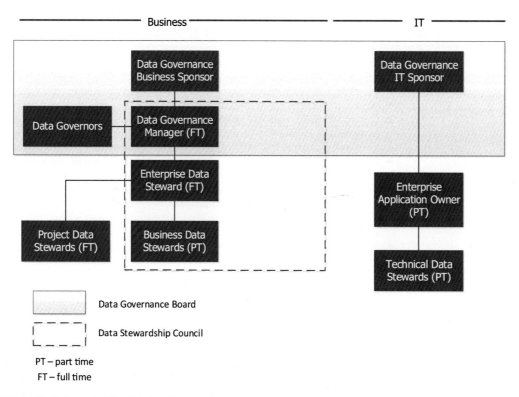

■ **FIGURE 1.4** The Business and IT view of the Data Governance Organization.

the Business sponsor can often be the Chief Financial Officer (CFO) as people in finance are used to having to follow strict rules and often feel considerable pain when data is not governed properly. Another alternative is the Chief Operating Officer (COO) or Chief Risk Officer (CRO).

The Data Governance Manager runs the Data Governance Board. The "Enterprise Data Steward" runs the Data Stewardship Council. This role may be filled by the Data Governance Manager in small organizations, although it is often a separate individual who reports to the Data Governance Manager and is part of the DGPO.

Also, note that Technical Data Stewards don't magically appear—these people need to be assigned and made available by IT managers with sufficient authority to make the assignment.

Fig. 1.5 shows a different view (but the same structure as in Fig. 1.4) of the organization, including the reporting relationships within the DGPO.

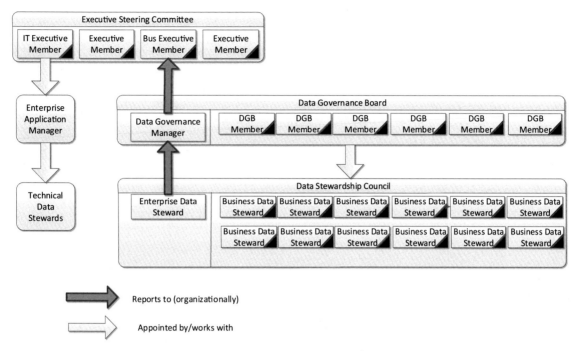

Reports to (organizationally)

Appointed by/works with

■ **FIGURE 1.5** Reporting relationships of the overall organization.

The primary difference between the two figures is that Fig. 1.5 shows the Executive Steering Committee, individual Data Governors ("DGB Member"), and Business Data Stewards. Additionally, it shows the reporting relationships of the members of the DGPO (Data Governance Manager and Enterprise Data Steward). Note also that the Data Governance Manager is proposed as being a direct report to a highlyplaced executive.

## SUMMARY

As stated earlier, Data Governance is all about how people work together to make recommendations and decisions about data. That is, the people are the most important part of the equation. The Business Data Stewards represent the largest population of those people as well as the most knowledgeable about data. They are, therefore, the keystone of any Data Governance Program.

The key to a successful Data Governance program is to set up and staff the organization needed as well as to understand and socialize the roles and responsibilities of the Data Governance participants. One of the most critical parts of the organization are the Business Data Stewards, who must work together to determine ownership, meaning, and quality requirements for their data. Without a smoothly functioning Data Stewardship Committee, Data Governance cannot produce the important data-related deliverables that are the most important measure of the program's success.

# Chapter 2

# Understanding the Types of Data Stewardship

## INTRODUCTION

The generic term "Data Stewardship" (as defined in Chapter 1: Data Stewardship and Data Governance: How They Fit Together) primarily encompasses two different types of stewards: Business Data Stewards and Technical Data Stewards. However, on occasion, there is a need to "fill in" with another type of Data Steward, the Project Data Steward. This is a support role, picking up some of the load when the Business Data Steward is unable to handle everything. In addition, Business Data Stewards may get help from Operational Data Stewards, yet another support role. In this chapter we will discuss and detail each of the different types of stewards, when and why they are necessary, and how they work together to achieve the goals of Data Governance. In Chapter 3, Stewardship Roles and Responsibilities, we will explain the detailed responsibilities of each type of Data Steward.

Fig. 2.1 shows how the different types of Data Stewards interact. Here is a brief summary of each type of Data Steward:

- *Business Data Stewards represent their business function.* In the case of business function—driven Data Stewardship, the Business Data Steward is responsible for the data owned by that business function. In the case of data domain—driven Data Stewardship (as described in Chapter 11: Governing and Stewarding Your Data Using Data Domains), the Business Data Steward participates in all Data Domain Councils that steward data of interest to their business function. Further, the Business Data Steward may serve as the Lead Data Steward for a Data Domain Council where their business function is the primary owner or producer of the domain data.
- *Operational Data Stewards are there to provide help to the Business Data Stewards.* Operational Data Stewards are usually people who work directly with the data (such as by doing input) and can provide

**Data Stewardship. DOI: https://doi.org/10.1016/B978-0-12-822132-7.00002-4**

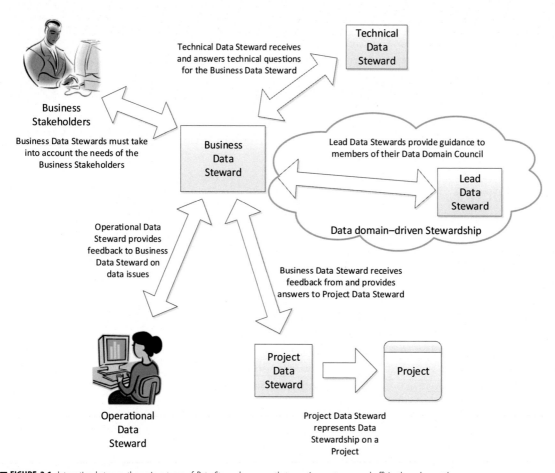

Business Stakeholders

Technical Data Steward receives and answers technical questions for the Business Data Steward

Technical Data Steward

Business Data Stewards must take into account the needs of the Business Stakeholders

Business Data Steward

Lead Data Stewards provide guidance to members of their Data Domain Council

Lead Data Steward

Data domain–driven Stewardship

Operational Data Steward provides feedback to Business Data Steward on data issues

Business Data Steward receives feedback from and provides answers to Project Data Steward

Operational Data Steward

Project Data Steward

Project

Project Data Steward represents Data Stewardship on a Project

■ **FIGURE 2.1** Interaction between the various types of Data Stewards ensures that questions get answered efficiently and correctly.

immediate feedback to the Business Data Stewards when they notice issues with the data (including declining data quality).

- *Project Data Stewards represent Data Stewardship on projects.* They report back to the appropriate Business Data Steward when data issues arise on the project or when new data must be governed.

- *Technical Data Stewards* are IT representatives with knowledge about how applications, data stores, and ETL (extract, transform, and load) processes work.

In the rest of this chapter we will look at each of these types of Data Stewards in more detail.

## BUSINESS DATA STEWARDS

So what do we mean by a Business Data Steward? A Business Data Steward is the key representative in a specific business area that is responsible for quality, use, and meaning of that data in the organization. Business Data Stewards make specific recommendations about the data to the Data Governors.

Business Data Stewards are typically individuals who know the data and work closely with it. People with titles like "Data Analyst" or "Business Analyst" are often good candidates to be Business Data Stewards. Of course no one can know everything about all the data. The Business Data Steward should know who to talk to in their area to get the information needed to fulfill the role. And once a Business Data Steward has gathered that information, the Business Data Steward (and not the person providing the information) is responsible for stewarding the data. Having access to other resources working with data means that the Business Data Steward has the authority to obtain some of the resource's time to help in the stewardship effort. If requests for contributions from other resources go unanswered or are refused, escalation to the Data Governors is appropriate.

### Choosing the Right Business Data Steward

Choosing the right person in the business area to be a Business Data Steward is crucial, not only for the success of the program, but also for the person's job satisfaction. As stated earlier, the people chosen to be Business Data Stewards need to know the data and the issues with the data. They should be aware of where the data is not meeting business needs, as well as business data elements whose meaning is not well-understood or a bone of contention. Most business areas have people who care about the data and can even be said to have a passion for the data. These people are good candidates for the role. In fact, many business areas have individuals that "everyone knows to go to" in order to get questions answered. They have become practiced at answering questions about meaning, business rules, what data to use for what purpose, and so on. In fact, these local experts often spend a good deal of time answering the same questions over and over. In many cases, Business Data Stewardship simply formalizes this role and these responsibilities. Formalization of the role provides the following benefits to the Business Data Steward:

- *Answer the question once.* Once a question has been answered and documented in the Business Glossary (in whatever form that takes), the Business Data Steward can encourage the person asking the question to "look it up."

- *Fewer arguments.* Since the Business Data Steward is a recognized authority on the data and has the ability to make decisions (with the backing of the Data Governor), there should be fewer arguments and less wasted time. Having this authority is a great incentive for getting people to buy into the role of Business Data Steward. It can be very frustrating to people who care about their data if all they can do is provide advice to others, who may then go off and do whatever they please anyway.
- *Repeatable process for changes.* If the data decisions that have been made (either by the owning business function Business Data Steward or by the owning Data Domain Council) are not working for one of the stakeholders, a repeatable process to engage with the decision maker(s), and revisit the decision will be in place. Following this process is more efficient and less confusing than the usual path of trying to figure out who should be involved, having many meetings, and usually struggling to get to a resolution that satisfies everyone.
- *Additional rewards and recognition.* The "data expert" role is rarely recognized as being of value and compensated for. With the formalization of this role, the individual's performance objectives (which usually are tied to compensation) can be adjusted and this expertise and responsibility formally recognized.

To summarize, it is quite appealing to people who care about their data to be in charge of it so that others can't use it in inappropriate ways or corrupt it.

---

### BEING A BUSINESS DATA STEWARD CAN *SAVE* YOU TIME!

Not everyone tapped to be a Business Data Steward is going to look on this assignment with joy. On the face of it, it is another "job" that is being heaped onto the usually already overworked individual. There are also new tasks to be learned, some tools to become familiar with, and meetings to attend. But to balance this out, quite soon the constant interruptions from colleagues and endless meetings about "your" data become a thing of the past as people learn to use the Business Glossary and engage with the Business Data Stewards using formally designed processes. A real-life example of this is the Actuarial Business Data Steward at an insurance company. She estimated that prior to Data Governance being instituted she spent about 40% of her time dealing with data questions and issues, rather than creating and running risk models. After approximately 6 months with Data Governance in place, she estimated that this had dropped to less than 10%. She became one of the biggest proponents of "getting stuff into the glossary" and then making other analysts use the tools to find their own answers.

## Characteristics of a Successful Business Data Steward

In addition to being interested (or passionate) and knowledgeable about the data, a successful Business Data Steward needs several other characteristics. These characteristics may well be harder to find than the data knowledge.

- *Writing ability*: Since Business Data Stewards are involved in writing up definitions and business rules, it would be most helpful if they are able to write well. Further, Business Data Stewards have an active role in drafting procedures; so again, being able to write well is huge plus.
- *Committed to improvement*: The best data stewards are the ones who strive for excellence and aren't satisfied with the status quo. It is extra work (despite the return on that investment) to drive to well-defined, high-quality data, but everyone is better off if this work is done. Obviously if a Business Data Steward isn't interested in an improved data environment, that Business Data Steward is not going to be very effective.
- *Good people skills*: Data stewards need to work together not only with each other, but with other stakeholders to try and reach agreements about meaning, location, and required quality of the data. This may mean setting up and leading meetings, collaborating with others, following up on issues, and publishing the results (i.e., writing). All of this requires leadership, organizational and facilitation skills, as well as a certain amount of political acumen. These skills are especially useful in the case of a Lead Data Steward for a Data Domain Council.

### STEWARDSHIP AND TRUST

One of the biggest "gotchas" in today's business world is a tendency to mistrust the data. Mistrust causes a lot of extra work (and potentially wasted effort) as data analysts check the data, trace it back to the source, and extract it into their own environments so they can manipulate it. Why do the analysts mistrust the data? It is because the data can so often be full of surprises. These surprises (as illustrated in Fig. 2.2) can be caused by many variables, including undocumented changes to business processes, transformation issues, source data problems, uncertainty as to what the data means, and changes to the technical applications and processes. Without assigned stewardship, there is little formal accountability for researching the impacts of changes, making the changes, or communicating the changes. IT personnel may well want to work with the business to figure out the impacts of proposed system changes, but they are unable to find anyone in the business willing to step up and work with them. Data Stewards (both Business and Technical) take much of the uncertainty out of these processes, and can greatly reduce the number of data surprises—and thus increase the level of trust in the data.

### NOTE

On occasion, there can be "stewardship" without a formal program. If there are critical processes that depend on the data, people will often "step up" and act accountable because the processes fail if they do not. This is especially true with Finance data. However, without a formal Data Stewardship program, that accountability can vanish if the individual goes on vacation, accepts another assignment, or retires.

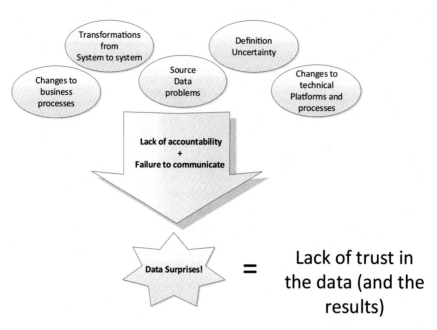

■ **FIGURE 2.2** Stewardship can prevent data surprises—and lack of trust.

### Business Data Stewards and the Data

As we said earlier, the Business Data Stewards steward the data most critical to the business function they represent and that they are most knowledgeable about. This connection must be determined (i.e., what data is the steward responsible for) and documented and available to everyone.

There are a number of approaches to connecting the Business Data Stewards to the data they steward.

- *Single owner.* In many enterprises, a business function is represented by a single Business Data Steward (or perhaps a small group). Individual business data elements are stewarded by the business function, represented by that function's Business Data Steward. This works well in a situation where ownership is relatively clear—that is, there is little need to discuss who owns various business data elements because the answer is fairly obvious. Certain data belongs to Finance, Marketing, Underwriting, Loan Servicing, Patient, Provider, and so on. In this situation, the responsibility is on the owning Business Data Steward to know who uses the data (stakeholders), and consult with those people before making changes.

- *Shared owner.* In an enterprise where data is used over a wide range of business functions and it is difficult for a single Business Data Steward to know or consult with them all, business data elements may have several (or more) business functions that need to steward them. The Business Data Stewards are responsible for stating that they need to be part of the decisions, and then participating in the discussions and voting on the result. This approach documents who the stakeholders are at the business data element level and sets up processes for involving them. However, it can lead to difficulties in maintaining the involved business functions or people, as each business data element can have its own set of participants in decision-making. In reality, this "solution" doesn't scale very well if you use it for all business data elements. However, it may work well for key data elements that are of high importance to multiple business functions.
- *Data domains.* As we will see in great detail in Chapter 11, Governing and Stewarding Your Data Using Data Domains, data domains bundle sets of related business data elements together into a "data domain." Business data elements are related to a single data domain. Decisions and questions are brought to the decision-making body for the data in that data domain. This body is called the Data Domain Council and is made up of Business Data Stewards from all the business functions that need to have a say in the stewarding of the business data elements in that data domain. In addition, the make-up of the Data Domain Council includes appropriate roles to ensure that there is uniform participation, and that the council is run efficiently. However, determining the appropriate hierarchy of data domains, which business functions need to participate in each Data Domain Council, and the assignment of business data elements to the right data domain is a major undertaking. It requires a large commitment from the enterprise and relatively mature Data Governance effort.

Table 2.1 summarizes these three approaches.

## The Key Role of the Business Data Steward

Although there are many other types of stewards (as described in the rest of this chapter), the Business Data Stewards are the authorities on their data in that they know what the data is supposed to represent, what it means, and what business rules are associated with it. The Business Data Stewards coordinate their work with many others in the enterprise, including the Technical Data Steward and business stakeholders. The stakeholders' concerns must be taken into account when decisions are made about that data. The relationship between Business Data Stewards, Technical Data Stewards, and stakeholders was illustrated in Fig. 2.1.

**Table 2.1** Advantages and Disadvantages of Various Approaches to Organizing Data Stewardship

| Data Stewardship Approach | Advantages | Disadvantages |
|---|---|---|
| Single owner | • Simple to set up<br>• Appropriate for getting started<br>• Easy to locate individual decision maker | • Business Data Steward must know and consult with all stakeholders<br>• Does not handle widely shared data well |
| Shared owner | • Able to handle and document widely shared data that requires multiple stewards<br>• Can work well for a very limited set of multiple owner data elements (the exception case) | • Requires more up-front preparation to determine stewards<br>• Complex, with each business data element having a different set of stewards<br>• Hard to maintain as personnel changes occur |
| Data domain | • Fairly stable population of data stewards associated with each data domain<br>• Handles multiple ownership and changing ownership (see Chapter 11: Governing and Stewarding Your Data Using Data Domains) efficiently<br>• All stakeholders are explicitly represented in the decision—making process. | • Determination of data domains can be difficult and complex<br>• Requires some sort of supervisory guidance for each Data Domain Council<br>• Mature Data Governance effort is needed to set up, run, and maintain the Data Domain Councils |

**NOTE**

An "Information Chain" is a supply chain for data. It shows where the data originates, how it is modified and stored, and where it is used. The Information Chain is an important concept because data must be managed across the entire life cycle. Many thought leaders recognize the concept of an Information Chain producing data as similar to a supply chain producing physical products. At its most granular level, the information chain is "technical lineage," and includes the physical location of the data within in each data store as well as the transformations that take place to the data as it flows through the systems and applications.

The Business Data Stewards work closely with Technical Data Stewards and Business Stakeholders to influence the data along the entire "information chain" (the flow of data from source to various targets such as Business Intelligence) as shown in Fig. 2.3. The partnership of Data Stewards and Stakeholders makes it possible to manage the data as it flows through the enterprise.

## TECHNICAL DATA STEWARDS

Technical Data Stewards are IT personnel who have an important role in supporting Data Governance. But where Business Data Stewards are associated with data domains or specific data elements and represent a specific business function, Technical Data Stewards provide support and are associated with specific systems, applications, data stores, and technical processes such as Identity Resolution (for Master Data Management), data quality rule enforcement, and Extract, Transform, and Load (ETL) jobs. This relationship can be more clearly seen in Fig. 2.4. Technical Data Stewards are the people to turn to in order to understand *how* the data is created, manipulated, stored, and moved in technical systems. They can answer questions about how data got to be a certain way. Business Data Stewards are associated with Technical Data Stewards

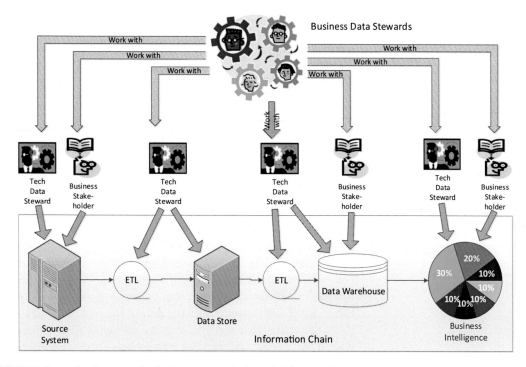

■ **FIGURE 2.3** Business Data Stewards work with others to manage the data in the Information Chain.

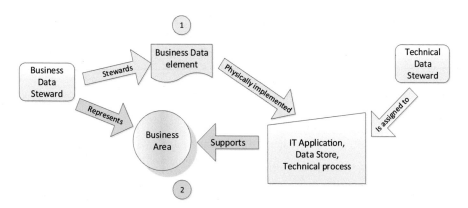

■ **FIGURE 2.4** The relationships between Business and Technical Data Stewards.

through the IT application or technical processes the Technical Data Steward support. There are two paths for this association:

1. The IT asset (application, data store, technical process) supports the business area represented by the Business Data Steward.

2. A business data element stewarded by the Business Data Steward is physically implemented in the IT asset supported by the Technical Data Steward.

As an example, consider a Card Membership system where data profiling revealed a significant anomaly in the distribution of birth dates. Although most days of the year had approximately the same number of members born on that day, the number of members born on December 31 was over 150-times higher than any other day. The Technical Data Steward for that system explained this anomaly: the previous system (from which the data was converted) contained only the birth year. During the conversion to the new system, December 31 was used as the default date. In another example, it was discovered that there were over 4000 car "body types" (e.g., 4-door sedans, pickup trucks, etc.) listed for insured automobiles. The Technical Data Steward explained that the field in the application that captured the description of body type was a free-form text field with no validation, so agents could enter whatever they wanted. Further, the Technical Data Steward revealed that it really didn't matter that the data in the body type field was a mess, since this data *was not used* by the application—instead, the body type was extracted from the automobile's VIN number by another part of that same application.

As you can see, this sort of information is not only valuable, but critical to a robust Data Governance or data quality effort. With additional knowledge about the system data the data consumers can make better choices about what fields to use—and what fields to fix. Having this knowledge increases the trust in the data. In many organizations there are IT personnel who can answer questions as they come up, but Technical Data Stewards are very different from these "casual" contributors because Technical Data Stewards are:

- Assigned by IT management. Working with Data Governance is considered an important part of their job, and not a "do it when you have time" task.
- Responsible and accountable for providing answers in a timely manner. They understand the importance of the Data Governance and Data Stewardship efforts and their role in those efforts.
- Part of the Data Stewardship team. That is, they are not being asked random questions in a vacuum; they are kept up to date on Data Stewardship activities, and data management tasks are planned and integrated into their schedules. If the Technical Data Stewards are concerned about the level of their involvement and

ability to get the work done, they have a chain of command (including the Data Governance Manager) to make those concerns known to.

## PROJECT DATA STEWARDS

Ideally there should be Data Stewardship representation on all major projects to provide support and make decisions about data meaning, usage, quality needed, and business rules. However, especially in companies with multiple projects going on at once, it simply isn't practical to have the Business Data Stewards present at all meetings and work sessions on the possibility that they will be needed. To help take the load off the Business Data Stewards but still involve them where they are needed, you can use *Project Data Stewards*. A Project Data Steward is an individual who is trained to recognize issues and questions that require input from the Business Data Stewards, and who brings that information to the Business Data Steward. The Business Data Steward then provides input, which the Project Data Steward brings back to the project. Project Data Stewards are assigned to projects, and depending on the project's size, may cover multiple projects.

Project Data Stewards can be analysts already assigned to a project (if they have the proper training), a member of the Data Governance Program Office, or even a contractor. Major projects are expected to fund the extra cost of Data Stewardship involvement, so it is important that the project methodology include the Data Governance tasks so that the estimate and budget will include those costs.

But what about smaller projects that typically have small budgets? Small projects can usually achieve what is needed by making use of an analyst on the project or a small to moderate percentage of a Project Data Steward attached to the Data Governance Program Office. In fact, in my last Data Governance Management role, we funded a single full-time person to supply this service to small projects. She was well-liked and well-respected throughout the company, having worked there more than 30 years, and was welcomed onto the projects.

### PROJECT DATA STEWARDS ARE *NOT* BUSINESS DATA STEWARDS

There is a major difference between a Business Data Steward and a Project Data Steward—the Project Data Steward is *not* responsible for the

*(Continued)*

**(CONTINUED)**

decisions about the data. This distinction is important because once a Project Data Steward gains some experience and gets to know the data, there can be a tendency to start making decisions on his or her own. This sort of behavior must be nipped in the bud because any "decision" made by the Project Data Steward does not carry the authority of the Business Data Steward or the Data Governance Program. The Project Data Steward *is* responsible for:

- Recognizing and recording issues and questions that require the input of the Business Data Steward.
- Coordinating the list of issues and questions with other Project Data Stewards, because multiple projects may well come up with the same issues and questions.
- Presenting the list to the appropriate Business Data Steward(s) and recording decisions and input.
- Providing the results as input back into the project.

## OPERATIONAL DATA STEWARDS

Operational Data Stewards are "helpers" for Business Data Stewards. Operational Data Stewards can step in on some of the duties that mesh with their jobs. For example, they can help ensure that data creation rules are followed, or assist with researching issues. Oftentimes, Operational Data Stewards are people who work on the front lines and see early opportunities where improved data quality would benefit certain groups. They may also notice behavior (such as always using a default value) that is damaging to the business. Business Data Stewards can designate Operational Data Stewards to help them. Though the Business Data Steward remains responsible for the data, Operational Data Stewards are often those who are responsible for collecting (and inputting) data accurately.

## SUMMARY

There are a variety of different types of Data Stewards, including Business, Technical, Project, and Operational Data Stewards. Each type of steward has a set of responsibilities as summarized in Table 2.2. These stewards all need to work together (as detailed in Fig. 2.1) to get the data fully stewarded.

**Table 2.2** Summary of Stewardship Responsibilities

| Steward Type | Responsibilities |
|---|---|
| Business Data Steward | • Primarily accountable for the data owned by their business function<br>• Participates in Data Domain Councils representing data of interest to their business function and may be the Lead Data Steward<br>• Supports Project and Operational Stewards<br>• Works with business stakeholders to make recommendations on data issues<br>• Manages metadata for their data<br>• Champions Data Stewardship to their business area |
| Technical Data Steward | • Provides expertise on applications, ETL, data stores, and other links in the Information Chain<br>• Assigned by IT leadership to support Data Stewardship |
| Project Data Steward | • Represents Data Stewardship on projects<br>• Funded by the projects and provide deliverables that belong to Data Stewardship<br>• Work with Business Data Stewards to obtain information about and make recommendations for the data stewarded by the Business Data Stewards<br>• Notifies Business Data Stewards about data issues raised by the project |
| Operational Data Steward | • Provides support to Business Data Stewards<br>• Recommend changes to improve data quality<br>• Help enforce business rules related to the data they use<br>• Often responsible for accurate input of data |

# Chapter 3

# Stewardship Roles and Responsibilities

## INTRODUCTION

Before we get into more detail on how to set up and run Data Stewardship as part of a Data Governance Program, we need to examine and explain the detailed tasks that the various types of Data Stewards perform as part of their participation. The tasks include not only what the Data Stewards do individually, but also include the tasks that they perform as a group (the Data Stewardship Council). Not only will this information let you start building job descriptions (if you're just starting out) while you read the rest of this book, but later sections will make more sense in light of the roles and responsibilities explained here.

Each of the types of Data Stewards has a set of tasks, which can be further classified into categories.

## THE DATA STEWARDSHIP COUNCIL

Although Business Data Stewards have many responsibilities as individuals (discussed later in this chapter), they also form the Data Stewardship Council, and have responsibilities as a *group*.

### What is the Data Stewardship Council?

The Data Stewardship Council is a formal group of Business Data Stewards whose primary purpose is to guide the overall Data Stewardship effort for the enterprise. Although there are a number of different ways of organizing Data Governance and Data Stewardship (with the primary ones being business function–driven and data domain–driven), there is always a need for a forum to drive the consistency of the effort. Reaching a consensus on what should be the common processes and goals of Data Stewardship is critical both for avoiding confusion and for having common metrics. This is true even though many of the decisions the Business Data Stewards make are local to their business function or data domain. It is also true even though the Data Governance Board may establish some of these processes and goals because they rarely do so at the granular level needed for execution. That is usually left to the

> **NOTE**
>
> The structure of Data Governance and Data Stewardship shown throughout this book is the *recommended* structure. It may not be possible to achieve the recommended structure right away due to a lack of funding, personnel, or interest. However, the goal should be to move toward the recommended structure as the effort matures.

Data Stewardship. DOI: https://doi.org/10.1016/B978-0-12-822132-7.00003-6

Business Data Stewards, who must (as noted previously) cooperate and coordinate their efforts.

## Membership in the Data Stewardship Council

The recommended overall structure of Data Stewardship is shown in Fig. 1.4 (within the dotted line box). Fig. 3.1 shows a sample (in this case for an insurance company) of how the Data Stewardship Council might look, with each box representing a business function. The structure is the same regardless of which way (business function or data domain) your Data Governance effort is organized, but the membership in the council may be slightly different. The membership can be summarized as:

- For business function–based Data Stewardship, the membership must consist of one or more Business Data Stewards representing all the appropriate business functions.
- For data domain–based Data Stewardship (as described in Chapter 11: Governing and Stewarding Your Data Using Data Domains) business functions that supply a Lead Data Steward for a Data Domain Council should be represented by that Lead Data Steward. For functions that do not supply a Lead Data Steward, a Business Data Steward from that business function should be part of the Data Stewardship Council. In any case, all data-owning business functions must be represented.

There are a couple of things to note about the structure of the Data Stewardship Council. First of all, the council is led by the *Enterprise Data Steward*, a role which may be initially filled by the Data Governance Manager, but ideally should be a role staffed by a dedicated person in the Data Governance Program Office. Note also that each business function (such as Insurance Services) may be further broken down into component parts such as Actuarial, Claims, and Underwriting Operations. This may be necessary in order to designate Business Data Stewards who can manage the key data for that component of the business. In this case (a real example), there was no single Business Data Steward who could be responsible for all the Insurance data, so it had to be broken down as shown.

Put another way, the assignment of Business Data Stewards depends on the structure of your business and the complexity of the data you need to manage. For example, a major healthcare provider has business functions around membership and eligibility. However, they provide their services to widely varying types of customers such as corporate programs and government programs. The different types of

---

**NOTE**

There may be a misconception that the group of Data Domain Council Managers (referred to in Chapter 11: Governing and Stewarding Your Data Using Data Domains, as the "Data Domain Management Committee") can substitute for the Data Stewardship Council. However, that is simply false. The Data Domain Council Managers are primarily charged with guiding the actions of the Business Data Stewards in reaching decisions around critical items such as business data element definitions. The purpose of their management committee is to standardize the ways they manage their Data Domain Councils. They lack the business expertise to represent their council members as an alternative to the Data Stewardship Council. The Data Domain Council Managers may participate in the Data Stewardship Committee meetings in order to understand the business drivers for the Business Data Stewards.

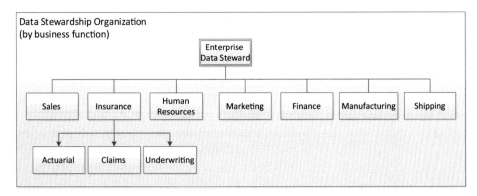

**■ FIGURE 3.1** A sample structure for the Data Stewardship Council.

programs have considerable variation in the data collected as well as the rules that must be applied to safeguard that data. Thus, different Business Data Stewards are needed to represent corporate program membership/eligibility and government program membership/eligibility despite the fact that the business functions (membership/eligibility) seem to be similar.

## Responsibilities of the Data Stewardship Council

The responsibilities of the Data Stewardship Council include:

- *Focus on ways to improve how an organization obtains, manages, leverages, and gets value out of its data.* Data represents a valued asset, and the Data Stewardship Council should be looking for ways to improve the quality of the asset and use the data for competitive advantage.
- *Be the advisory body for enterprise-level data standards, guiding principles, and policies.* The standards and principles set guidelines that the Business Data Stewards (and others) need to use, so the council must have a say in drafting and modifying them. Recommending what policies are needed and what the policies need to say is also an important task because the Business Data Stewards are on the front-lines, and, thus, in a great position to see what policies are needed to make Data Governance a success.
- *Mediate or arbitrate the resolution of issues.* The Data Stewardship Council has to work together as a team to settle any data issues that

> **NOTE**
> Much of the work noted as the responsibilities of the Data Stewardship Council is carried out by the members of the councils—but is listed here as part of the Council responsibilities because it requires discussion and reaching consensus with other stewards due to its impact to the organization outside the owning business function.

arise. There can be many of these, including disagreements over meanings or rules, differing requirements for data quality, modifications to how data is used, and which business functions should own key data elements.

- *Communicate decisions of the Data Stewardship Council and Data Governance Board.* It doesn't make a whole lot of sense to institute Data Governance and Data Stewardship unless the decisions made about the data are communicated to the people who use the data. For example, if the Council determines that currently, certain data is not of sufficiently high quality to be suitable for a particular use, then the Council needs to identify the people using it in that way, and let them know that it is not appropriate.

- *Ensure alignment of the Data Governance effort to the business.* It is all too easy to start designing Data Governance protocols (including processes and procedures) that are out of alignment with what is important to the business. Make no mistake—doing so is a recipe for failure. If Data Governance is perceived as being a roadblock, out of synch with the business priorities, or simply irrelevant, the effort will quickly be dismantled and the resources put to more effective use.

- *Participate in and contribute to Data Governance processes.* The day to day processes for executing Data Governance and Data Stewardship are a little different in each company. The Council (as a group) needs to define and design the processes since they are mostly the people (or represent the people) who will be expected to follow them. They will also be expected to provide feedback on the processes to determine which ones are working, and which ones need to be changed or discarded. These processes—and the tuning of the processes—are a key part of the design and implementation of Data Governance. It is not a good idea to try and build the processes without the input of the Data Stewardship Council.

- *Communicate Data Governance vision and objectives across the organization.* In most organizations, the vision and objectives of Data Governance are new to the company, and few, if any, of the employees understand what is required. The Data Stewardship Council has to communicate the vision and objectives, especially into the business functions they represent. This constant communication is one of the most important things that the Council is responsible for.

- *Communicate the rules for using data.* Rigorous business rules around data are new to most employees, yet using the data according to the rules is everyone's responsibility.

- *Review and evaluate Data Governance performance and effectiveness.* The Business Data Stewards need to "buy in" to the performance and effectiveness measures, much as employees should have a say in how their performance is measured in other ways. The best way to have effective Business Data Stewards is to for them to *want* to participate, and that requires that they be part of the measurement process.

- *Provide input into Data Governance goals and scorecard development.* The Data Governance goals must align with the performance and effectiveness measures (the previous bullet point), so just as with those measures, the Business Data Stewards should have a voice in what the Data Governance effort hopes to accomplish (goals) and how progress is displayed to Management (scorecard).

- *Collaborate on Procedures.* Procedures state how results (dictated by policies) will be accomplished. Business Data Stewards must have input into the procedures because they are responsible for meeting many of the goals laid out and for executing the established procedures. If you just "hand over" procedures to the Business Data Stewards without getting their input, it will be more difficult to get them to cooperate.

- *Collaborate with other interested parties in the management of definitions and data issues.* In the case of business function–driven Data Stewardship, the Data Stewardship Council provides a forum for the Business Data Stewards to discuss and reach agreement (or at least consensus) on definitions of business data elements and data quality issues.
  - *Definitions*: Many people (commonly known as stakeholders) have an interest in how terms are defined, and it is especially important that the stakeholders have a common understanding of the data names and definitions. Managing definitions requires soliciting input from stakeholders during both the initial definition phase and for any changes to the definitions that are proposed.
  - *Data quality issues*: Managing issues with the data and data quality is a key job of the Data Stewardship Council. The impacts of the issues must be assessed, proposed remediation options must be developed, the impacts of the various remediation options must

also be assessed, and priorities must be established. This work is best done by members of the Council and identified stakeholders and with a well-defined workflow. Establishing the workflow for resolving issues requires discussion and agreement within the Council.

- *Enforces use of agreed-upon Business terminology.* When data users use different terminology to represent the same concept, confusion reigns supreme. As business data elements are named, given a robust definition, and have business rules defined, the elements should be used consistently across the organization and synonyms should be actively discouraged by the Business Data Stewards. That is, when a synonym is used in conversations, discussions, and documentation, the Business Data Stewards should insist that the correct term be substituted. This is especially important when the incorrectly used term has actually been defined to mean something different (e.g., Customer vs Client vs Account).

## DATA GOVERNANCE MANAGER

The Data Governance Manager runs the Data Governance effort and is the head of the Data Governance Program Office. While the Data Governance Manager has many tasks, those most associated with maintaining effective Data Stewardship include:

- Managing and ensuring adequate staffing levels for the Data Governance Program Office.
- Ensuring that all appropriate business functions are represented on the Data Governance Board and Data Stewardship Council.
- Obtaining appropriate involvement from support organizations. These can include Enterprise Architecture, the Program Management Office, IT application support, and Human Resources (for writing job descriptions, recruiting, and adjustments to Management By Objective (MBO) goals and compensation).
- Reporting to the Data Governance Board on Data Governance performance.
- Collaborating with leadership across the organization to identify business needs and implement Data Governance and Data Stewardship capabilities.
- Ensuring that Data Governance and Data Stewardship processes are inserted into and aligned with appropriate enterprise processes.

## ENTERPRISE DATA STEWARD

The Enterprise Data Steward is charged with running the day to day stewardship effort through the Data Stewardship Council. These responsibilities can be broken into three major categories, namely Leadership, Program management, and Measurement.

The Leadership responsibilities include:

- *Report to the Data Governance Manager.* The Enterprise Data Steward is part of the Data Governance Program Office, and as such, is part of the Data Governance Manager's staff.
- *Lead the community of Data Stewards through the Data Stewardship Council.* The primary responsibility of the Enterprise Data Steward is to provide leadership for the Data Stewards across the organization. In the absence of data domain–driven stewardship, the Enterprise Data Steward is *the* guiding role. Even with data domain–driven stewardship, leadership is needed for anything that crosses data domains and to drive best practices. Although the Business Data Stewards don't report functionally to the Enterprise Data Steward, the members of the Data Stewardship Council work closely with the Enterprise Data Steward.
- *Liaise with Data Governors/business leads, Data Domain Council Managers or their appointees as well as IT and Business project leads/PMOs to implement and maintain Data Stewardship.* The Enterprise Data Steward works closely with each of the roles noted:
  - The Data Governors (members of the Data Governance Board) as needed to guide the Business Data Stewards.
  - The Data Domain Council Managers to assist them with issues such as nonparticipation of Business Data Stewards or when a Business Data Steward becomes unavailable and must be replaced. The Enterprise Data Steward may also work to resolve issues that the individual Data Domain Council Managers cannot resolve on their own.
  - IT and Business Project Leads/PMOs. Both IT leads/analysts and Project Managers may not be familiar with the role that Business Data Stewards must fulfill both during data-driven projects and resolving "business as usual" (BAU) data issues. The Enterprise Data Steward is usually the person most well-versed in providing this information and education.
- *Work with the Data Governance Manager to develop the Data Governance vision and framework—both short term and long term.* Working closely with the Business Data Stewards, the Enterprise

Data Steward is in a unique position to understand and drive the framework that the Data Stewards work within. Even when some of that framework is provided by the data domains, there is a lot that the Business Data Stewards do that falls outside the data domains (as discussed in Chapter 11: Governing and Stewarding Your Data Using Data Domains).

- *Identify and initiate projects to implement the vision.* Although the Business Data Stewards (working together as the Data Stewardship Council) may propose projects to fix specific data issues, it is up to the Enterprise Data Steward to propose and initiate projects that drive forward the vision of Data Governance. These projects may include instituting an overall workflow to handle data quality rule violations, collaborating with the screen designers to create standards for data entry (which improves input quality), and working with IT to install tools that make the business data and metadata available to the enterprise as a whole.

- *Ensure all Data Governance work efforts are in line with overall business objectives and the Data Governance vision.* This primarily means focusing the efforts of the Business Data Stewards and DGPO staff on projects and efforts that are of highest importance to the enterprise. For example, if new metrics are proposed by the company executives, the Enterprise Data Steward may need to have the Business Data Stewards start work immediately on getting those metrics defined, temporarily stopping work on other business data elements or data issues they were working on.

- *Define prioritization criteria.* The Business Data Stewards are responsible for reaching an agreement on the priorities of competing projects that correct data issues. However, a standardized set of prioritization criteria are needed so that ranking is not done according to "who shouts the loudest." The Enterprise Data Steward is responsible for proposing and gaining agreement on these criteria, which may include reduced cost, increased income, probability of regulatory violations, inability to achieve business goals, and deterioration of data quality.

- *Provide direction to business and IT teams.* The Enterprise Data Steward is (or should be) aware of what is going on and what is needed to drive Data Stewardship forward. Ideally, that person should be the single point of contact for teams that need to interact with Data Stewardship either to get information needed or to provide the services needed.

- *Lead implementation of the Data Stewardship organization.* As organizational changes need to be made, including identifying the need for additional or replacement stewards, the Enterprise Data

**NOTE**

In cases where it is determined that new (and unstewarded) business data elements are needed, the Enterprise Data Steward can gather the appropriate members of the Data Stewardship Council together to determine which business function or data domain should own that element and move forward to define it.

Steward takes the lead on identifying what changes are needed as well as implementing those changes. In the case of data domain–driven stewardship, the Enterprise Data Steward works with the Data Domain Council Managers on any organizational changes.

The Program Management responsibilities include:

- *Design the processes and procedures for Data Stewardship.* The Enterprise Data Steward needs to collect specifications on how data should be managed from the Business Data Stewards and formulate them into a set of processes and procedures that the Business Data Stewards can use. Changes to those processes and procedures are unavoidable as steps that seemed to be a good idea initially may not work out as intended. The Enterprise Data Steward needs to make the necessary changes, get the buy-in from the Business Data Stewards (and Data Domain Council Managers where they exist), and republish as necessary.
- *Build and drive the agenda for Data Stewardship Council meetings.* The Enterprise Data Steward is responsible for collecting issues that need to be discussed, status updates, and other agenda items, scheduling Council meetings, and running the meetings themselves. Publishing the meeting minutes is part of this as well.
- *Maintain a repository of information and decisions.* The Enterprise Data Steward must ensure that the work product (documentation) produced by the Business Data Stewards is completed and published. The documentation can include:
  - Definitions, data quality requirements, and business rules that must be put into the Business Glossary.
  - New processes and procedures that are published and listed on the Data Governance/Data Stewardship website.
  - Presentations for information and training, published on the Data Governance/Data Stewardship website.
  - Rules for engaging Data Stewardship on data issues.

- *Improve overall enterprise data quality and reliability through process improvement.* This includes:
  - Develop and institute information lifecycle processes. Carefully planned, documented, and executed information lifecycle processes protect the quality of the data by ensuring that they are properly and completely captured and that the business rules for the data are consistently applied.
  - Improve the processes that capture and process the data. Although the focus of "Data Stewardship" is on data, poor quality data is often a symptom of broken processes. The Enterprise Data

**NOTE**

In the case of data domain–driven stewardship, the Data Domain Council Managers are responsible for ensuring that all the information generated as part of the operation of the Data Domain Councils are provided to the Enterprise Data Steward.

Steward is in a unique position to see the "big picture" on data quality problems, and work with the Business Data Stewards to look for opportunities to proactively improve the data as well as to identify the process issues and remediate them.

- *Review and manage issues, and meet with the business to understand user needs and technical feasibility.* Issue management includes keeping on top of the Issue Log, making sure that the issues are properly documented, impacts assessed, and priorities established. With this information, the Enterprise Data Steward can meet with the impacted groups and Business Data Stewards to work out a remediation plan.
- *Work with Data Governors and Business Data Stewards to facilitate the issue resolution process.* Act as a point of resolution prior to Data Governance Board or Executive Steering Committee involvement.
- *Provide counsel to projects to ensure the project is in line with the vision of the Data Governance program.* Projects (especially major projects) can have significant impact on the goals of Data Governance. For example, without guidance from Data Governance, critical business data elements may be misdefined or misused, and the proper representatives and tasks from Data Governance may not be involved. The Enterprise Data Steward can educate the project managers on what is needed and provide resources (in the form of Project Data Stewards, described later in this chapter) to the project to ensure that the goals of Data Governance are safeguarded.

The Measurement responsibilities include:

- *Define, implement, and manage Data Governance metrics.* The Data Stewards have some responsibility in helping to define the metrics, but the Enterprise Data Steward takes "point" on getting the metrics defined and implemented—as well as actually running the measures to generate scorecards.
- *Track, monitor, and publish Data Governance scorecards.* Scorecards are generated periodically and provide information on how Data Governance is doing in achieving its overall goals as well as the level of participation (see Chapter 8: Measuring Data Stewardship Progress: The Metrics).

## BUSINESS DATA STEWARDS

The Business Data Steward's responsibilities can be broken into three major categories, namely Business Alignment, Data Lifecycle Management, and Data quality and risks.

The Business Alignment responsibilities include:

- *Collaborate closely with other Business Data Stewards.* This collaboration will depend on how Data Stewardship is organized.
  - The Data Stewardship Council is the primary forum where the Business Data Stewards work together across the enterprise. In an organization that uses data domain—based stewardship, the Data Stewardship Council is largely made up of the Lead Data Stewards from the Data Domain Councils.
  - A Data Domain Council (see Chapter 11: Governing and Stewarding Your Data Using Data Domains) is a working group that manages a set of data domains. Within each of these working groups, Business Data Stewards manage the data (and metadata) that are associated with their data domains. For example, the definitions of business data elements are determined and updated within the Data Domain Council for the data domain to which the business data elements are attached.
- *Aligned to a business function.* Business Data Stewards represent a business function, which is different from a portion of the organization. For example, in an insurance company, there might be Business Data Stewards for Claims, Actuarial, and Underwriting— even though there might not be a portion of the organization called "Claims," etc. As will be discussed in Chapter 4, Implementing Data Stewardship, organizing the Business Data Stewards this way makes them relatively unaffected by reorganizations.
- *Responsible for Data Governance execution in their functional area.* Each Business Data Steward represents (along with the Data Governor) Data Governance and Data Stewardship in their business function. Business Data Stewards provide visibility into what is going on in their business function, and must actively ensure that policies, processes, and procedures are followed—escalating to the Enterprise Data Steward if there is an issue.
- *Identify and define key business data elements.* Since it isn't possible to bring all the data under governance at once, Business Data Stewards must identify the most important data (key business data elements). As discussed in Chapter 6, Practical Data Stewardship, a standardized process can be developed and used to identify the key business data elements. Once identified, the Business Data Stewards are responsible for:
  - *Defining the business data element definitions.* The Business Data Stewards are responsible for establishing business definitions for the data they steward that meet the requirements for robust definitions established by the Data Governance Program Office.

- *Creating a standardized and unique name for the business data elements.* The name must meet the naming standards established by the Data Governance Program Office. Ideally, the name is unique across the enterprise.

- *Establish the requirements for data quality in order for the data to be usable for the purposes intended by the business.* This step often comes after the definition, at a point where the physical source of the data has been at least tentatively identified so the data quality requirements (rules) can be used to test the quality of the data.

- *Communicate the definition and any other known metadata to the Data Governors and stakeholders.* This may include business data quality rules, any stated limits on what the data can be used for, and the proper way to derive the data (if appropriate).

- *Provide input for Data Governance metrics.* As stated earlier, the Enterprise Data Steward is responsible for putting together the Data Governance metrics, but the Business Data Stewards provide input into that process. As with most other types of metrics, it is difficult to expect the Business Data Stewards to "buy in" to the metrics if they have no say in what the metrics consist of.

- *Represent interests of Data Governors.* When the Data Governors have issues or concerns about the data, it is the responsibility of the Business Data Steward to review those items with the other members of the Data Stewardship Council or the Data Domain Council to get feedback and make recommendations.

- *Work with Data Governors to ensure the business users have a practical understanding of the data.* It is important for all the data analysts and other data users to understand the data, what it means, and what business rules it must follow. This understanding will help the analysts use the data properly as well as spot potential issues early and bring them to the attention of the Business Data Steward. Under these circumstances, the data analyst and data user population become the "eyes and ears" of the Business Data Stewards, leading to a more effective governing and stewarding of the data.

- *Participate in process and standard definition.* The Business Data Stewards are in a good position to define efficient processes and standards that are not too onerous to follow. Since they will need to adhere to the processes and standards, it is important to get their input into the process definition. The Enterprise Data Steward then takes this input and creates the processes and standards.

**NOTE**

In the case of business function–driven Data Stewardship, the Business Data Stewards agree on which business function "owns" the business data elements, and that Business Data Steward writes the definition and determines the other metadata in collaboration with the stakeholders. In the case of data domain–driven Data Stewardship, the Data Stewardship Council (largely comprised of Lead Data Stewards) usually go through proposed business data elements, agree on which data domain they belong to, and then verify that with the members of the Data Domain Council. At that point, the members of the Data Domain Council create and agree on the name, definition, and other appropriate metadata. As with business function–driven Data Stewardship, there is usually one of the business function Business Data Stewards who has a large stake (often the producer) and, thus, takes the lead in that work.

- *Ensure that data decisions are communicated and business users understand the impacts of the decisions to their lines of business.* It is important that decisions about the data—and their impacts—are communicated to the people who use the data. The quality of the data and the quality of business decisions can seriously deteriorate if the decisions about the data are not communicated to the data users. For example, if an issue is discovered with the quality of birth dates in a particular system, that needs to be communicated to people using those birth dates, perhaps with a recommendation on where they can get reliable birth date data.

- *Provide business requirements on behalf of aligned function.* The Business Data Stewards need to provide their business function's requirements for the quality and usage of the data so that issues can be surfaced and projects considered to ensure the data meets those requirements.

Data Lifecycle Management responsibilities include:

- *Facilitate the Data Governors through the change control process.* The Data Governors have a role in approving recommendations made by the Business Data Stewards, and, thus, are part of the change control process workflow. However, they often need input and guidance from the Business Data Stewards to effectively perform that role.

- *Coordinate business requirements and requests specific to the stewarded data business area.* This responsibility includes not only establishing priorities within a business function, but reviewing requirements and requests to ensure that there are no duplicates and identify where they can reasonably be combined into a single work stream.

- *Work with their Data Governor to own data metrics for compliance with Data Governance policies and standards.* The Business Data Stewards need to work with their Data Governor to take ownership as well as responsibility for the metrics used to measure compliance with what is required by Data Governance policies and standards. No one else can do this because it is the Business Data Stewards who understand what the data means, how it should be used, and how the quality needs to be protected and improved.

- *Participate in conflict resolution.* Resolve issues when able or manage issues throughout the escalation process. Different business areas use data differently, and these differences can lead to conflicts about definition, appropriate data usage, and required data quality. As these conflicts arise, the Business Data Stewards responsible for the business data elements in question must take a leadership role in getting them resolved to the satisfaction (if possible) of all stakeholders. However, it is not always possible for the stewards to resolve conflicts at their level, in which case the issues must be escalated to the Data Governors with the Business Data Steward's recommendations. The Enterprise Data Steward can guide this process, but the Business Data Stewards must be accountable for getting conflicts resolved.

- *Assess enterprise impacts related to data changes.* As decisions are made about appropriate data usage, required data quality, and what the data means, these decisions have impacts on the enterprise, as shown in Fig. 3.2.
- *Organize and participate in Data Stewardship working groups.* It is often necessary for a small subset of the Business Data Stewards to cooperate in identifying correct usage of data as well as resolving issues around data use. The Business Data Stewards need to work with their peers in these Data Stewardship working groups. Doing so is more efficient than involving the entire Data Stewardship Council or Data Domain Council as some of the Business Data Stewards have little interest or stake in a particular data usage or issue.
- *Work on behalf of Data Governors to ensure consistency of data usage and share best practices.* The Business Data Stewards carry the

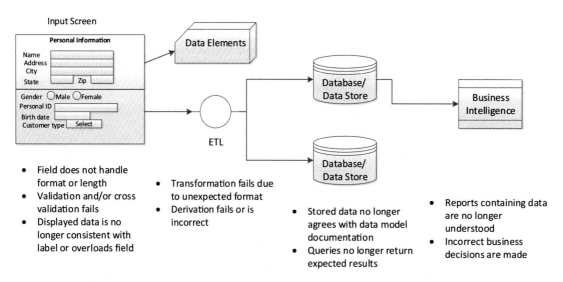

**■ FIGURE 3.2** Decisions about data have impacts across the entire information chain.

authority of the Data Governors to ensure that everyone in their business function is aware of best practices around data. This work includes ensuring that everyone knows that new uses must be reviewed by the Business Data Steward.

- *Work with the business stakeholders to define the appropriate capture, usage, and data quality business rules for all business data elements and business data element derivations within their data business areas.* Having these rules defined—and having everyone aware of them—is key to preventing the misuse of data such as when an analyst simply decides to use data in a way it was never intended (thus, violating the usage rules) or for which the quality of the data is not sufficient. The Business Data Stewards must work with the data users to identify data that meet the business needs or that can be adjusted to meet those needs.

---

**PRACTICAL ADVICE**

Successful stewardship of data requires managing the metadata. To manage the metadata effectively, a few key tools and processes are necessary. Primary among those tools are a metadata repository with a business glossary as either an integrated part of the repository or as a separate tool. These tools enable the stewards to store and retrieve definitions, business rules, and other critical pieces of information about the data the steward is accountable for.

The data quality and risks responsibilities include:

- *Define and validate data quality rules.* The Business Data Stewards need to define the data quality rules based on the needs of all users (stakeholders) of the data. These rules are used to guide the creation of the system-level data quality rules used for examining the data (data profiling) and regularly monitoring and ascertaining how closely the data adhere to the defined rules.
- *Work with the business to define acceptable levels of data quality.* "Acceptable" levels of data quality are based on "context," that is, what the data will actually be used for. Thus the Business Data Steward needs to understand the uses that the data will be put to, and also be aware whenever additional uses are planned for the data. This awareness reflects back to the previous statement about best practices including notifying the Business Data Steward whenever data usage changes.
- *Monitor the data quality metrics, and define improvement opportunities.* Closely aligned with defining the acceptable level of

data quality is monitoring the metrics on data quality—that is, how closely the data quality matches the data quality rules within what was defined as "acceptable." Any time the data quality appears to be falling below acceptable levels, the Business Data Stewards need to evaluate the situation, decide if there is really a problem, and whether there is a business case for additional action to improve the quality. The business case for improvement (a cost/benefit analysis) must then be analyzed to determine if it is strong enough to bring the data quality back up to acceptable levels.

- *Define a valid list of values (reference data) for data elements used across the enterprise.* One of the key difficulties of data that is shared across multiple business areas is reaching a consensus on what valid values should be allowed at the logical level. These discussions often highlight subtle differences in data meaning that may lead to breaking a business data element into additional business data elements. These discussions are often coordinated by the Enterprise Data Steward or the Lead Data Steward for a data domain to ensure that all data needs are met.

## PROJECT DATA STEWARDS

The responsibilities of Project Data Stewards include metadata, data quality, and Data Governance project alignment responsibilities. The metadata responsibilities include:

- *Work with the Data Stewardship Council to determine the appropriate responsibility for the project business data element.* The Project Data Stewards spend a lot of their time reviewing the data-related project proposals with the appropriate Data Steward. This may be either the Business Data Steward from the owning business function or the Lead Data Steward for the owning data domain. In cases where it is not clear which business function or data domain owns or should own the business data element, the Data Stewardship Council will make that determination.
- *Maintain the names and descriptions of the business data elements being used in a project.* As business data elements are exposed and discussed during a project, the Project Data Steward has the responsibility to ensure that a robust name and description is supplied for each element. That is, the name follows business data element naming rules, and the description is as complete as possible, stating the best estimate of what the data element means, how it is used, and how it is collected. Having a robust name and description is necessary to ensure

that the appropriate Business or Lead Data Steward has a clear understanding of what data the project is proposing to use.

- *Review the business data element name and description with the appropriate Data Steward and get a business definition.* Data definitions that meet Data Governance standards must be provided by the Business Data Steward of the owning business function or (via the Lead Data Steward) by the owning Data Domain Council. The Project Data Steward must be familiar with the standards and evaluate the proposed definitions for conformance to the standards.
- *Collect and document project-proposed business derivations and calculations.* In the case that the project data is the result of a derivation or a calculation, the project subject matter experts should propose the derivation or calculation or request that the appropriate Data Steward do so. The Project Data Steward must ensure that the derivation conforms to the standards.
- *Review the project-proposed derivations and calculations with the appropriate Data Steward.* The appropriate Business Data Steward or (via the Lead Data Steward) Data Domain Council can agree with the proposed derivation or state what the derivation should be.
- *Deliver Data Steward decisions to the project for incorporation in the project plan.* Decisions made by the appropriate Business Data Steward or Data Domain Council—including definitions, derivations, data usage rules, and other metadata—must be communicated back to the project by the Project Data Steward.

**PRACTICAL ADVICE**

As Project Data Stewards gain experience, there is a danger that they may begin to make recommendations about the data themselves, rather than consulting with the appropriate Data Stewards. This must not be allowed. The Project Data Stewards do *not* own the data or the responsibility for the data, and, thus, *cannot* make decisions about the data. The Enterprise Data Steward must be watchful for signs that the Project Data Stewards are not consulting with the appropriate Data Stewards.

**PRACTICAL ADVICE**

In reality, multiple projects may be trying to use the same data. In that case, multiple Project Data Stewards may be working on the same data.

*(Continued)*

**(CONTINUED)**

The Project Data Stewards need a coordination mechanism (such as a weekly meeting) to review the business data elements of interest to their projects and ensure that they aren't doing the same work. In addition, the Project Data Stewards must ensure that the projects are using the data consistently.

The data quality responsibilities include:

- Collect and document data quality rules and data quality issues from the project. Project discussions will often expose known issues with data quality as they relate to the intended usage. Alternatively, questions may arise about whether the quality of the data will support the intended usage. In such cases, the Project Data Steward should collect and document the data quality rules that define what is expected of the data by the project.
- Evaluate the impact of the data quality issues on the project data usage and consult with the Data Governors or Business Data Stewards where appropriate. The consultation should discuss whether the perceived issues are real, and assess how difficult the data issues would be to fix. The Business Data Stewards may suggest other sources of higher-quality data for project usage. The assessment will also feed into the decision on whether to expend the work effort needed to profile the data in depth.

**PRACTICAL ADVICE**

A major data quality issue, coupled with a lack of another data source, may have a significant impact on the project. In extreme cases, the project may actually fail due to poor data quality that was not discovered before the project started. In such cases, the project scope may need to be expanded to fix the data quality issue. The data quality fix may expand the scope of the project to the point where it is no longer economical or feasible. Clearly it is better to know that *before* the project has gotten underway. To put it succinctly, there is no sense beginning a project until some level of data inspection is conducted and the quality of the data is assessed.

- *Consult with the appropriate Data Steward and project manager to determine if data should be profiled based on data quality rules and expectations collected on a project.* Although the rules may not be well known (or known at all) people who have requirements almost always have assumptions and expectations about what the data will look and act like. One of the nastiest surprises that can occur on a project is that data assumed to be fit for purpose is actually not of sufficient quality to serve the purposes of the project. Consultation with the Business and Technical Data Stewards serves to quantify the risk that the data quality is insufficient for the project's purposes. The Project Data Steward can then work with the Project Manager to schedule a data profiling effort, adjusting the project schedule to allow for the extra time needed. As mentioned earlier, it is better to identify the need and profile the data prior to laying out the project schedule as it can take a significant period of time to profile the data.

## DATA PROFILING

*Data Profiling* is the process of examining the contents of a database or other data source and comparing the contents against the data quality rules (rules that define what is considered "good quality" in the data) or discovering those rules. Ideally, any project that makes use of data should profile that data. This is especially true of projects that make use of data of questionable quality. Adding data profiling to a project that has not included it in the project plan can lead to significant delays. But not knowing what shape your data is in will lead to much bigger problems. Data profiling is a many step process that requires collaboration between IT, Business Data Analysts, data profiling tool experts, and the Data Governance Program Office. These steps can include:

1. Determining what data to profile. Once the project has determined what business data it will need, that business data has to be mapped to its physical sources.
2. Preparing the profiling environment. Data profiling is rarely—if ever—performed on the production server using the operational data. Instead, the data must be migrated to a profiling environment. This involves setting up the environment (server, disk, and database engine), creating the data structures, and migrating the data. This is largely an IT task, and it is not uncommon for it to be a challenge to accomplish.
3. Ensuring that sensitive data is properly protected in the profiling environment. There are often policies and stringent rules about moving data outside of the transaction system where it is collected and protected by various security considerations. Often these policies require masking or obfuscation of the data when moved. This is essentially *changing* the data and hiding some or all of the contents in the new environment. However, doing so usually precludes profiling the data, since you are not actually examining the data.

*(Continued)*

### NOTE

The Business Data Stewards should either already know the condition of the data or they should insist that the data be profiled. Making the Business Data Stewards accountable for the data also makes them accountable for demanding data profiling be performed where they feel it is warranted. Of course, if the Project Manager refuses to spend the time and expense, this must be recorded in the project risks to document the fact that the steward was ignored.

**(CONTINUED)**

4. Running the profiling tool and storing the results. The data profiling tool expert performs this task, and if all goes well, this usually takes only a day or two, depending, of course, on the complexity and amount of data.

5. Analysis of the results. This is the most resource-intensive task as the results of the profiling have to be reviewed with the appropriate Business Data Stewards. The Business Data Stewards must determine whether any potential issues are *actually* issues and work with the Technical Data Stewards and the Project Manager to formulate what it would take to remediate the issues. This typically requires close examination of the profiling results and a clear understanding of both the data quality rules and the characteristics of the actual data as captured by the profiling tool.

6. Document the results. The profiling results and analysis are documented in the tool, and may also need to be published in the project documentation.

As you can see, Data Profiling is somewhat involved and can take time. However, the time saved due to project delays usually outweighs the cost of the profiling. And as stated earlier, you either know the data is of high quality (because you have inspected it before) or it is simply foolish to proceed with the project without inspecting the data.

**NOTE**

It *is* possible to profile data without a tool, but tools are better. They can show you things that you might not be looking for, propose rules you might not know about, and store the results in a reusable form that can save time later. But the act of profiling is essentially one of comparison; what you have versus what you expect.

- *Assist the data profiling efforts by performing data profiling tasks related to data quality.* If properly trained, the Project Data Stewards can do some of the analysis and guide the work of others to ensure that standards are followed and the results are properly documented in the appropriate tools.

The Data Governance Project Alignment responsibilities include:

- *Inform and consult with Business Data Stewards (including Lead Data Stewards), Data Governors, and the Enterprise Data Steward about definitions and data quality rules and issues that result from a project.*
- *Work with project managers and project members throughout the course of a project in a collaborative manner while ensuring that Data Governance related concerns are addressed for each project.*
- *Where possible, align with projects that utilize a Project Data Steward's previous experience and expertise.* Leveraging a Project Data Steward's previous experience can lead to a shortened learning

curve, making the Project Data Steward more of an asset to the project.

## TECHNICAL DATA STEWARDS

Technical Data Stewards have these responsibilities:

- *Provide the technical expertise around source systems, extract, transform, and load (ETL) processes, data stores, data warehouses, and Business intelligence tools.*
- *Explain how a system or process works (or doesn't).* The Technical Data Stewards are frequently the individual(s) assigned to support a system, and know the "guts" of the system. In addition, the Technical Data Stewards have a historic perspective on "how things got the way they got." For example, an odd distribution of birth dates was the result of a conversion from an earlier system and the choice made for defaults during that conversion.
- *Check code, CopyLibs, internal database structures, and other programming constructs in search of how the information is structured, how the data moves, and how the data is transformed within a system or between systems.*
- *Assist in identifying where business data elements are physically implemented in a system.*

## OPERATIONAL DATA STEWARDS

Operational Data Stewards have these responsibilities:

- *Ensure adherence to data creation and update policies and procedures while creating new values or modifying existing ones.* The Operational Data Stewards are often the front-line people putting in new data, new valid values, and updating existing information—or supervising people who are doing this work. They may also be the people resolving mismatches (false positives and false negatives) in the management of Master Data. This situation presents an opportunity to ensure that the creation and update policies and procedures are followed.
- *Assist Business Data Stewards in the identification and collection of data metrics.* Often the metrics for measuring conformance to policies, procedures, and standards involve gathering information about the data. For example, the metrics might include mandatory capture of key business data elements, or the usage of only valid values for certain fields. It can be a fair amount of work to gather this information as inputs to the metrics, and the Operational Data

Stewards can assist with this work by running the queries and reporting back the results.

- *Assist the remediation project team with changes to data, application processes, and procedures.* Project teams often need "hands on" help with changes to data, application processes, and procedures. Typically, it is best to have these changes made by someone familiar with the processes and data. The Operational Data Steward can step in and help with this, again taking some of the load that would otherwise end up on a Subject Matter Expert (SME) or even the Business Data Steward.
- *Assist Business Data Stewards in performing data analysis to research issues and change requests.* Researching issues and change requests can involve knowing where the data is, what the data is being used for, and digging into the data to see what is going on. Operational Data Stewards can take on much of this work, usually under the direction of the Business Data Steward.
- *Identify and communicate opportunities for data quality improvement.* Operational Data Stewards are often closer to the data than the Business Data Stewards, using it on a day to day basis. They are, thus, in the unique position to see where the quality of the data is insufficient for the need. The Operational Data Steward can open an issue or (depending on how Data Governance is set up) report the issue to the Business Data Steward for resolution.

---

**THE DIFFERENCE BETWEEN OPERATIONAL DATA STEWARDS AND BUSINESS DATA STEWARDS**

For people who are new to Data Stewardship, it can sometimes be confusing to try and figure out the difference between an Operational Data Steward and a Business Data Steward. This difference is most clear when following a business data element through a business process. In a nutshell, the Business Data Steward is responsible for the business data element regardless of the process it is used in. That is, it is the Business Data Steward that would be turned to in order to understand what the business data element means, the business rules associated with it, and the data quality requirements. The Operational Data Steward is responsible for making sure that the data is input accurately, and that the data being input meets the requirements of the business data element. Unlike the Business Data Steward, that responsibility can change as the process progresses.

*(Continued)*

**(CONTINUED)**

A simple example should help make all this clear. As shown in Fig. 3.3, there are several stages to hiring and managing an employee's onboarding and benefits. The figure shows the business function (or data domain) responsible for fulfilling each role.

- *Initial onboarding.* In this stage, a person is hired and quite a lot of information is gathered, including their birth date and marital status. The Business Data Steward (or data domain) representing Benefits is responsible for the definition, valid values, and business rules around these business data elements. However, the Operational Data Steward is responsible for inputting the data correctly. The system into which the data is input may also be considered an Operational Data Steward since it will be enforcing the data entry rules such as (for example) the birth date being a valid date for which the employee's age falls within a certain range.
- *Report to work.* When the new employee reports to work on the first day, documentation must be provided (in most countries) of the right to work in that country. In the United States, this is referred to as "I9 documentation." In this example, both the Business Data Steward and the Operational Data Steward come from Recruiting. That is because Recruiting is responsible for the definitions and other metadata surrounding the business data elements needed to prove the right to work. In addition, Recruiting is responsible for receiving those documents from the employee *and entering the information accurately into the system.*
- *Life Change Event.* As things change in the employee's life (called a "life change event") additional data may be needed. For example, if the employee gets married, their marital status needs to be updated, and information about the beneficiary spouse (including birth date) must also be collected. Again, it is Benefits who is responsible for specifying and understanding the business data elements. However, in this example, the employee provides the data, and the Human Resources Shared Services Group is responsible for collecting, validating, and updating this information—and, thus, both are Operational Data Stewards.

## LAYING OUT A DATA STEWARDSHIP RACI MATRIX

As you develop the duties, processes, and breadth of your Data Stewardship effort, it can be helpful to develop a RACI (responsible, accountable, consulted, and informed) matrix. A sample is shown in Table 3.1. As with any RACI matrix, the processes are listed down the left side, and the various roles (such as Business Data Steward) are listed across the top. For a given role in a process, the appropriate

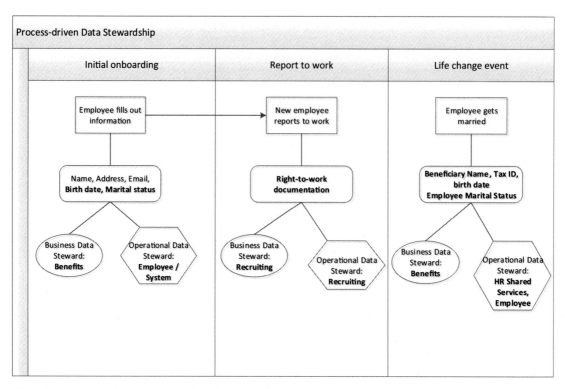

**Process-driven Data Stewardship**

| Initial onboarding | Report to work | Life change event |
|---|---|---|
| Employee fills out information | New employee reports to work | Employee gets married |
| Name, Address, Email, Birth date, Marital status | Right-to-work documentation | Beneficiary Name, Tax ID, birth date Employee Marital Status |
| Business Data Steward: **Benefits** / Operational Data Steward: **Employee / System** | Business Data Steward: **Recruiting** / Operational Data Steward: **Recruiting** | Business Data Steward: **Benefits** / Operational Data Steward: **HR Shared Services, Employee** |

■ **FIGURE 3.3** Illustrating the difference between the Business Data Steward and the Operational Data Steward.

letter (R, A, C, and I) is noted at the intersecting cell. There can be only a single value of "A" (accountable) for any row.

The value of the RACI matrix is that it clarifies who does what—and who is responsible or accountable for ensuring a task/process is completed. What you'll notice about the sample is that it contains a lot of processes—and the list of processes is added to periodically as the various roles associated with Data Stewardship engage in more efforts. For example, as you'll see in Chapter 7, The Important Roles of Data Stewards, Business Data Stewards are often involved in many different types of efforts, including data quality improvement, valid value harmonization, and privacy. The sample RACI includes some of that, though not everything. For example, the tasks and roles involved in MDM are not included in this RACI matrix, but would need to be added if your enterprise is involved in MDM and include the Business Data Stewards in that effort. Of course, your RACI matrix is likely to have the responsibilities laid out differently—it seems like every enterprise does things a bit differently.

**Table 3.1** A Sample RACI Matrix

| Process | Business Data Steward | Technical Data Steward | Business System Owner | Exec Steering Committee | Enterprise Data Steward | Data Quality Analyst | Data Governance Manager | Data Governor | Compliance Analyst |
|---|---|---|---|---|---|---|---|---|---|
| Write policies | | | | A | | | R | | |
| Approve policies | I | | I | R, A | | | I | | |
| Write procedures | C | | | R, A | | | | | |
| Train Bus Data Stewards | C | | | R, A | | | | | |
| Choose Data Governors | | | | R, A | | | C | I | |
| Choose Data Stewards | I | | | | I | | C | R, A | |
| Assign ownership of BDE | R, A | | | | C | | | | |
| Define DQ rules of BDE | R, A | C | | | | C | | | |
| Identify physical location of BDE | C | C | R | | | A | | | |
| Evaluate DQ Results | R | R | | | | A | | | |
| Formulate remediation of DQ failures | R | C | C | | | A | | | |
| Authorize DQ improvement project | C | C | | A | I | | I | R | |
| Determine harmonization of valid value attributes | R | R | | | A | | | | |
| Assign sensitivity of BDE | R | | | | | | | | A |
| Create classification of Info Security rules | I | | | | | | | | R, A |
| Assign regulated Info security class of BDE | I | | | | | | | | R, A |
| Profile PDE and assemble results | | R | | | I | R, A | | | |

A, Accountable; BDE, business data element; C, consulted; DQ, data quality; I, informed; PDE, physical data element; R, responsible.

## SUMMARY

There are a large number of responsibilities that are split up among the various types of Data Stewards as well as the Enterprise Data Steward and the Data Stewardship Council.

The Enterprise Data Steward leads the stewardship effort, and, thus, has some leadership responsibilities. The Business Data Stewards bear primary responsibility for the data owned by their business function or the Data Domain Council they are a part of, are supported with some of the "hands on" work by the Operational Data Stewards, and depend on the Technical Data Stewards for technical information. In addition, the Data Stewards have responsibilities as a team (the Data Stewardship Council).

# Chapter 4

# Implementing Data Stewardship

## INTRODUCTION

As you begin to put together your Data Stewardship effort there are some things you need to find out, much like surveying the land before deciding what to build on it. The first thing is to get the word out on what Data Stewardship is and find your organization champions who will help you drive it. You also need to understand how your business is organized, ascertain who owns data, and who just uses what others own (stakeholders). Finally, there needs to be a determination made about whether you are going to approach the implementation via the direct interaction of Business Data Stewards representing each business function, or (as explained in Chapter 11: Governing and Stewarding Your Data Using Data Domains), implement data domains that logically group business data elements and have Business Data Stewards from the business functions making joint decisions about the data in that data domain. As explained in Chapter 11, Governing and Stewarding Your Data Using Data Domains, there are advantages and disadvantages to using data domains, the primary disadvantage being that success requires a more mature organization, ideally with some experience in Data Governance. Because of this need for maturity and experience in Data Governance, many organizations begin with business function–driven Data Stewardship and switch to data domain–driven Data Stewardship after establishing a functioning Data Governance effort.

In addition to determining the organization structures, there is the very important task of finding out what resources the enterprise already has. For example, a survey of the data analyst community might uncover a data dictionary that someone put together, a set of data quality specifications that people are using to ensure the data supports their needs, and even a set of tools in IT that can be leveraged for Data Stewardship. These tools might even be just sitting idle.

> **NOTE**
>
> For business function–driven Data Stewardship, the business functions which own data will need to supply Business Data Stewards who then determine and work with their stakeholders. For data domain–driven Data Stewardship, owning business functions and stakeholder business functions will need to supply Business Data Stewards who work together in the Data Domain Council.

### THE MEANING OF DATA OWNERSHIP

Data "ownership" means several things. First of all, it means that the owning business function is largely responsible for establishing the

*(Continued)*

Data Stewardship. DOI: https://doi.org/10.1016/B978-0-12-822132-7.00004-8

**(CONTINUED)**

meaning (definition) and business rules (such as creation, usage, and data quality rules) for the data. That is, the owning the business function is responsible for establishing the metadata for the data it owns. I say "largely" because the business function that owns the data must take into account the needs of all the stakeholders. If you have implemented data domain–driven Data Stewardship (see Chapter 11: Governing and Stewarding Your Data Using Data Domains), the business function should have a lead role (and most often supplies the Lead Data Steward) for the data in the data domain that contains that data. The data domain should also have participation from Business Data Stewards representing the business functions that are stakeholders.

It also means that decisions about changing the metadata are the sole responsibility of the owning business function (for business function–driven Data Stewardship) or a combined effort of the data domain to which the data is associated. Finally, data ownership means that maintaining the quality of the owned data is the responsibility of the owning business function.

## CHAMPIONING AND COMMUNICATING DATA STEWARDSHIP

One of the most important things you need to do to ensure the success of Data Stewardship is to get the word out that it exists, what it means, and why it is important. The reasons for this are fairly straightforward. The Business Data Stewards are highly knowledgeable about their data (or should be), but no one can know everything or be everywhere at once. Especially in a large company, there are many data analysts, and some may have information the Business Data Steward lacks. If the data analysts (and other data users) are aware of Data Stewardship and how it operates, as well as who the Business Data Stewards are, then they can:

- *Bring up matters or data issues to the appropriate people.* In some companies this may even mean having the data analysts open their own issues in the Issue Log (see Chapter 6: Practical Data Stewardship).
- *Offer solutions and known work-arounds for data issues.*
- *Make available data dictionaries, lists of valid values, queries, data quality specifications, and other artifacts that have been useful to them.*
- *Advise people to contact the Data Stewardship function when the analyst believes that a Data Stewardship procedure is not being*

*followed.* A good example of a data analyst stepping in was the incident where an insurance data analyst who had sat in one of our sessions heard that one project was planning to redefine the business data element "Close Ratio" because they didn't feel the current definition was accurate. That analyst advised the project lead that she needed to contact the Business Data Steward, and provided the name of that person. The Business Data Steward then worked with the group to figure out what the shortcomings were, and ended up renaming (to "Unique Quote to Close Ratio") and redefining the business data element by adding more specificity to the definition. In addition, several addition data elements (such as "Agent Unique Quote to Close Ratio") were defined and added to the Business Glossary as well.

## The Data Stewardship Message

The first step in communicating and championing Data Stewardship is to be prepared to talk about it to anyone who will listen. This requires a consistent message about its value, your vision, and what Data Stewardship consists of. You also need to be prepared to answer the common questions that everyone will have, such as:

- How does this affect *me*? This question often has multiple parts, such as what do you expect me to start doing, start doing differently, or stop doing. Put another way, what is the cost to me (change is always looked at as a cost).
- What is in it for me? That is, what benefit do I get from changing my ways?
- Who are you, and why should I listen to you?

The Data Stewardship message should push the ideas of metadata (definitions, derivations, creation and usage business rules) and improvement of data quality. In addition, the message must stress that data needs knowledgeable and acknowledged decision makers. To put it another way, Data Stewardship needs three central components:

- Documented, comprehensible knowledge about data (metadata).
- Cultivation of knowledge about data for the purpose of getting more value out of data (data quality).
- A framework for making decisions about data (Data Governance).

You also need various versions of your message, from a set of sound bites all the way up to full presentations. Fig. 4.1 summarizes this "pyramid" of communication.

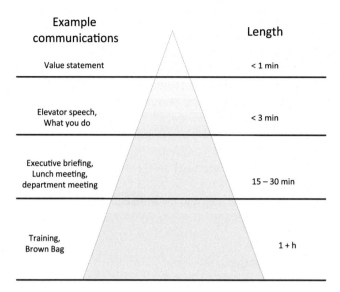

■ **FIGURE 4.1** Communications come in various sizes, as shown on the "Communication Pyramid."

The various-length presentations are useful under the following circumstances:

- *Under a minute*: When you have very little time, it is best to focus on a value statement—how you are going to improve the enterprise, preferably in ways that matter to the people you are talking to. Done correctly, this can pique someone's interest enough to allow you to have more of their time.
- *Under 3 minutes*: This is the classic "elevator speech" in which you need to get your point across very quickly. You need to be prepared to tell an executive or other important person enough of what you do and why it is valuable to pique their interest. My favorite example was the day I got on an actual elevator with the new COO. When he asked me what I did, I managed to tell him enough (including how it would impact his favorite initiative) by the time the doors opened on the fifth floor that he asked me get on his calendar for a half hour so he could hear more.
- *15–30 minutes*: While the "elevator speech" must of necessity be delivered extemporaneously, these longer presentations are often better done with a few slides that you can leave behind. They are typically presented in executive briefings, short lunch meetings, or meetings of the direct reports to executives. For example, I was invited in to talk to the direct reports of the Executive VP of

Insurance Services to explain to them why they should appoint resources to support Data Governance and Data Stewardship, as well as support an internal metadata definitions project that some of their analysts wanted to do (which Data Stewardship could then leverage). I started with a brief rundown of the overall goals of Data Governance, followed by what Data Stewardship was and the importance of it, mentioning that it required assigned stewards from the business. I then finished by noting how many of their key initiatives would benefit from a strong understanding of their data, which tied directly to the metadata initiative. Of course, being able to present this information required some research into what the members of the audience considered important (the key initiatives).

- *1 hour and up*: Longer presentations start to move into the territory of training, presenting material at a level and depth needed by participants in the Data Stewardship and Data Governance programs. For example, a one-hour presentation on Data Stewardship should be standard delivery fare for new Data Governors so they understand the role of the data stewards in the overall process. Such training is critical because the Data Governors appoint the Business Data Stewards and must understand their duties and the type of person needed. "Brown bag" presentations are often close to an hour in length, and the presentations given to the IT developers were 1.5 hours long. In many companies, people who attend these presentations are given educational credit for their attendance.

Finally, you can make use of the regular communications vehicles that your company provides. These may include newsletters and various informational websites. A good communications plan (discussed at length in Chapter 6: Practical Data Stewardship) should include all these types of communication vehicles.

## Preparing the Data Stewardship Message

As part of communicating about Data Stewardship, you'll be making presentations to a variety of different groups, including:

- Executives, both from business and IT.
- Managers who tend to have roles as Data Governors or to whom the Business Data Stewards report functionally.
- Business Data Stewards.
- Subject Matter experts, both from business and IT.

It is important to prepare for these presentations, including taking these steps:

- Identify the important message(s) that you want to deliver. One of those messages will be to address the value that Data Stewardship brings, including how your audience will benefit from the effort. These value statements will be different depending on the audience, but any audience will be looking for this information to understand why they should participate, cooperate, and collaborate with the effort.
- Identify your audience. As I'm sure you're aware, the various audiences will require "tuning" on the level of detail, and their focus will be different as well. For example, executives tend to focus on the affects to the enterprise or subsidiaries, whereas Business Data Stewards and subject matter experts are focused on what is needed from them individually.
- Identify how long you will have to present. Clearly you'll need to pace the presentation differently, adjust the level of detail in the verbal presentation as well as the number of slides, and strive to finish within the allotted time.
- Customize the message for the audience. These variations will occur not only due to the type of audience and the time, but also the area of the company that the audience works in (see the sidebar "Customizing the Message").

---

**PRACTICAL ADVICE**

"Elevator speeches" are hard because you need to grab the subject's attention in a short time. One piece of good advice is to look for the "universal truth" that relates to what you do and how that matters to your target. When you find the universal truth that connects you, you'll usually find the persuasive message you want to relay. For example (the universal truth is underlined):

"You know how everyone agrees that we must carefully manage our data and ensure its quality is sufficient for all the things we want to use it for? That's what I help the company to do by working with the business and IT to create and run an organization dedicated to that purpose. My name is David Plotkin. I'm a Data Governance Manager."

---

**CUSTOMIZING THE MESSAGE**

One key tenet of effectively communicating anything—including Data Stewardship—is to customize your message for the audience. Customizing the message was illustrated in "The Data Stewardship message" section, specifically about the 15–30 minute message. Customizing the message

*(Continued)*

**(CONTINUED)**

for the audience is especially important when discussing Data Stewardship because Data Stewardship is often a foreign concept to many people. In addition, different audiences will have different relationships to Data Stewardship and thus different levels of detail are needed. Before talking to business people, take time to find out about the initiatives underway or being considered by that business function, and to understand how the success of such initiatives depends on data. Also pay particular attention to pain that the business is feeling with their data. That is, research what problems the business function has with its data, and ask what data issues have gotten in the way of their success in the past. If you focus on how Data Stewardship will help drive key initiatives or has the potential to relieve some of the data pain that they are feeling, it makes the message far more effective because it is directly relevant. Speaking about the relationship of Data Stewardship to their initiatives also shows that you cared enough to find out about their business and didn't just deliver a canned presentation. For example, in the case of the insurance executive's meeting, they were struggling with various reports that showed differing amounts for what appeared to be the same calculated result for paid claims. I discovered (and presented) that the basic problem was that each report defined and calculated this number differently, that there was no formal accountability for either the report or the definition/calculation, and no mechanism for fixing these issues—unless, of course, they participated in the Data Stewardship effort. I pointed out that the Data Warehouse they were building would have the same problems unless they took the time to define and get consensus on their terms and rules. I also told them that if they would implement Data Stewardship procedures, they would have a structured way to determine what dimensions and facts were needed, and ensure that all of the facts were defined and calculated in a consistent way—and documented in an accessible and shared repository.

Something else to keep in mind is that when presenting to IT (especially developers) there is a huge opportunity to gain an active and enthusiastic community of gatekeepers. Developers often feel the pain of being given requirements that lack the information they need to do a good job of locating and using the right data, as well as checking its validity. If you provide the developers with the tenets of doing proper Data Stewardship, they can push back when they are handed half-baked requirements and they can involve the Data Governance organization to help improve the efficiency of finding and using the right data, as well as coding the new requirements. It is the equivalent of the "old days" when I was managing the data modeling group at a large pharmacy chain. We maintained the logical and physical models, and generated the DDL to create and modify the database structures. Of course, it was important that the database structure be in synch with the models. We enlisted the aid of the Database

*(Continued)*

**(CONTINUED)**

Administrators (DBAs), who were often given requests by developers to add a column here and there. This was a pain for the DBAs and caused all sorts of deployment issues because these changes had to be deployed to over 400 stores. It also often led to creating columns that already existed or were created in the wrong table because the developers didn't understand the structure of the data. The DBAs then had to undo their work. The DBAs worked with us and became the gatekeepers of the database—and would refer any request for new columns or other database structural changes to our group. We would work with the developer to understand the need, and if it was legitimate, we would change the model, generate the new DDL and hand it off to the DBA for implementation. It was a beautiful example of teamwork, not only protecting the integrity of the database (and the models) but also getting the notoriously over-worked DBAs out of the business of hand-coding DDL for these small changes.

## GAINING SUPPORT FROM ABOVE AND BELOW

It is really imperative to have support for the Data Stewardship initiative from both management (above) and staff (below). The support from management should be fairly obvious—as with most efforts that span the enterprise, there will be some resistance, and management support is needed to make it clear that ignoring the effort (or worse, actively opposing it) is not ok. In addition, it usually takes clear and obvious high-level support to get employees to believe that the organization is very serious about the implementation of Data Stewardship. Further (as will be discussed in Chapter 5: Training the Business Data Stewards), Data Stewardship often involves cultural changes, and only the executives can make those happen. Finally, if the rewards and incentive system is going to be adjusted to encourage active participation in Data Stewardship, high-level management support is needed for that too.

Support from staff is less obvious but just as important. The ideal situation is to build a ground swell of support in the organization, and that requires winning the hearts and minds of the data analysts who use the data and feel the pain. That pain—which stems from the lack of definitions and standardized derivations, poor or uncertain data quality, and no guidance or rules for creation and usage of the data—serves as incentive to the data analyst community to participate and support the Business Data Stewards. Much like the developers, the data analysts can be your eyes and ears throughout the organization, and can bring data-related issues to the Business Data Stewards for a solution. The data analysts directly benefit from better defined data, better quality data (including rules for what constitutes good quality data), and data with rigorous rules about creation and usage. Make them aware of this benefit and they will be your allies. Fail to do so, and they can end up looking on the Data Stewardship efforts as more overhead and a roadblock to getting their work done.

Support from below can provide you with champions of Data Stewardship throughout the organization. These champions will help you get out your messages of success. If the data analysts are happy with the improvements in data quality and how the data is used, they trumpet those successes. That is, they tell their colleagues how these new techniques delivered value and recommend that the Business Data Stewards be engaged whenever there are data issues, including uncertain meaning and perceived poor quality.

---

**PRACTICAL ADVICE**

If you're good at getting out the message about the value of Data Stewardship and how important it is for the data analysts to participate and support it, you may find yourself in the position of "overwhelming demand," with many data analysts bringing multiple issues to be dealt with. This situation can develop rapidly in organizations with a lot of data problems. At the first glance having people bring a multitude of data problems to the Business Data Stewards might appear to be a good thing, but that is not necessarily true. If the Data Stewardship effort is overwhelmed, and there start to be long delays in dealing with issues that are brought up by the data analysts, the data analysts may get frustrated and stop participating because they don't see any results. What to do? The first thing is to have the Business Data Stewards prioritize the issues. That usually involves having the Business Data Stewards talk to the analysts who raised the issue in the first place to:

- Determine the impact that the issue is having on the data analyst's work and how important work is to the business.
- Get the data analyst's understanding of the scope and work effort needed to resolve the issue. It is even possible for the Business Data Stewards to recruit the data analyst's help in getting the issues resolved. That is, if the issue is important enough, the load can be spread to include the people most adversely affected by it.

---

## UNDERSTANDING THE ORGANIZATION

Organizations have a structure, typically represented as an organization chart. They also have a culture which affects how decisions are made. It is imperative that you have a good understanding of both of these facets of an organization in order to set up and run an effective Data Stewardship organization.

## The Organization Structure

Since Data Governance and Data Stewardship are all about caring for the data and making and enforcing decisions about the data, it is critical to understand which business functions own data, and what data they own. It is also important to understand how the organization makes decisions and at what levels of the organization those decisions are made. Understanding this is critical so that participants in Data Governance (such as the Executive Steering Committee, Data Governance Board, and Data Stewardship Council) can be selected from the right decision-making levels.

The first step in sorting out the organization's decision-making levels is to understand how the organization is structured. The structure can be relatively straightforward, as illustrated in Fig. 4.2.

The complexity of the organization chart is not necessarily a function of the size of the company. Instead, it tends to vary by the number of business lines the company is in, though size often correlates with a large number of lines of business and how many layers of management the organization has in place. For example, one large company manufacturers engines and also runs a major TV broadcast network. Such companies often treat each of their subsidiaries as separate entities (which may have independent Data Governance implementations), with just a limited scope of overall corporate Data Governance to support regulatory-mandated reporting of financial (and other) results.

When building up a Data Stewardship function, however, you need to look past the strict structure of the business units and focus on the business *functions*. How do business units differ from business functions? A business unit is a structural part of the organization, that is, a division or a

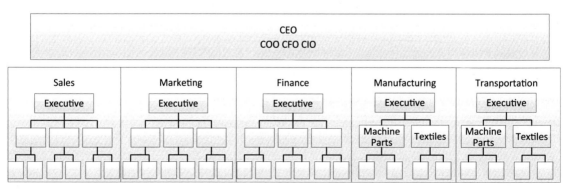

■ FIGURE 4.2 A fairly straightforward organization chart.

department in the overall company. A business unit often has its own budget and management structure as well. On the other hand, a business function is an area of the business responsible for the execution of a particular set of business responsibilities. On the face of it, they may sound the same, but they are not. Business units change frequently through reorganizations. I worked in one company that had a membership department and an insurance department. In less than a year, the two departments were bundled together into a "Product" department, and then broken apart again. This kind of fluidity can play havoc with the assignment of Business Data Stewards if based on the business units because each restructuring may change the make-up of the Data Stewardship Council. On the other hand, business functions rarely change unless the basic nature of the business changes (the company gets into a new business area it had not been in before). If you base the Business Data Stewards on business function, they don't have to change even when reorganizations occur. That is, basing the Business Data Stewards on business function rather than business unit makes Data Stewardship more stable. For example, the membership and insurance Business Data Stewards did not change as a result of the aforementioned reshuffling of the company's departments.

Focusing on business functions means that restructuring is largely irrelevant. For example, if the transportation department for textiles was suddenly reorganized to be under manufacturing for textiles, the transportation Business Data Steward(s) wouldn't change because the ownership of the transportation data still resided in the transportation business function.

Basing stewardship on business function also provides more flexibility. For example, Fig. 4.2 shows a company that has two main lines of business, manufacturing machine parts and textiles. While the data around these business areas are likely to be quite different, notice that the company also has a Transportation division which is also split into departments for Machine Parts and Textiles. But warehouses are warehouses, and trucks are trucks, so the data there is likely to be quite similar and the company could well benefit from having common definitions and quality requirements across the two departments.

**PRACTICAL ADVICE**

Even complex organizations tend to have fairly standardized functions, such as Finance, Sales, and Marketing. These are good places to start a Data Stewardship effort. First of all, Sales and Marketing are often able to quantify the pain they suffer from poor data. For example, a large insurance company marketing organization paid out $24,000 each month to an outside firm to standardize addresses and recognize when two of pieces of mail were going to the same person (no Customer Master Data Management existed). In addition, a sample count revealed that they also paid out about $3000 per month mailing to outdated addresses. The business and technical data stewards for this data worked together to:

- Add enforcement at data collection to allow only valid addresses.
- Purchase outside data on valid addresses.
- Perform address standardization on existing addresses.

The result was that in just five months of eliminating these costs, the company had earned back the money that had been invested in improving the data.

Finance is another good place to start a Data Stewardship effort because the Finance department not only has standardized definitions and calculations for external reporting but is also used to having rigorous governance of its data. The financial analysts often have the authority to force the reporting groups within the company to standardize and improve the data being reported. Rigorous governance is such an integral part of Finance that in many organizations the Data Governance function may fall under the Chief Financial Officer (CFO).

As shown in Fig. 4.3, a single overall business function may have multiple Business Data Stewards as well. A large and complex business area (such as Insurance Services) may handle several categories of data (such as Actuarial, Underwriting, and Claims) and often requires one or more Business Data Stewards from each because no one person is familiar

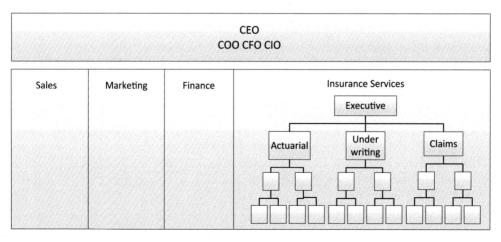

■ **FIGURE 4.3** A single business function may have multiple stewards, such as this example for an Insurance company.

with all three sets of this widely disparate data. Again, the point is that the organization chart is not a strait jacket when it comes to Data Stewardship, and is often not the best way to designate Business Data Stewards.

Things start getting more complicated when an organization is highly complex, or has the same function occurring in multiple subsidiaries, as shown in Fig. 4.4. An organization structure like this can often grow out of a vigorous "growth by acquisition" strategy. For example, creating accounts takes place in all three business functions, and in this particular case, the accounts were extremely similar and followed the same rules, such as that an account cannot exist without an identified customer. When this kind of organizational structure exists, it invites different business units to adopt different definitions and business rules for what amounts to the same types of data. In such cases, it is even more critical to have Business Data Stewards from each business function to ensure that consistency is enforced where it is likely to be beneficial.

In this example, a large bank grew by acquiring other banks, and keeping systems and business functions that were superior to the existing systems and functions. This did, however, lead to the odd situation where first mortgages

**NOTE**

In theory, a Business Data Steward can come from any level of the organization, as they are designated as having the authority as well as roles and responsibilities detailed in Chapter 3, Stewardship Roles and Responsibilities. But it is often advisable for the Business Data Stewards to be chosen from the ranks of people who already have some decision-making authority, as long as those people meet the requirements for being an effective Business Data Steward. Thus there is a balance between someone who knows a lot about the data (because of their experience regardless of whom they report to) and someone who has direct power to make decisions because of whom they report to.

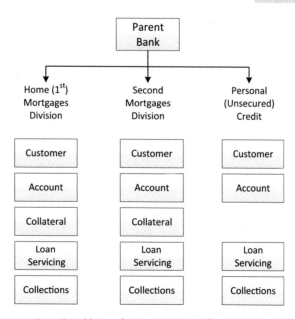

■ **FIGURE 4.4** An organization where very similar or identical business functions take place in different subsidiaries, which leads to data overlap.

were issued from one subsidiary (and system), second mortgages were issued from another, and personal credit (which has no collateral) was issued by a third. As you can probably imagine, the vast majority of the metadata that described the data used by the three systems was (or should have been) the same, yet issuing a combined first and second mortgage was next to impossible. Each business function owned the data it produced, and the only way to move toward standardization was by joint ownership. The three Business Data Stewards worked closely together to reach a consensus on meaning and business rules. A side benefit of this arrangement was that the three stewards were able to determine the data quality and find quality gaps between the systems. Close coordination between the Business Data Stewards also enabled the matching of customer/account holders across the systems. This last was possible because in a banking environment, SSN (social security number) or other government-issued identifier was a valid identifier for the account holders and was always (well, almost always) collected when the account was opened. Of course, if the enterprise has done master data management on its customers, having a master customer is possible even without an official identifier—provided the quality of the data is sufficient (see Chapter 7: The Important Roles of Data Stewards, for more on this).

Establishing Data Stewardship gets even more complicated when the company is divided up by country or region, each with different regulations, languages, and customs. A sample of such an organization structure is shown in Fig. 4.5.

The typical implementation in a situation where each country, region, or subsidiary company operates with a great deal of autonomy is that each of these entities has to establish its own Data Governance and Data

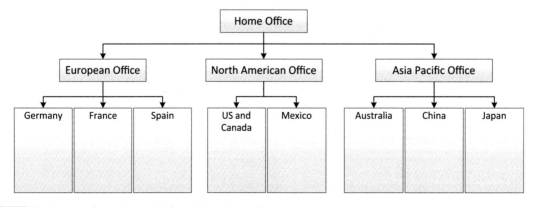

■ **FIGURE 4.5** A more complex organization chart for a multinational corporation.

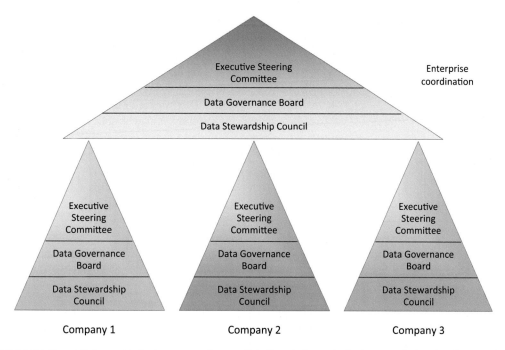

■ **FIGURE 4.6** Data Stewardship for a multinational company usually must add the Enterprise layer to handle the common business data elements and management of data that must be common.

Stewardship in a way that may be mostly independent of the other entities. Once this occurs, an international Data Governance organization needs to look across the key business data elements and focus on those for which there is a solid business reason to have a common definition and business rules across the entire enterprise. To achieve the goal of having commonality across key business data elements, it may be necessary to modify the metadata (such as the definition) in each entity to match the definition required at the corporate level. Another solution may be to define the set of common business data elements and a derivation rule from each entity's data to the common data. A Data Stewardship organization to support largely autonomous companies is shown in Fig. 4.6.

## The Culture of an Organization

It is important to understand the organizational culture if you want to be successful at implementing a Data Stewardship program because Data Stewardship almost always requires significant cultural change. This is especially true if you have been hired in from outside to implement Data

Stewardship. The rigorous establishment of decision rights for data is often a new experience for the organization as a whole as well as for those that use the data. So is establishing and enforcing processes for dealing with data issues. The data analysts may consider it normal to have endless discussions to reach consensus, or to simply do what they please with the data. Data Stewardship changes all this. People have to perform differently and behave differently than they did previously. It may be quite a shock for the data analysts to discover that the Business Data Stewards have the authority to state what the data that is owned by the Steward's business function (or data domain) means, how it is calculated, and what the quality, creation, and usage business rules are. That is, the concept of data decision-making may be foreign to the corporate culture, and that has to change. Changed behavior has cultural impacts. This is especially true in companies where achieving consensus is a requirement for every decision. While Business Data Stewards should try to get people to work together, understand data in similar ways, and achieve consensus with their stakeholders, ultimately the Business Data Stewards are responsible for the making recommendations and decisions, whether consensus is achieved or not.

Of course, you aren't going to be able to change the culture right away, nor would you want to. You need to understand the current state before trying to make changes. Analyzing the current culture really helps to understand where issues will arise. In companies where decision making by designated individuals (who may be peers of the people they are making decisions *for*) is inconsistent with the company's culture, executive support is even more important. The company's leaders must put out the message that this new way of doing the "business of data" is accepted and supported by upper management, and is in the best interests of the enterprise. This same message must be repeated by the Business Data Stewards and by the Data Governance Program Office whenever there is pushback from people in the organization.

## ORGANIZING THE DATA STEWARDS

Business Data Stewards are organized into a Data Stewardship Council, which works with the Data Governance Board, subject matter experts and stakeholders to make decisions about data. Fig. 4.7 shows the relationship between the Executive Steering Committee, Data Governance Board, and Data Stewardship Council. The Data Governance Program Office is shown across the bottom. The members of the Data Governance Program Office are recommended to be part of the business (rather than IT), and to report to the sponsoring business executive.

**NOTE**

For business function—based Data Stewardship, the Data Stewardship Council is comprised of the Business Data Stewards representing the business functions. For data domain—based Data Stewardship as explained in Chapter 11, Governing and Stewarding Your Data Using Data Domains, the Data Stewardship Council is comprised of the Lead Data Stewards (who also have the role of Business Data Stewards representing their business function) from the Data Domain Councils. The key point is that regardless of which way you set up your Data Stewardship function, the Data Stewardship Council is needed to provide a mechanism for collaboration.

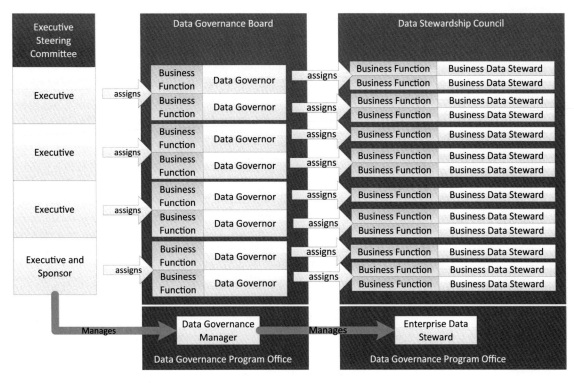

**■ FIGURE 4.7** The interaction between the various levels of the Data Governance participants and organization.

## FIGURING OUT YOUR STARTING POINT

As you kick off a Data Stewardship effort, you are going to be focusing on data, metadata, improving data quality, clear and repeatable processes, and implementing a robust toolset for documentation and information. The good news is that you rarely have to start from scratch; there is a good chance that people who regularly work with the data have been collecting this sort of useful information for their own use. If you can locate this information, you'll have a body of work to build from.

### Figuring Out What You've Got: The Data

To govern and steward your data, you are going to have to know about the following items:

● *What data you have.* Initially, this information will be more in terms of data groupings (e.g., Finance, Sales, Customer, Product, and so on) than specific data elements. And while you will quickly reach the point of stewarding individual business data elements, it is still very useful to have an idea of what groupings of data are important to your enterprise. Understanding the groupings not only will help you know which business functions should be supplying Business Data Stewards, but also (see Chapter 11: Governing and Stewarding Your Data Using Data Domains) provide guidance on what data domains you will need.

- *Where the data comes from.* Data doesn't just sit in one place, it flows through the enterprise. This flow, known as the "Information Chain," includes capture (via outside files or source systems), movement and transformation (via extract, transform, and load, or ETL), storage (in intermediate databases and operational data stores), summary and aggregation (in data warehouses, data marts, and data lakes) and being used for decision-making (via business intelligence). Of course, there is not just one Information Chain in an enterprise, and the chains may branch off in varied (and often complex) ways. A simple information chain is shown in Fig. 4.8.
- *What parts of the organization are responsible for source data capture, ETL, and reporting?* Typically, various IT groups are responsible for "chunks" of the Information Chain, including the source systems, ETL,

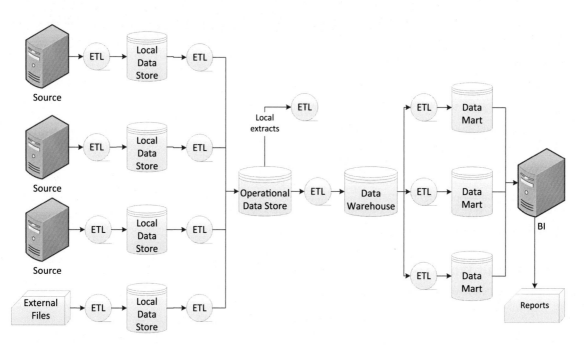

■ **FIGURE 4.8** Information flows through an enterprise in the "Information Chain."

data stores, and the Business Intelligence reporting environments. These IT groups (along with Enterprise Architecture) can help you figure out how the data flows, what occurs in the various source systems, where files are consumed or produced for outside sources, and the key reports produced (which will help you understand what data is most important to the organization). Knowing who they are and establishing a good working relationship with them will go a long way towards understanding the data and how it is used.

## BUSINESS PROCESSES AND THE INFORMATION CHAIN

The Information Chain is in place to support the flow of business data for business processes. Understanding these business processes is important in order to make sense of the technical systems and processes in the Information Chain because the technical systems and processes support the business processes. That is, without the business processes, there is no reason to even have the Information Chain. When analyzing the purpose and details of an Information Chain, the first step is to understand the business process supported by the Information Chain. Oftentimes, Information Chains linger long after the business process has changed or been discontinued—and if that happens, the Information Chain needs to be modified or eliminated altogether.

An example of the relationship between the Information Chain and Business Processes may help. Fig. 4.9 shows an Information Chain (in the top box) and the Business Processes supported by the Information Chain (in the bottom box). This example—which is based on writing an insurance policy—shows how the processes necessary to assess the risk, offer a policy, sell ("bind") the policy, and report on what has been accomplished line up to the various systems and infrastructure (such as source systems, as well as a Data Warehouse and Data Marts) to support the needs of the business. Note also how the business process flow often branches off to other business processes (such as the Policy Maintenance Process), which are themselves supported by an Information Chain. In this example, the business process makes a distinction between creating a policy and servicing/ maintaining it, even though the same system is used for both.

## PRACTICAL ADVICE

In an enterprise of any complexity, you are not going to get all the information related to the flow of data through the organization at once. However, you can focus on the data and Information Chain for major areas of the business on a one-by-one basis, and come up to speed

**NOTE**

Once Business Data Stewards have been designated, a significant portion of their job is to create and manage metadata. When new sources of metadata are discovered (e.g., another analyst offers a spreadsheet of definitions) the new sources should be referred to the appropriate Business Data Stewards.

incrementally. The priority of digging into the available data will often be dictated by high-visibility projects and issues. Also, don't forget that Enterprise Architecture often maintains diagrams that illustrate various Information Chains and how they interact. Enterprise Architecture may also be able to provide a good high-level schematic of the enterprise as a whole, which is crucial before starting on any given piece of the overall Information Chain.

## Figuring Out What You've Got: The Metadata

Metadata is critical to a Data Stewardship effort. In fact, in many ways "Data Stewardship" is also "Metadata Stewardship." Much of what you need to discover and document about your data is its metadata. The chances are good (because metadata is so useful to the analysts making use of the data) that those same analysts have collected the metadata they need in various ways, and documented the metadata in everything from home-built desktop databases to spreadsheets. The key is to find the metadata, collect it, and validate it with the Business Data Stewards.

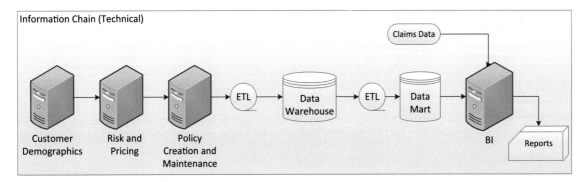

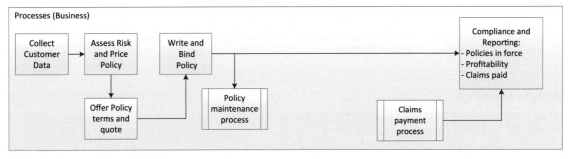

■ **FIGURE 4.9** An Information Chain exists to support Business Processes.

The important parts of finding existing metadata include:

- *Finding Definitions.* Many analysts collect data definitions. They usually also collect lists of valid values and their meanings, so that they can evaluate and use the data that consists of code values. Report writers/managers can also be a good source of data definitions. This is because people who receive the reports usually turn to the reporting group whenever they don't understand the report or think that some result looks suspicious or incorrect. Although the people who construct the reports are often initially *not* experts on what the data means, they begin collecting and documenting this information in self-defense so that they can answer the questions that invariably come their way. People who input the data may also understand the data definitions, and, in fact, this is the ideal case. If the people who perform data input understand what they are inputting, they are often the first to become aware that something is not correct in the data.
- *Finding Derivations.* Analysts also collect data derivations, which are rules about how a quantity is calculated or otherwise derived. These rules are often embedded in program code, and thus require a different kind of research and documentation than definitions.
- *Where is the metadata being kept*? Most of the people who collect metadata for their own uses store it away in spreadsheets or something similar. Gathering up copies of these documents, keeping up with the latest versions as they get updated, and cross-indexing between multiple spreadsheets or other tools to locate the duplicates can be a painful task. Ideally you'll want to convince the providers of the metadata to start using a shareable resource (such as a business glossary) and updating that resource via a set of procedures designed to protect the integrity of the metadata. This would eliminate most of the "housekeeping" required to keep current as the metadata changes in all the various tools and documents. The ideal situation is that metadata is kept in a single, enterprise-wide repository, whose use is enforced by the Data Governance Program Office.
- *Is anyone managing and validating the metadata and by what means*? It is often true that the people who are collecting metadata for their own purposes simply jot it down in a spreadsheet (or some other tool). But groups of analysts may discuss and validate the metadata, perhaps to create a single consolidated list of business data elements with definitions for their department. The validation effort usually consists of reaching a consensus, or perhaps asking the person that they all agree is the best expert on the data (sounds like a Business

**DEFINITION**

What is metadata? In her book *Measuring Data Quality For Ongoing Improvement*, Laura Sebastian-Coleman defines metadata: Metadata is usually defined as "data about data" but it would be better defined as explicit knowledge, documented to enable a common understanding of an organization's data, including what the data is intended to represent (definition of terms and business rules), how it effects this representation (data definition, system design, system processes), the limits of that representation (what it does not represent), what happens to it as it moves through processes and systems (provenance, lineage, information chain, and information lifecycle), how data is used and can be used, and how it should not be used.

Data Steward, doesn't it?). In fact, these localized groups of data experts are really silos of Data Stewardship that come to exist within isolated business functions. Discovering these groups can give you a big step up in the formation of enterprise-wide Data Stewardship.

---

**PRACTICAL ADVICE**

At one large bank where I worked, the data analysts across the company could dial into a weekly meeting where data and metadata were discussed. The discussions revolved primarily around what data was available, what it meant, how it was derived, what issues were known, and where it was stored. They could send in questions, and the attendees would provide input and answers. The Enterprise Data Steward attended these meetings and would collect this intelligence, then work with the appropriate Business Data Stewards to find answers, validate the provided information, and get the metadata into the business glossary.

---

- *How is IT tracking its metadata?* Many of the tools that IT uses—including ETL and data profiling tools—produce a considerable amount of metadata. In general, these tools store the metadata internally in some sort of repository. Most modern tools support extracting this metadata into another tool (such as a metadata repository) for use (see Fig. 4.10). More advanced IT departments may indeed go this extra step to make the lineage, data profiling results, and physical database structures available even to those who don't use these tools. But even if your IT department doesn't externalize the metadata, just knowing what tools they use for these purposes will make it more straightforward to get at metadata that is important to use in the Data Stewardship effort.
- *Are there any data dictionaries for legacy systems available?* One of the most difficult tasks to accomplish is to understand the meaning and usage of data in older systems. These systems often form the backbone of corporate processing, but just as often the people who understood them have long since retired or left the company. Any documentation you can find, even if it is out of date, can help with the understanding of the data captured, used, and stored in these systems. Data dictionaries from older systems often reside in printed binders, stashed away on some dusty shelf, so it may be a bit of treasure hunt to locate them. Generally, though, it is worth the effort.
- *Does the current project methodology support capture and validation of metadata?* Capturing and validating metadata is a critical part of a

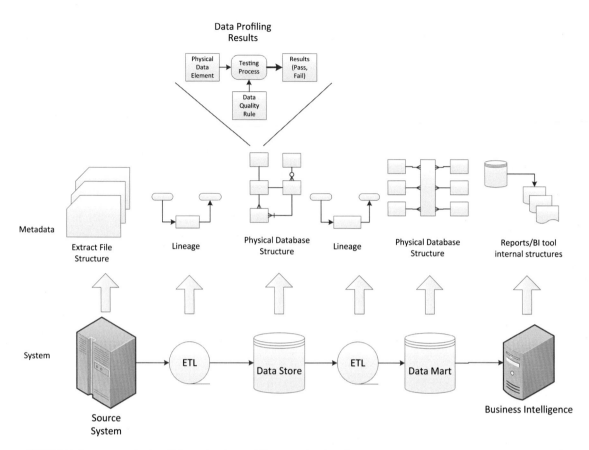

**■ FIGURE 4.10** Extracting metadata from IT data tools make it available to a much wider audience.

project. Even if you can't find documentation on metadata from older systems, ensuring that you capture the metadata as part of projects can start to make up for the lack of documentation. Projects often expose new data to scrutiny, questioning meaning, attempting to ascertain whether the data actually represents what the documentation says it does, and examining the quality of the data to ensure that it can be used for the project's needs. As these investigations proceed, a lot of important metadata is discovered. If the project methodology demands that the metadata be captured and validated, then project documents become an important source of metadata. Ideally the project methodology would capture this information in easily-available form (such as a business glossary), rather than in printed documents that are put in folders and placed on a shelf. Unfortunately

**NOTE**

One of the most important jobs for the Data Governance Program Office is to work with the Project Management Office (PMO) to establish the Data Governance and Data Stewardship deliverables for projects by working with the PMO. Establishing the deliverables includes information such as at what stage of the project the deliverables must be completed, who has sign-off authority, and how the deliverables are to be leveraged for future use. In addition, the project managers must be trained to include the deliverables and budget in their project plans, and call on Data Governance to provide resources to represent the interests of Data Governance on the project (Project Data Stewards).

this level of sophistication is rare in companies that have not already implemented Data Stewardship.

## Figuring Out What You've Got: Data Quality

Improvement of data quality is not only a very important goal of Data Stewardship and Data Governance as a whole, but one of the more important ways of measuring how successful your stewardship effort is. Improving the quality of data so that it becomes more useful and presents less risk to the enterprise can reap huge benefits. One of my favorite stories is from Con-Agra, the huge food (among other things) company. Most shipment is done by loading product onto pallets, and then loading those pallets onto trucks. Not surprisingly, the size of the pallet determines how many pallets can be loaded onto a truck, and the size of the product boxes determines how much product can be loaded onto a pallet. However, the product and pallet size data was of poor quality, which led to the suspicion (as well as the observation) that trucks were not leaving fully loaded. Improving the quality of the pallet size data (by actually measuring and recording the pallet size) and product box dimensions allowed for more efficient loading, enabling 19 trucks to do the work that required 20 trucks previously. That is, every 20th truck was essentially free. The cost-savings benefit dwarfed the cost of improving the data quality.

Since improving Data Quality is so important, it is one of the early tasks that the Business Data Stewards will want to focus on. It is usually not too hard to convince them of this priority, as they live with the pain of poor data quality on a daily basis. The pain includes hunting down data that is of sufficient quality, extracting and "correcting" data to get it up to the required level of quality, or simply not being able to produce the deliverables required. Very often a good starting point for working on data quality in Data Stewardship is to find out why analysts are extracting data into their own computers from source systems or official data stores. Quite frequently the reason is to manipulate the data in ways the analysts have deemed necessary to get the quality up to the level needed.

To get started on the data quality aspects of Data Stewardship, you need to ask the following questions:

- *Is anyone collecting data quality rules, and where are they documented?* Data quality rules state what is meant by "good quality data" and will be discussed in much more detail in Chapter 7, The Important Roles of Data Stewards. They can vary from simple (this column must never be null) to highly complex. Although sophisticated data profiling tools can often propose possible data quality rules based on the data itself, it is very important to collect a set of data quality rules from the Business Data Stewards (with help from the Technical Data Stewards) that can be tested against the data. The data quality rules should be placed in a central business rule log or glossary where they can be managed by the Business Data Stewards who work with the Data Quality Analysts. Any time there is a poor match between the data quality rule(s) and the data itself, this can lead to a data quality issue being raised.

- *What data quality issues have been raised and documented?* Data quality issues give a very real sense of where the pain points are in the data picture of the enterprise. Of course just because someone classified an issue as a data quality issue doesn't mean that the Business Data Stewards need to be involved in correcting the issue. For example, I once saw a data quality issue raised because an entire table was empty. And while a big batch of missing data is a "data quality" issue, in fact, the cause was that a job didn't run correctly, and IT needed to correct it. So use a trained eye as you look at "data quality" issues. Once you sift out the issues that are clearly technical (job didn't run, table space was too small, column was missing) you should have content-related issues remaining that need to be addressed by the Business Data Stewards and Data Quality Analysts. You can then categorize these and start examining how often they occur, along with input from the Business Data Stewards and Technical Data Stewards on root causes and impacts to the business. There are a variety of places where data quality issues could be documented, so you'll need to know where to look. Possibilities include:
  - *A real data quality issue log or business glossary.* This is rare unless Data Governance has been implemented and procedures are in place to collect data quality issues and put them only in the log or glossary. As we'll see in Chapter 6, Practical Data Stewardship, the business glossary may be a good place to store data quality issues, as the issues can be related to the data they apply to and the rule that was violated.
  - *The IT issue-tracking tool*, sometimes called a "trouble ticket system." Data quality issues end up here a lot when there is nowhere else to record them. Unfortunately, these issues often get lost among the purely technical issues. In addition, IT often then gets forced into taking responsibility for fixing issues that should belong to the business and require business input.
  - *The QA issue-tracking tool.* Data Quality issues can come up as new discoveries during QA testing of systems. This is especially true if test cases have been written based on the expected data results.

Further, the more competent QA tools can be customized to provide an ideal environment to record data quality issues and track progress and workflow in finding and implementing a solution.

- *Project documentation.* If data quality issues come up as part of a project, they may be recorded in the project documentation. On occasion, projects may be tabled or canceled because the quality of the data is so bad that it simply can't be used for the project's purposes. This may lead to a whole new project to fix the poor-quality data.

- *Are there any projects "in flight" to fix data quality issues?* If poor data quality is making it difficult or impossible for the company to do business the way it wants to, one or more projects may have been initiated to correct the data quality issues. It is very important to locate these projects early in the Data Stewardship effort. The benefit of engaging Data Stewardship on data quality improvement projects is very high. These projects also point directly at data quality issues that are so important (and so high profile) that the company is willing to spend significant amounts of money on them. Helping to enable these projects shows a clear and rapid return on investment (ROI) for the Data Stewardship effort and leads to buy-in from people who might otherwise ignore the effort. In addition, engaging Data Stewardship can help prevent the same data quality issues from occurring again.

- *Does the current project development methodology support capture of data quality rules and issues?* As mentioned previously, projects often expose new data (and old data) to scrutiny, examining the quality of the data to ensure that it can be used to meet the project's goals. As the projects progress, a lot of information about data quality (and lack thereof) is discovered. If the project methodology demands that the data quality rules be captured, validated, and compared to the data (data profiling), then project documents become an important source of both data quality rules and data quality issues. Ideally the project methodology would capture the data quality issue (as a function of the rule violated) in an easily-available form such as a log or the business glossary.

- *Is anyone doing data profiling?* Data profiling consists of examining the contents of a database and providing the findings in a human-readable form. Most data profiling is done using tools designed specifically for that purpose. The tools are quite sophisticated, and can discern possible data quality rules from the data, as well as point out the outliers. For example, the tools might ascertain that a particular column contains only positive numbers formatted as money, or that the contents of a column are unique with just a few exceptions. Most profiling tools also enable you to enter specified data quality rules ("the contents of this column must never be null") and then tell you how often that rule is violated. The point of data profiling is to try and spot data quality issues proactively and analyze those issues. Data profiling requires an environment, as well as the effort to set up the table structures and port the data to the environment. In addition, there is considerable expense for the tool and efforts by both the Business Data Stewards and the Technical Data Stewards to analyze the results. Thus it is not something that is done on a whim. If you discover that data *is* being profiled, it is likely to be important data for which data quality issues are a significant problem. This would therefore be a great place to focus Business Data Steward's data quality improvement efforts.

## Figure Out What You've Got: Processes

Data Stewardship establishes and enforces repeatable processes for managing data. However, even in the absence of a Data Stewardship program, organizations often have already established processes. Finding, documenting, and possibly formalizing these processes—and the business reasons for the processes—can give a Data Stewardship program a jumpstart. For example, one organization has to report its data to a state agency. To avoid having the data rejected by the state agency (which could affect funding for many programs run by the company), the organization instituted a set of over 100 data validation checks on the load to the Data Warehouse. The organization established a set of processes for specifying, creating, and testing new data validation checks, as well as a robust set of business processes (including accountable personnel) for remediating errors that were reported by the checks. The business processes include analyzing the errors to identify the source and root cause, working with the users of the source system to correct the data, training the users in order to prevent future occurrences, and tracking number and distribution of the data errors. As you can see, this process could easily be leveraged by Data Stewardship, and the accountable personnel could even be considered either Business or Operational Data Stewards.

## Figure Out What You've Got: Tools

A full-fledged Data Stewardship effort benefits significantly from a robust toolset. Tools include a Metadata Repository, a Business Glossary, a Data Profiling tool, and some sort of web-based collaboration tool to post issues, handle communications, and so on. Of course, licensing all these tools could be quite expensive, and many Data Stewardship efforts have little or no budget when they first get started.

Before you throw up your hands in despair, talk to the IT people, especially those responsible for software licensing. It is possible that you already have some or all of these tools and not even realize it. For example, at one company where I worked, we had licensed the entire tool suite from a prominent vendor known for their ETL tools. However, it turned out that the suite also included a data profiling tool, a business glossary tool, and even a metadata repository. None of these tools were "best in breed," but we could start using them without any added expense, and some of them were even in production and sitting unused.

Many companies also have Microsoft SharePoint or its equivalent, and use this type of tool to create department websites. Data Stewardship can do the very same thing, again, for little or no cost. It does require a certain amount of expertise to use SharePoint (or equivalent) effectively, but such expertise usually exists in the company if the tool is widely used. We even used a SharePoint list as our starting business glossary. Again, it wasn't the ideal solution due to the limits of the tool, but it was better than a shared spreadsheet!

Another important tool is some variation on a data quality dashboard to show what is being worked on and the level of quality in various data quality dimensions such as timeliness, validity, integrity, completeness, and others. While it is possible to cobble together something out of a spreadsheet and whole bunch of macros, if you already have a business intelligence tool (all of which can generate dashboard-style reports), you can feed the results from data profiling into the BI tool and generate dashboards.

## SUMMARY

There are many steps to getting Data Stewardship going. Understanding your organization and its culture, getting the message out and gaining support, and surveying what resources exist are all tasks you need to undertake at the beginning. But performing them gives you a clear baseline for your efforts from which progress can be measured.

# Chapter 5

# Training the Business Data Stewards

## INTRODUCTION

Data Stewardship does not just happen. It takes people and support for the function. Business Data Stewards are much more effective if they are trained to carry out their responsibilities and tasks. Just as importantly, sustaining Data Stewardship over time requires overall support for the role. When new Business Data Stewards are brought on board, they need training, and existing Business Data Stewards need to receive ongoing reinforcement. In addition, new business functions can get their Business Data Stewards up to speed quickly if an organization prepares itself to take a comprehensive approach to (and has robust curricula for) Data Stewardship.

It is a best practice to create a repeatable course that can be given to both the original Business Data Stewards and to any replacements that come along. This course is an introduction and overview to the responsibilities of Business Data Stewards as well as how they interact with others involved in Data Governance.

In addition, it is usually advantageous to create several smaller courses that can be given just before Business Data Stewards take on a new responsibility. These shorter courses focus on particular skills and responsibilities. For example, it doesn't make much sense to train the Business Data Stewards to perform their data profiling responsibilities if they aren't actually going to profile data until six months or a year later.

Don't skimp on the effort put into training Business Data Stewards. They are key players in Data Governance, and if they are not well trained, the results obtained will generally be of lower quality, take longer, and be less consistent.

One important thing to keep in mind when training Business Data Stewards is to not waste the training opportunity. The common causes of training failure are:

- Teaching the wrong skills. Only teach the skills they need, don't waste time training them for things they won't use. For example, if the Business Data Stewards are not going to run a data profiling tool, then it is pointless to teach them how to do so. On the other

> **NOTE**
>
> Keep in mind that different Business Data Stewards have different skills based on their experience and background. As a result, some Business Data Stewards will need training on topics that others do not. For example, if there are Business Data Stewards that are practiced at performing analyses for data profiling, you can work with them to develop courses to educate the less experienced Stewards. Taking the approach of leveraging the knowledge of some Business Data Stewards to train the rest leads to an increase in the overall level of Stewardship performance.

**Data Stewardship. DOI: https://doi.org/10.1016/B978-0-12-822132-7.00005-X**

hand, they *are* likely to analyze the results coming out of the tool and make recommendations for corrections and process improvements, so those skills *should* be taught (see Fig. 5.1). Of course, ensuring that only the right skills are taught means that you must understand what those skills actually are, and this book should make that clear.

- Teaching at the wrong skill level. Business Data Stewards are heavily involved with improving data quality. However, the theoretical concepts of data quality (such as the theory behind improved data quality as discussed in the Introduction to the book, *Journey to Data Quality* by Yang W. Lee et al.) are not terribly important. Instead, Business Data Stewards must understand the life cycle of their data, the information chains of data within their own organization, and the techniques on how to conduct root cause analyses and error-proof new systems. Thus the focus of the training should be on the practical "doing" of data quality improvement and other Business Data Stewardship activities.

- Teaching at the wrong time. "Just in time" training (training close to the time someone will apply these concepts) should be the goal of any training program. This is especially true if the skills being taught aren't familiar to the Business Data Stewards. For example, when we taught new project managers what was needed to include Data Stewardship as

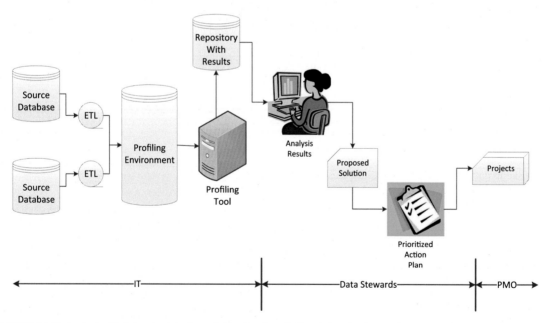

■ **FIGURE 5.1** Teach only the skills indicated as belonging to Business Data Stewards. They don't need to be trained in the skills of IT or the Project Management Office (PMO).

part of their project plan, those project managers who didn't build a project plan until several months after the training had already forgotten about us and did not include Data Stewardship deliverables, resources, and funding in their plan. We dealt with this by conducting an overall high-level training as part of the Project Manager (PM) on-boarding, with a refresher for new PMs (until they got used to including us) during the planning phases of any new project. That is, we used a combination of an introduction to get them familiar with the idea and "just in time" reinforcement.

- Teaching the wrong audience. This one seems pretty obvious, but again, if you don't have a clear idea of what duties various participants will be performing, you will waste your time and theirs teaching them skills they will never use. For example, it makes little sense to teach information producers how to do data profiling—while it makes a lot of sense to teach information producers how to safeguard quality when entering data.
- Addressing the wrong objective. You need to gauge what your audience is ready for, and teach at that level. For example, at first you might need to provide lots of background, essentially "selling" them on the ideas, and convincing them of the value ("why"). But later, you'll need to focus on "what" and "how"—the ends that need to be achieved and how they will be achieved. Teaching an audience the "why" when they are ready for the "how" will just bore them and convince them that the whole thing is a waste of time.

To sum up, in order for training to be successful, you need to train the right audience in the right skills at the right skill level at the right time and for the right reasons (to achieve the right objectives). In the case of Business Data Stewards, they must immediately learn what Data Governance and Data Stewardship are all about, why they are crucial to the effort and what value they add, their key early responsibilities, and the processes and procedures that they will either apply immediately or participate in creating in the early stages of the effort. Training should focus heavily on the practicalities of getting the work done and documented. It should also focus on the responsibilities that every Business Data Steward will be called upon to perform right away; namely defining key business data elements and managing them on an ongoing basis, managing data issues, and working together as a cohesive group.

## THE CURRICULA FOR TRAINING BUSINESS DATA STEWARDS

There are a lot of topics that can be covered when training Business Data Stewards. Though they are all discussed here, you will want to tailor your training to avoid the pitfalls discussed previously such as training too early. As discussed previously, you'll probably want to break the lessons up into multiple parts, and deliver them as needed.

## The Basic Principles

The basic principles around Data Stewardship are a good place to start training. Of course, you'll need to customize the information for your own use and your own company. For example, if poor data quality is hampering your company's ability to do business and maintain a competitive advantage, you will want to focus on that when you discuss why Data Governance and Data Stewardship are important. On the other hand, if data quality is not perceived as a problem (and believe it or not, there are many companies where this is true), but there is confusion about definitions, then the focus should go there instead. Much of the information in the lesson headings listed here is presented elsewhere in this book or can be extracted from presentations held at major conferences.

The lesson headings for Basic Principles are:

- What is Data Governance?
- Why is Data Governance important?
- What is Data Stewardship?
- The importance of Data Stewardship and what happens without it.
- Where Data Stewardship fits in the overall Data Governance initiative.
- The detailed structure (operating model) of the overall Data Governance organization.
- The detailed structure of the Data Stewardship Council.
- The types of Data Stewards: Business, Technical, and Project (and Operational if you choose to use them). If you choose to implement data domain–based Data Stewardship (see Chapter 11: Governing and Stewarding Your Data Using Data Domains) then there are several more roles (such as the Lead Data Steward) to discuss.
- Why these particular stewards were selected, and who selected them.
- Major roles and responsibilities of Business Data Stewards:
  - Metadata: definitions, derivations, data quality rules, creation and usage rules, and protecting metadata quality.
  - Stewardship and ownership: What they mean and the levels of decision making.
  - Data quality: What it means and establishing data quality levels in context.
  - Master Data Management: The many ways that Business Data Stewards participate.

- Reference Data Management
- Information Security, Privacy, and Compliance.
- Data Lakes and big data.
- Business Process Risk.
- Data Lineage.
- Major roles and responsibilities of Technical Data Stewards:
  - The overall role of IT in Data Stewardship and tools
  - Technical explanations of how and why programs work the way they do.
  - Information about physical database structures and ETL.
  - Interpretation of production code.
  - Data Lineage.
- Meetings, web support, and logistics.
- General principles of Information Management.

## METADATA FOR KEY BUSINESS DATA ELEMENTS

One of the most critical things that Business Data Stewards need to do is establish the key business data elements and create an enterprise-wide accepted definition for each business data element. Just as important (for calculated data elements) is a standardized derivation rule so that the business data element is always derived the same way. As you can imagine, having a standardized derivation rule eliminates a great deal of confusion and efforts to try and reconcile different reports that use the same business data element. Finally, the data quality, creation, and usage rules must be defined, and eventually, the physical location of the business data elements must be located and documented. See Chapter 6, Practical Data Stewardship, for more information on how to create robust metadata.

Creating, gathering, and documenting metadata is a crucial part of Business Data Steward training because creating rigorous metadata is not something that most data analysts are familiar with. Further, it is important to have a standardized set of guidelines for performing the work and evaluating the quality of the result.

## USES OF DATA

It is important to teach Business Data Stewards how to determine how data is used throughout the enterprise. Decisions about the data have impacts on source systems, ETL, data stores, and reporting. These impacts need to be understood. For example, a decision to standardize on a single set of valid values (e.g., for Marital Status) could require modifications to source systems or at least a set of conversion rules that will need to be implemented in ETL prior to being loaded into a Data Warehouse.

Data is everywhere in an enterprise and affects all aspects of an organization. Data also crosses organizational boundaries and is easily reproduced and repurposed—making data more difficult to manage than other organizational assets. Given this situation, it becomes a challenge to narrow down what data to review, manage, improve, monitor, and govern. There are a variety of models for understanding how data is used across an organization and its Information Chains. Understanding the relationship between Information Producers and Consumers is one way, and Supplier–Input–Process–Output–Customer (SIPOC) is another. A combination of both is probably necessary in most organizations if you hope to make real progress. Put another way, the starting point for managing and governing data needs to be documenting knowledge and understanding how data exists and moves through an organization. Once the overall Information Chain is understood, the Information Producers/Consumers and SIPOC can be applied to the links in the Information Chain.

## Information Producers and Consumers

Information Producers include anyone who inputs or imports data. These producers can come from all levels of an organization—from data entry clerks to the executives themselves. Producers can include those outside the organization, from customers who put data into a web page to those who input data at a third party that provides purchased data. The responsibilities of information producers are to understand and abide by enterprise data standards and policies for valid values, acceptable usage, and controls. They must also understand and follow data management processes and procedures as well as understand and support data management business goals and objectives.

> **NOTE**
> Of course, those outside the organization would seem, at first glance, to have a problem with understanding and following data standards, processes, and procedures. In the case of third-party information producers, these must be made clear in the contract between the organization and the third party. In the case of customers, the input system itself must be set up to enforce these requirements in a clear (and friendly) way.

Information Consumers are those that use the data for analysis and to run the business. They may also be internal or external, and can be considered an important customer of Data Governance because of the increased insight and operational improvements that Data Governance enables. They are also, of course, the customers (stakeholders) of the information producers. Information consumers also come from all levels of the business.

Information consumers have a number of responsibilities, including escalating data issues, understanding and abiding by enterprise data standards, acceptable usage, and controls. As with information producers, they must also understand and follow data management processes and procedures as well as understand and support data management business goals and objectives. The major difference in the responsibilities of information consumers is to understand what constitutes proper sources for data, and use those sources correctly.

There is often a disconnect between information producers and consumers, which causes information producers to produce or collect information that is either insufficient or of too low quality (or both) for the needs of information consumers. This disconnect is often the result of not treating data as an enterprise-wide asset. The key lesson to be taught here is that the specifications given to information producers need to take into account the requirements of information consumers, even when those consumers are not part of the business unit that is collecting the data. For example, in one large insurance company, the information producers that collected data that was used to create new homeowner's insurance policies did not collect the birth dates of the home owners because the policies weren't priced using the age of the homeowner. Without their birth dates, it wasn't possible to reliably identify customers as part of the Master Customer effort, which had a large impact on a variety of other enterprise efforts. However, when asked to collect the birth dates, the information producers refused because doing so meant taking extra time, and they were paid based on policy throughput. Data Governance had to get involved to get both their attitude and their compensation requirements adjusted.

## Using SIPOC to Understand Data Use

Another way to look at the flow of information is via SIPOC (Supplier – Input – Process – Output – Customer), as shown in Fig. 5.2. This set of terms comes from the process world, primarily Six Sigma. SIPOC has the capability to become a tool for understanding the uses of data in an enterprise much in the same way as a Data Flow diagram. By understanding where the data comes from (Supplier), what it is used for (Customer), and what is done to the data on its trip from supplier to customer (Process), you can:

- Understand the requirements that the customer has for the data.
- Understand the rules governing how the data is provided.
- Determine the gap between what is required and what is provided.
- Trace the root cause of data failures—both of type and of quality.
- Create requirements for modifying the processes that move the data.

The SIPOC principle can be applied at many different levels of detail. At a high level, for example, Claim data is used by Actuarial to assess risk. At a detailed level, a rule for calculating a data element can result in an unexpected number because of a condition that was not anticipated.

**NOTE**

The disconnect between Information Producers and Information Consumers is sometimes referred to as the "Silk Road Problem." Long ago, the Chinese produced silk, but did not know who bought it or what their requirements were. The Europeans bought the silk, but did not know where it came from or how to ask for changes in color or weave. Only the Persians—who actually moved the silk from the Orient to Europe—were aware of both ends of the transaction. The problem with the Silk Road was that the Chinese did not know how their silk was being used, and, thus, could not produce it the way the customer wanted. The Europeans had the opposite problem—they knew what they wanted, but did not know how (or who) to ask for it. By connecting the needs of the consumer to the producer, the Persians ensured that the Chinese could sell more silk, the Europeans could buy more silk, and the Persians could make more money transporting more product. This story also shows that when the incentives are correct, the producers will provide what the consumers need.

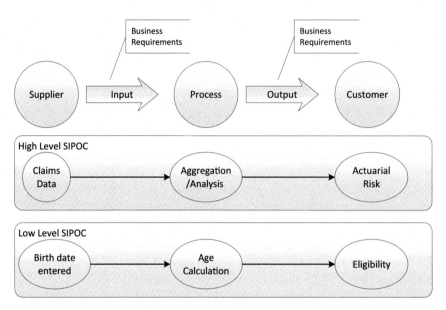

■ **FIGURE 5.2** SIPOC illustrates the flow of information through an enterprise in steps.

In this model, each step in the information chain is broken down into components that supply information as input into a process, and the output from the process is supplied to the customer. The customer may be the supplier to the next link in the process, and so on. By analyzing the flow of data in this way, the needs of *all* the customers in the chain are understood, and the supply of data as well as the output of the processes can be analyzed to ensure that it meets all the enterprise's needs. Examples of high-level and low-level SIPOC are provided in Fig. 5.2.

## INTRODUCTION TO DATA STEWARDSHIP PROCESSES

Successful Data Stewardship depends on well-defined and repeatable processes. Working with well-defined and repeatable processes—which may be foreign to many stewards—must be introduced and constantly reinforced during training. The processes include using an Issue Log (see Chapter 6: Practical Data Stewardship) and workflows (also in Chapter 6: Practical Data Stewardship) with approval steps and time limits for these steps. Stewards must be made to understand that these processes and their workflows will lead to an efficient management of the data and a higher quality product than ad hoc methods.

The initial training should include some examples of basic processes such as:

- Defining and updating key business data elements.
- Opening and working issues with business processes.
- Collecting and remediating data quality issues (see Fig. 5.3 for a sample process using regular DQ metric reports to identify and prioritize issues).
- Defining and executing Data Stewardship Procedures.
- Working with other stewards to reach a solution on data problems.
- Providing input for Master Data Management (see Chapter 7: The Important Roles of Data Stewards).
- Supplying Information Security classifications (see Chapter 7: The Important Roles of Data Stewards).

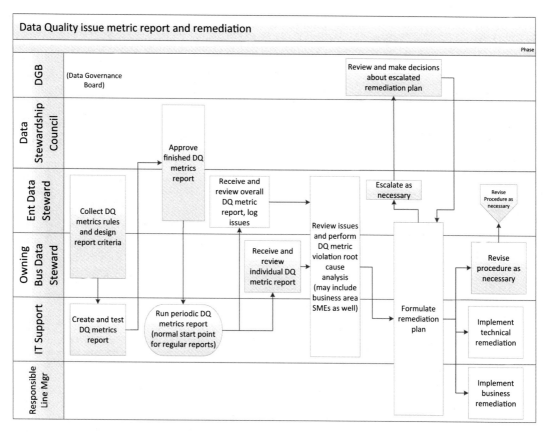

■ **FIGURE 5.3** A procedure for defining Data Quality metrics reports and handling issues. The vertical "swim lanes" show the various actors (such as the Enterprise Data Steward) who take part in the procedure, and the rectangles specify the individual steps, connected by flow arrows.

## TOOLS OF THE TRADE

The training must also focus on how to use the Data Stewardship toolset, including:

- A Data Stewardship Web Site. As will be discussed in Chapter 6, Practical Data Stewardship, this is a key artifact that ties other tools together and serves as a reference for everything that involves Data Governance and Data Stewardship.
- A Data Governance Wiki. Data Governance and Data Stewardship have many terms that may be unfamiliar to the general population. As these definitions are worked out, they need to be published in a Wiki. Business Data Stewards should know how to look up items, provide links to their coworkers, and either directly update the Wiki or make a request to have an update made (depending on how you set up the update procedure).
- A Business Glossary. A Business Glossary is a key deliverable of Data Stewardship both in providing content and in deciding what should be documented. This tool holds the business metadata documentation such as the list of key business data elements and their links to other important metadata, definitions, derivations, and all business rules. In addition, some tools allow for semantic classification of the terms, logical lists of valid values, and more. Business Data Stewards should know how to look up items, provide links to their coworkers, and take part in adding and updating the metadata.
- A Metadata Repository. Whereas a Business Glossary handles the logical/business metadata, a Metadata Repository handles the physical metadata such as database and file structures, lineage and impact analysis (based on ETL), and making the connection between the physical data and the business data elements stored in the Business Glossary. Unlike other tools, Business Data Stewards are not normally expected to make updates to the Metadata Repository, but should learn how to use it to look at databases and understand where data elements come from

**NOTE**

Whereas it is possible to build "homegrown" tools for the Data Stewardship Web Site, the Wiki, and even the Business Glossary, it is rare to do so with a Metadata Repository. That is due to the complexity of the metamodel and the complex functionality underlying the tool, including connectors to read database structures and ETL definitions. Instead, it is almost always necessary to license a commercially available tool. In many cases, it is possible to license a combined Business Glossary/Metadata Repository or to integrate a Business Glossary with a Metadata Repository by using an application programming interface (API).

**THE ROLE OF IT IN MANAGING TOOLS**

After reading through the list of technical tools needed to properly support Data Governance and Data Stewardship, you may be wondering where the support for these tools will come from. IT has an important support role for commercial tools such as a Metadata Repository and

*(Continued)*

**(CONTINUED)**

probably the Business Glossary. Servers need to be purchased and installed, the software licensed, installed, and maintained, and issues with underlying databases/repositories dealt with in a timely manner. In addition, some of the more complex Metadata Repositories require considerable expertise to customize as well as needing batch jobs set up and run periodically to update the metadata.

All of these tasks are typically handled by IT, which will need to assign and train one or more resources to support the Data Stewardship effort. Note that these tasks are *not* the same as what is expected from Technical Data Stewards; instead some of these tasks are for developers, while others are for system maintenance and DBAs. As you consider adding tools to support Data Stewardship, make sure to engage IT early to enable them to estimate, budget, and properly staff to provide production support. Keep in mind that Data Stewardship tools must also be considered a necessary part of the enterprise applications they make useful. For example, a Data Warehouse is not usable if there is no data dictionary and business glossary that allows the end users of the Data Warehouse to know what data elements they are looking at, what they mean, how they are derived, and so on.

## TRAINING FOR DATA QUALITY IMPROVEMENT

Improving data quality provides much of the driving force—and visible results—for Data Governance and Data Stewardship. At some point, therefore, Business Data Stewards need to be trained in how they can play an important role in a data quality improvement effort. Key points to train Business Data Stewards in include:

- Framework for data quality:
    - How the organization defines quality data.
    - What data quality rules are, and how to define them.
    - Detection and documentation of data quality issues.
    - How to do root cause analyses.
    - How business process improvement increases the quality of data.
    - Data cleansing, and when it is appropriate.
    - Ongoing logging/measurement of data quality levels.
- Principles of data profiling and the roles of Business Data Stewards in analyzing the results:
    - Viewing, investigating, and rendering decisions on the profiling results (what's a problem and what's not).
    - Analyzing the quality of the data for both newly governed data and existing governed data:

**NOTE**

"Data Profiling" in this context means not only running a profiling tool and analyzing the results, but also performing ongoing data analysis to confirm that the quality of the data continues to meet the stated data quality goals. These goals can change over time as the uses of the data change, causing data that was once considered to be of good quality (because it met the then-current needs) to now be considered to be of insufficient quality.

- For newly governed data, Business and Technical Data Stewards need to establish data quality criteria based on the data usage and do a level of analysis to determine whether the data meets those quality criteria.
- For existing governed data, Business and Technical Data Stewards need to plan and execute (with support from IT) ongoing data measurement and analysis to ensure that the quality of the data does not diminish. If the data usage changes (and, thus, the data quality needed changes), the data should be handled as newly governed data, as described in the previous bullet.

## SUMMARY

If Business Data Stewards are well trained and learn the skills they need just before using them, the overall Data Stewardship effort will be both more effective and more efficient. In addition, as major efforts like data quality improvement get underway, Stewards need to be trained on how to participate in those efforts as well.

Good training for Business Data Stewards is the same as good training for any other subject. It must include clear goals, appropriate level materials, exercises for reinforcement, tests for comprehension, and the ability to apply what you've learned. Appendix B shows outlines for two training plans, namely Training Technical Data Stewards and Training Project Managers. Note how much of the material is repeated between the plans—including instructing the trainees on what Data Governance is and why it is important to them.

# Chapter 6

# Practical Data Stewardship

## INTRODUCTION

If done properly, Data Stewardship achieves its goals while providing job satisfaction and a sense of adding value to the participants. They work together as a team, see the results of their efforts and end up doing less, but more effective, work. If not done properly, Data Stewardship can overwhelm the stewards, leading to frustration and "push back" from them. The key is to focus on the practical and fundamental aspects of Data Stewardship. These include determining the key business data elements (BDEs), assigning stewardship for them, creating quality metadata (such as a business definition and business rules), creating and following a set of repeatable processes, and putting procedures in place to streamline the logistics of working together.

The day-to-day Data Stewardship work often revolves around issues that have been raised and that must be dealt with. A well-managed issue log can provide structure to this work and ensure that the issues are resolved in a timely manner. Other tools such as a Data Stewardship web portal, Wiki, Business Glossary (with a workflow engine if possible), and Metadata Repository (MDR) can guide the Data Stewardship work and ensure that decisions are documented and published to the enterprise. Key to the documentation and publication of decisions is a Data Stewardship communications plan that should leverage common enterprise communications (web articles, newsletters, and brown bag presentations) as well as create specialized Data Stewardship communications for participants in the effort. A roadmap provides a timeline, tasks that must be accomplished, and the interdependencies of those tasks. It is also crucial that projects include a Data Stewardship component—and the elements of the "work breakdown structure" must include the necessary stewardship tasks.

## THE BASICS

The starting point for Data Stewardship is almost always to choose the key business data elements (BDEs) that are worth spending time on, creating robust definitions and derivations, as well as business rules for

> **NOTE**
>
> A "work breakdown structure" (WBS) is a project management tool that lists the tasks that must be accomplished during the project along with the resources necessary, the estimated duration and start/end of each task, and the dependencies of the tasks. For example, you can't start the task to analyze the results of data profiling until the data profiling tool has been run and the results returned. One of the more important objectives of adding Data Stewardship into the project methodology is to define the Data Stewardship-related tasks and their dependencies and add them into the template used to create the WBS.

Data Stewardship. DOI: https://doi.org/10.1016/B978-0-12-822132-7.00006-1

creation, usage, and quality. Of course, to do all this, you need to do one of two things:

- For business function—driven Data Stewardship: Assign a Business Data Steward to the key BDEs. The assigned/owning Business Data Steward makes the decisions about the BDEs and creates the metadata.
- For data domain—driven Data Stewardship: Determine the owning data domain so that the Data Domain Council (see Chapter 11: Governing and Stewarding Your Data Using Data Domains) can make decisions about the BDEs and create the metadata.

## Choosing Key Business Data Elements

As mentioned in Chapter 2, Understanding the Types of Data Stewardship, bringing business data elements (BDEs) under governance requires some effort. First of all, the Data Stewardship Council (whether comprised of Business Data Stewards or Lead Data Stewards from the Data Domain Councils) must decide on an owner for the BDEs. Next, the BDEs need to be defined, the creation and usage business rules ascertained, and the data quality rules documented. Often, the data has to be examined ("profiled") to find out whether it meets the data quality rules, which means that the physical instantiation of the BDEs must be known or determined. In addition to all this "set up" work, established procedures must be followed to achieve agreement and consensus from the stakeholders.

Since most companies have thousands of BDEs (and many more physical data elements), the very first thing you need to do is establish the most important (key) business elements (KBEs) to focus on. If you think of the work done to bring BDEs under governance as an "investment," then it is reasonable to determine KBEs by the return on that investment. That is, how important is it to the company that particular BDEs be governed? Which BDEs are worth spending the necessary time on? Or, to put it bluntly, what is the business case for spending time on these BDEs when there is so much else to do?

What follows are some types of BDEs to consider in making this determination.

### *Financial Reporting Data*

Data which is reported to the financial community—and from which investment decisions may be made—must be governed. The good news is that Finance experts typically understand this requirement and have usually defined their BDEs, including the derivation rules. They are often frustrated by the fact that other sections of the enterprise use the same terms to mean different things, therefore Finance officials often welcome Data Governance because it provides the opportunity for them to own their data and enforce their decisions, including having a common definition and derivation across the company. The Finance department is often a good place to start working on Data Stewardship because of this.

### Risk and Regulatory Reporting Data Elements

Many industries—especially financial services and insurance—are heavily regulated and need to provide reports to regulators that prove that regulations are being followed and that best practices in managing risk are being adhered to. In recent years regulators have started to require information on how data is governed, and if the organization cannot provide that information (or are not governing their data to the satisfaction of the regulator) an issue may be raised by the regulator that will then need to be addressed. Having a rigorous governance process and a clearly defined set of tools for recording decisions about regulatory data is key in answering questions from regulators and documenting exactly how the reported results were calculated.

To properly govern risk and regulatory reporting data, a number of things are necessary, including:

- Understanding the data that appears on a report. Regulations are notoriously bad about defining exactly what is needed, and often the company's lawyers and regulatory experts must step in to clarify the options and provide additional details.
- Linking the data on the report to one or more BDEs. These BDEs provide business definitions and derivation rules, as well as showing what part of the organization is accountable for the business metadata.
- Linking the data on the report to the physical data elements used to populate the report. As noted earlier (Chapter 2: Understanding the Types of Data Stewardship), fully governed data requires the BDEs and the physical data elements. The ability to show the physical data elements *and their lineage back to a trusted source* can provide a high level of comfort to the regulators that data integrity is being maintained and that the data is being properly governed.

Risk and Regulatory report data is often where many Data Governance efforts begin. This is not only because these reports are important, but also because it is fairly straightforward to show the value of properly governing this data. For example, at a large bank fines were levied by

> **NOTE**
> A hierarchy (established by the organization and "acknowledged" by the appropriate regulators) of the reports that must be filed is often needed. A large bank might need to file more than 1000 reports, and a technique for prioritizing them (such as in tiers) may be needed to break down the work to be done into manageable components.

regulators over several years due to violation of anti-money laundering rules. However, once these data elements were given a high priority, it was discovered that the rules were not being violated—it just *looked like they were because of poor quality data*. In this case, a direct monetary return could be attached to bringing the data under governance which included tracing the information chain and locating where the poor quality was introduced. The monetary return was exactly the value of the fines that no longer had to be paid.!

### Business Data Elements Introduced by Company Executives

It should come as no surprise that terms (BDEs) that figure prominently in presentations given by company executives need to have a high priority. You would think that when highly placed individuals in the company use terms regularly they would have a clear idea of what the terms mean and how they are measured. But that is rarely the case. In one example, the president of a large insurance company introduced a new metric that *everyone in the company was going to have in their bonus program*. The metric was calculated by dividing one number by another. However, when questioned, she was unable to fully define either of the two terms involved despite having set a numerical goal to be reached. On another occasion, a senior executive created a presentation that explained how a "prospect" moved through the sales funnel to become a "lead," an "opportunity," and finally a "customer." However, except for "customer," none of the terms were defined, nor was there any way to determine when the change in state occurred. This situation needed to be addressed quickly as well by providing definitions of each term and the trigger event that caused the change.

### Data Used by High-Profile Projects

Large projects should have representation from Data Stewardship (i.e., Project Data Stewards), and the data used by high-profile projects should have a high priority for being brought under governance. Also, high-profile projects present the opportunity to bring data under governance in a managed way with the limited scope of the project, as discussed later in "Adding Data Governance to the Project Methodology" section. Ungoverned data raises the probability that the project will fail, or at least take longer and cost more than was originally predicted. High-profile projects catch the attention of important people when these failures occur. Examples of high-profile projects may include replacement of aging enterprise-critical systems, systems that provide distinct competitive advantage and analytical systems such as data warehouses and data lakes, especially when multiple failures have occurred in the past.

### *Allowing the Business Data Stewards to Decide*

One way to identify KBEs that is often overlooked is to let the Business Data Stewards decide what elements are important enough to be worthy of their attention. As the data experts, the Business Data Stewards are in a good position to know what business data elements should be dealt with that would benefit their business function.

One case that is often ignored is where a stakeholder Business Data Steward will request the owning Business Data Steward to take on BDEs that are troublesome for the stakeholder. In fact, this happens quite often because the owning Business Data Steward may not realize what issues the stakeholders are facing.

---

**SUBTLE DEFINITION DIFFERENCES CAN BE IMPORTANT**

We've all had business people tell us that writing down definitions for key BDEs is unnecessary because "everyone knows what it means." At a macro level this may occasionally be true, but detailed definitions and derivation rules can point out subtleties that are important. Robust definitions and derivations often explain differences in reported numbers and help resolve nagging inconsistencies. A good example is the definition of "Delinquency Date" that I encountered at a large bank. Two reports purported to show how many loans (and the total value of those loans) were "delinquent"—that is, payment on the loan was overdue. Yet the two reports, one from Loan Servicing and the other from Risk Management, showed two different sets of numbers. Each report identified a different number of loans and the value of those loans differed as well. Both reports calculated the delinquent loans the same way—comparing whether the loan payment was received by the payment due date. So how could they be different? The answer lies in the derivation of "delinquent loan." One report defined a loan as delinquent as of the payment due date; the other report defined it as of *the next day*. Once this difference was discovered, the Business Data Stewards agreed on a common definition and derivation, and the reports were reconciled. Once the agreement was in place, the Risk Management group stopped using their report and began using the Loan Servicing report instead.

Another example involves the count and value of financial transactions on a travel agency website. Two different groups reported vastly different numbers, yet on the face of it their definition for a financial transaction (to pay for reservations) was the same. It wasn't until the Data Governance group delved into the discrepancy that things became clear. In one group, any attempted transaction was counted and the count was triggered any time an attempted payment occurred whether the payment was successful or not. In the other group, only successful transactions were

*(Continued)*

**(CONTINUED)**

counted. Since credit card transactions are frequently rejected due to incorrect data being entered (such as the card number, expiration date, etc.) the counts were quite different. As it turned out, both numbers were important. The successful transactions represented actual financial commitments, while the total transactions represented costs to the travel agency as each transaction cost them money regardless of whether it was successful or not. As is usual in such cases, the term was broken up into two separate terms (*Attempted Financial Transaction* and *Successfully Completed Financial Transaction*) with different business functions owning each term. An important lesson can be learned from this story. Whenever there is a strong disagreement on what a BDE means or how it is derived, it is likely that two arguing groups are actually talking about different BDEs. This occurs frequently when the BDE name is too generic (as in "Financial Transaction") and can be resolved by making it more specific (as in "Attempted Financial Transaction" and "Successfully Completed Financial Transaction"). Another example can be found in Appendix A.

## Assigning the Responsible Business Data Stewards

As KBEs are identified by the Business Data Stewards (with guidance from the Data Governance Program Office), the first thing that needs to be done is to assign a business function or data domain (see Chapter 11: Governing and Stewarding Your Data Using Data Domains) that will be responsible for that BDE.

It is often clear which business function or data domain should own the BDE. Many data elements are collected by, and for, a single business function. For example, the policy information collected by an insurance company is collected by the Underwriting business function. It is Underwriting that needs the data to run their business and must be able to define and derive that data in order to run their business. That isn't to say that the data isn't used by other business functions that are considered to be stakeholders. That same policy information may be used by the Accounting business function to bill customers and by the Data Management group to manage master customer data. When determining an owning business function or the owning data domain, there are some key questions:

- *Whose business will fundamentally change if the definition or derivation of the BDE were to change?* There is a huge difference between just *using* a BDE and driving your business with it. Accounting, Finance, Master data management, risk management, and other groups may use the data. However, if the definition or derivation changes, these groups can make a small change to the way they use the data and continue on as before. Usually only a single business function will be significantly impacted by any change. Put another way, which business function owns the core business processes that most depend on the BDE? For business function—driven data stewardship, that business function would own the BDE. For data domain—driven stewardship, it would be one of the data domains for which that Business Data Steward has the role of the Lead Data Steward (see Chapter 11: Governing and Stewarding Your Data Using Data Domains) in the Data Domain Council. The other users of the data are represented as stakeholders in the managing Data Domain Council as well.

- *Where within a business process does the data originate?* Using the Information Chain concept, if the group that originates the BDE is responsible for it then ownership is clear. With a well-documented Information Chain, the owner can see the implications of the various uses of the BDE.

An example may help here. An insurance company identified their agents using a three-digit code. This Representative ID was used in all sorts of ways including by Finance to pay commissions on policies sold. Unfortunately, as the company grew, they found that they were running out of codes. The need therefore arose to expand the field, which was a major undertaking. It seemed reasonable to expect the owning business function to pay the costs, which led to the unusual circumstance that no one wanted to own the field. The argument was made that Finance owned the field because they cut the commission checks, and without the code they couldn't do that. But paying commissions is not a core Finance process—that is, Finance could continue to operate just fine without cutting the checks. On the other hand, keeping track of the agents—and what they sold (and getting them paid for it)—was very definitely a core Underwriting process. Without an upgrade to the code, Underwriting would not be able to identify agents, associate policies with the agents, and make sure that Finance had the data needed to get the agents paid. The end result would be that the agents would leave the company and start selling someone else's insurance—perhaps policies from a company that would pay them. In addition, all the existing policies would no longer have agents to manage them, leaving the company with the major headache of handling existing customers with a rapidly shrinking work force. Given these facts, Underwriting had to take ownership of the Representative ID and pay for the change.

**NOTE**

The previous example "works" with data domain—driven data stewardship as well. In that case, the data domain (with its Data Domain Council) would have the Underwriting Business Data Steward as the Lead Data Steward, but the stakeholder Finance Business Data Steward would be a member as well.

This example also brings up another important role, that of a "stakeholder." All decisions have impacts, and it is important for the Business Data Stewards to understand the impacts. To do so they need a clear idea of who uses their data, and need to consult with those users to understand the impact that a decision would have on that usage (via a well-documented Information Chain). The users of the data—that is, those who are impacted by a decision—are the "stakeholders." In the parlance of RACI (responsible, accountable, consulted, informed), the stakeholders need to be consulted about a proposed decision. In the delinquent loan example, Risk Management was a stakeholder as they based many of their Risk reports on the value of delinquent loans, and that would change with the new definition. In the Representative ID example, Finance was a stakeholder as they need to be able to accept the longer code, translate it into real people, and then cut the checks.

## Naming Business Data Elements

Naming the BDEs is an important task for Business Data Stewards. Following a naming standard and creating a name according to a rigorous set of rules helps identify duplicates, as well as helping users understand the term simply from the name and minimizing the chaos that occurs when the names are too general. A basic set of BDE naming standards should include:

- Must start with a noun or a noun with a valid modifier in front of the noun (e.g., Accrued Interest)
- May have one or more qualifiers that will bring uniqueness to the name (e.g., Accrued Interest Override)
- Should end in a "class word" that indicates the type of data element. Examples include "Amount" (to indicate a monetary amount), "Number," Indicator (a Boolean Y/N, T/F), and Percent. See Appendix C for a suggested list of class words.
- All names are unique. If you are having trouble naming two different terms uniquely, you need more specific modifiers to more clearly identify them.
- Abbreviations should not be used (e.g., Amt., Adr.). If you abbreviate a word in some names and not in others, you reduce the chance of finding duplicates.
- Acronyms should be avoided and *only* used if they are well-known in the industry.
- Avoid variants of the same term based on time periods or currencies.

## Creating Good Business Definitions

As stated in Chapter 3, Stewardship Roles and Responsibilities, one of the primary responsibilities of Business Data Stewards is to provide business definitions that clearly define what the BDE is, and why it is important to the business. These definitions must meet the standards for a high-quality business definition.

A repeatable process must be established for identifying BDEs and creating definitions for them, as discussed later in this chapter. The definition goes through various statuses, and different people contribute to the process as it moves to a finalized definition.

---

### THE CHARACTERISTICS OF A GOOD BUSINESS DEFINITION

So what is a good business definition for a BDE? We've all seen the bad ones—just the name of the BDE, or the name with the words switched around. But a good business definition should include the following to be complete and useful:

- *The definition of the term, using business language.* The definition should be concise and describe the meaning of the BDE. That is, we want to know (through the definition) how the business talks and thinks about the BDE, and *not* how it is named and resided in a database.
- *What purpose the term serves to the business—how the business uses the information represented by the BDE.* The importance of the term to the business helps to clarify what the term means.
- *Must be specific enough to tell the term apart from similar terms.* This requirement often leads to qualifying or specializing a generically named term. This was what happened in the previous example with Financial Transaction, which became "Attempted Financial Transaction" and "Successfully Completed Financial Transaction."
- *Should link to already-defined terms that are used in the definition* (see Fig. 6.1 and notice the underlined terms in the definition). The key here is not to define (again) other terms which are already defined, but simply provide a link to those embedded definitions.
- *Where appropriate, should either state the creation business rules or link to them.*

There are certain questions you can ask yourself to determine how complete and accurate a definition is. First of all, completeness: after reading the definition, does it leave you asking another question or wanting more detail? Next, can you provide a specific example that would *not* fit the definition as it stands? Finally, could someone new to the organization understand the definition? You do have to be careful with

*(Continued)*

**(CONTINUED)**

this last question. It does *not* mean that someone who is completely unfamiliar with the industry should be able to understand the definition. Instead, all that should be necessary to understand the term is a general background and familiarity with other common terms.

Business Term: Representative ID

Poor definition: The identifier for a representative (generally, it is not acceptable to use the term in its own definition).

Good definition: Uniquely identifies the Agent or another representative who is directly responsible for a new or a renewed Insurance Policy. Data about a new account is filled in by the agent during the initial data entry process for the policy. Identifying the representative is crucial to measuring the productivity of the agent as well as for use when compensating the agent. This data is not captured when a customer logs in and fills out the insurance information directly using web-based access.

Note that ISO (International Standards Organization) has published a definition of a good definition—International Standards Organization. (2004-07-15). *ISO/IEC 11179-4 Information Technology — Metadata Registries (MDR) Part 4 Formulation of Data Definitions*. (2nd ed.). Section 4.1 provides requirements, such as that the definition be stated in the singular; that it state what the concept is, not only what it is not; be stated as a descriptive phrase or sentence(s); and that it be expressed without embedding the definitions of other data or underlying concepts. Section 4.2 additionally provides a set of recommendations, such as that the definition state the essential meaning of the concept; be precise and unambiguous; that it be able to stand alone, and that it be expressed without embedding rationale, functional usage, or procedural information.

## Defining the Creation and Usage Business Rules for a Business Data Element

Defining the creation and usage business rules is key to ensuring that (not surprisingly) the data is created *only* when it is appropriate to do so, and used only for the purposes for which it was designed. Fig. 6.1 shows an example of a defined BDE with its listed business rules. Since the quality of the data (and the perceived quality) are often negatively impacted by improperly creating data or using it for purposes for which it was not designed, having and following the creation and usage business rules can go a long way toward protecting the quality of the data.

The creation rules for a BDE state the specific conditions under which an instance of the data can be created. They may include:

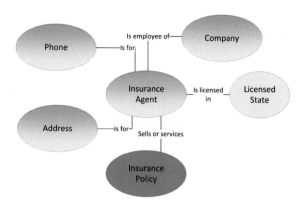

**Creation Business Rules**
· Must be assigned a unique identifier
· Must have verifiable licensure in at least one state
· Can only be created by Underwriting
· Must have a valid phone number
· Must not be represented in the system already

**Usage Business Rules**
· Valid to use only if license istill valid (expiration date is blank)
· For House Account, servicing agent is assigned by Underwriting
· Agent must be assigned to all policies written by that agent

■ **FIGURE 6.1** Business rules for a BDE. The conceptual model shows how the BDE Insurance Agent is related to other important BDEs, such as the Licensed State.

- At what point in the business process the data must be created or captured, and any circumstances under which it may *not* be created.
- What other data must be present and available prior to creating the data.
- Which business function is allowed to create the data.
- What approval process (if any) is needed before the data can be used in production.

The usage rules state how (and for what purpose) the data is allowed to be used. These rules may include:

- Validity tests that must be applied and passed before the data can be used.
- Relationships to other data that must exist.
- What business processes must use the data and the way in which each process uses the data.

---

**TIP**

It can be very helpful to show the conceptual model of the relationships between major pieces of data when defining and stating the business rules for the BDE. See Fig. 6.1 for an example.

---

## Defining the Derivation Rules

The values of many data elements are derived. Some of these derivations are direct numerical calculations, such as "Loan to Value" in banking. For each derived data element, it is critical that a single, well-documented equation be used to calculate the quantity consistently across the enterprise. Otherwise different reports purporting to display the same calculated quantity will not agree. It is also crucial that the component parts of the calculated quantity are themselves consistently defined (and if derived, derived in a consistent way). For example, what is the value of "loan" in the equation? Is it the original mortgage value with closing costs and points? Without closing costs and points? The Loan Delinquency Date is another calculated quantity—the Due Date of the payment plus a contractually agreed-upon grace period. But the Due Date itself is a derived quantity—based on the origination date of the loan and the period between payments.

Some business data elements (especially those with a specified set of valid values) may also be derived based on a triggering event. Some are relatively simple—an insurance policy status is considered "active" if the current date is less than the expiration date of the policy. Other data elements are more complex to derive. At the same insurance company, a Person was considered a "Customer" if they were actively doing business with the company, had ever done business with the company, or showed a willingness to do business with the company. The tricky part of the definition was that last bit—the willingness to do business. Sales (who owned "Customer") defined willingness to do business as someone who had received a quote on a policy. That is, when looking at the sales funnel, a Person moved from Prospect to Customer when they received a quote. This definition made it not only important to know when a particular person received a quote, but also to be able to identify a person uniquely *before* they were a customer.

## SETTING UP REPEATABLE PROCESSES

Having a set of repeatable Data Stewardship processes is one key to a successful Data Stewardship implementation, and ultimately leads to better management of data (which is, after all, the goal of Data Stewardship). One of the biggest issues with current data management is that people all tend to manage data differently. Having a set of repeatable Data Stewardship processes helps bring consistency to overall data management. With documented processes, everyone is aware of how to proceed to get a specific job done, what the steps in the workflow are, and who is responsible for each step in the process.

**NOTE**

In Chapter 5, Training the Business Data Stewards (Fig. 5.3) we saw a sample repeatable Data Stewardship process.

As the Data Stewardship effort matures, you'll find that you are adding processes as needed. The essential processes are listed below, although your organization will require others as well:

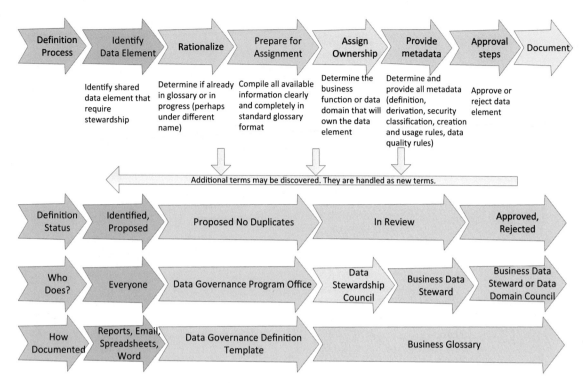

**■ FIGURE 6.2** The flow (across the top) of the process to identify, assign business function owner, define, and approve a new business data element.

- Bring new business data elements under governance (see Fig. 6.2)
- Manage the Business Glossary (see Fig. 6.3)
- Evaluate and find resolutions for data quality issues
- Resolve a Data Governance request or issue (see Fig. 6.4)
- Manage policies, procedures, and metrics
- Coordinate the work of multiple Project Data Stewards
- Manage the Issue Log

**WORKFLOWS**

In order to track the progress of repeatable processes efficiently, Data Stewardship is going to eventually need a tool with configurable workflow capabilities. Manually tracking statuses and attempting to shepherd processes through the required steps is both tedious and error-prone. In addition, a tool with workflow capabilities can automatically perform

*(Continued)*

**NOTE**

There are a variety of ways to document processes. While Fig. 6.4 uses "swim lanes," Fig. 6.2 uses a straightforward flow, and Fig. 6.3 uses a set of "Use Cases." You should pick the format that works best your audience and for the nature of the process that you need to document.

**(CONTINUED)**

certain tasks, such as moving a process to a secondary approver if it has sat too long in the primary approver's queue (e.g., if the primary approver is on vacation) and making sure that the right people execute the appropriate steps. Further, reports generated from the tool can show how many processes are at what stage, and if there is a bottleneck (e.g., one particular approver who takes a long time to do their work).

*(Continued)*

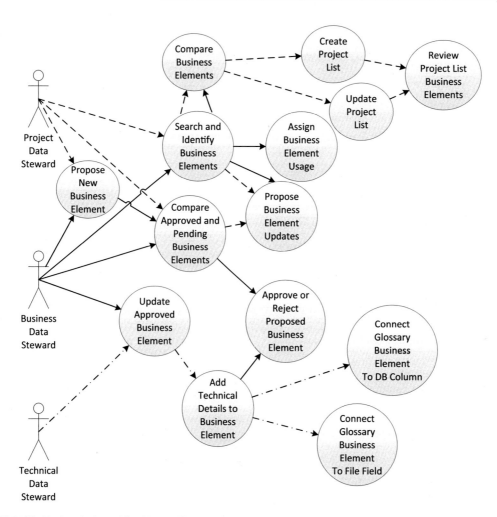

■ **FIGURE 6.3** The Use Cases (with actors) for adding, modifying, and removing business data elements (referred to as "Business Elements" in the diagram) in the business glossary, as well as mapping the business data elements to the physical data elements.

**(CONTINUED)**

The workflow tool must be configurable because the workflows change over time and because different kinds of tasks require different levels of workflow rigor. For example, a two-step approval process may prove to be too cumbersome, and the Data Stewardship Council could decide to dispense with one of the steps. Fig. 6.5 shows an example of a new data element moving through the approval process.

The details of how to build workflows is covered in the "Automating processes with workflows" section.

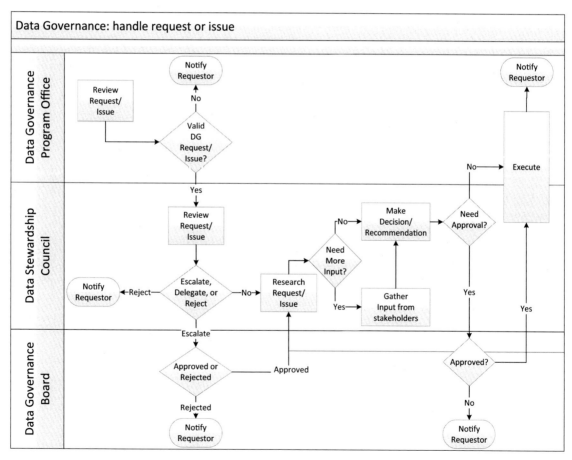

**Data Governance: handle request or issue**

■ **FIGURE 6.4** A "swim lane" diagram that shows the steps and decision points for managing a Data Governance issue or request. The horizontal swim lanes indicate which role(s) are responsible for each step in the process.

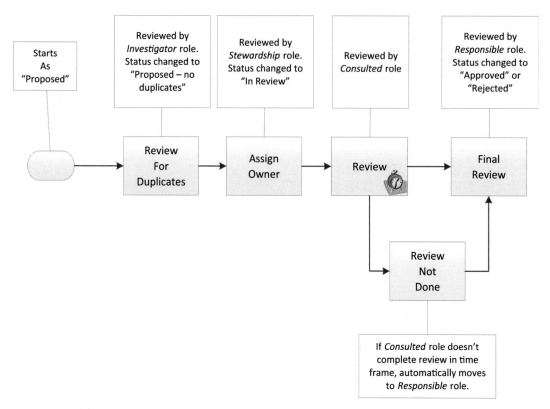

**FIGURE 6.5** Workflow for approval of a business data element in the Business Glossary.

## DEFINING THE SCOPE OF DATA STEWARDSHIP IMPLEMENTATION

One common question that often comes up at the beginning of a Data Governance implementation is whether to implement all at once (across the enterprise) or with a focus on a specific line of business. There are a number of considerations to making a decision.

Considerations which tend to point to the "all at once" solution are:

- Small company. A small company is usually better off implementing all at once because of the advantage of having standardized data management and decision processes. In a small company the Business Data Stewards will often know each other, and can more easily work together if they all have the same goals and procedures.
- Many or all business units have data problems. If data problems are common across the business units, there is considerable advantage to

approaching and solving those problems in a common way. These include having common roles with standardized responsibilities, and standard procedures. The data problems usually affect more than a single business unit so being able to work closely together with a common understanding on how to proceed provides considerable value.

- Many or all business units are involved in a larger data project, such as a new data warehouse or data lake, or replacement of a large application (such as a customer relationship management (CRM) system). The standardized interaction of the responsible and accountable roles ease misunderstandings and confusion, and lead to a cleaner and more well-understood solution.

- Upper management mandates a companywide rollout. In this case, of course, there is little choice, but at least with upper management support there is a good chance that the appropriate committees and individuals will be able to engage in Data Stewardship properly.

Considerations that point an implementation that is focused on a specific line of business or a small set of business units include:

- Project(s) isolated to a single or small number of business units. These projects will benefit from having the participants using the tenets of Data Stewardship, including performing the special tasks and achieving the milestones associated with Data Stewardship.

- Key business units with large data problems. If the most serious data problems are limited to a small number of key business units, the other business units (who may not have data problems) may not wish to participate in a large-scale Data Stewardship effort. Unless there is executive support for a full-scale rollout, it is probably best that those business units who *need* Data Stewardship should implement it. This approach is most effective when there is little interchange of data between business units, so that the fact that different business units are managing their data in different ways isn't too much of a burden. Of course the good outcomes that result from Data Stewardship often convince other business units to join in, and that is good too.

- Highly independent business units, not all of whom are ready for Data Stewardship. If the executive in charge of a business unit is convinced that Data Stewardship is a good way to go, but other executives are not ready for it, then it may be advantageous for the one business unit to start up their own Data Stewardship effort. It is, of course, not as effective to perform Data Stewardship in a silo, but if the overall company isn't ready to commit, there is little choice.

## UNDERSTANDING HOW THE BUSINESS DATA STEWARDS INTERACT WITH THE DATA GOVERNANCE PROGRAM OFFICE

The Data Governance Program Office staff needs to work closely with the Business Data Stewards on an ongoing basis. One key to a successful collaboration is to respect the Business Data Steward's time. Frequent or purposeless meetings can quickly sour the steward's willingness to participate in the Data Governance program. And while high-level support from the executives can mandate this participation, it is much better to have the stewards participate willingly. This is far more likely to happen if the demands on their time are limited to a reasonable amount and each meeting that is held is purposeful and clearly results in value added for the Data Stewardship effort.

---

**TIP**

You should never have a meeting without an agenda—nor should you have an agenda without goals. With goals (and an agenda that drives toward those goals) you can state what should be achieved in the meeting—and whether those goals were actually achieved. Business Data Stewards are far more likely to attend a meeting that has goals they are interested in and where they understand why their attendance is necessary.

---

## Regular Meetings with the Data Stewards

The key guidance for meetings is that you don't schedule a meeting every time an issue comes up. Instead, regular general meetings should be scheduled for items like:

- *Developments and issues related to the overall Data Stewardship effort*: These can include organizational changes, new lines of business, new demands being placed on Data Stewardship by the executive steering committee, and major data-related issues that require a concerted and coordinated effort by the Data Stewards.
- *Training and updates on Data Stewardship tools*: New tools or major updates to existing tools may require that the stewards be brought up to date on tool usage, including moving existing manual processes to an automated tool. Training is critically important, and should be done as close to the time of the tool change as possible.
- *New and improved processes and procedures*: As new processes and procedures are worked out, or existing ones are revised to make them

more robust or efficient, the Data Stewards need to be made familiar with these changes. It is best to review such changes as a group if possible, because the group dynamics can lead to valuable feedback on the efficacy of the changes.

- *Planning for major enterprise efforts that require Data Stewardship participation*: Major data quality improvement efforts, Master Data Management projects, and Data Warehouse or Data Lake initiatives all require significant input from the Business Data Stewards. Without careful planning and analysis of the level of effort and timing, the Business Data Stewards can be overwhelmed. Meeting as a group—and including the project managers where possible—can help alleviate this risk and set realistic expectations. In addition, such meetings can make the overall stewardship effort more efficient since they provide an opportunity for stewards to apply their past experience to these new situations.

**IN THE REAL WORLD**

Periodic "assignment meetings" are needed to assign ownership of new key BDEs. As discussed previously in the "Choosing Key Business Data Elements" section, new BDEs can pop up from many sources, and it is important to get ownership assigned early in the process. How frequently the assignment meetings are needed depends on the rate at which new BDEs need to be brought under governance, but it is not unusual to have meetings weekly or every two weeks. The frequency of the assignment meetings will also depend on where you are in your governance process. As the Business Data Stewards get more experienced in determining ownership, the process will go faster, and meetings will not need to be held as often.

A good set of steps to follow for assignment meetings starts with gathering up potential names and as good a definition as possible for the BDEs. These should then be forwarded to the members of the Data Stewardship Council, along with an invite to the assignment meeting. The Business Data Stewards (or data domain Lead Data Stewards) who have an interest in the BDEs would then show up to the meeting, those that don't have any interest would not have to attend. For example, if there are a set of Insurance BDEs, the HR Business Data Steward would not need to attend. This approach keeps the audience to a small number of interested parties, rather than forcing everyone to attend. The Business Data Stewards who do attend can then agree on ownership.

Note that if the attending Business Data Stewards realize that someone is missing who might well need to be an owner, the Enterprise Data Steward (who runs these meetings) can circle back with the missing party to see if they agree on the ownership assignment.

## Using Interactive Forums

A great deal of the rest of the work and coordination between the Data Governance Program Office and the Business Data Stewards can be done through an "interactive forum." That is, instead of holding meetings that many cannot attend, items can be posted on an interactive, web-based "bulletin board" such as a SharePoint site, and responded to at the convenience of the stewards. Examples of items that lend themselves to this sort of management are:

- Input on metadata definitions and derivations
- Creation and usage rules review
- Data quality rules review
- Evaluation of data profiling results
- General requests for feedback on issues

Using an interactive forum might work something like this:

1. A Business or Technical Data Steward or member of the Data Governance Program Office would open an issue or discussion point on the forum and request feedback. Depending on how Data Governance was set up, a stakeholder, designated subject matter expert, or impacted data analyst might also be able to open an item.
2. Members of the Data Stewardship Council would be notified about the open issue or item. This would most probably work by subscribing the members of the council to the list so they would get automatic notifications.
3. The members of the council would provide their feedback at their convenience, and the Enterprise Data Steward would monitor the discussion and provide periodic summaries or propose remedies.
4. If the issue had to be escalated, the Enterprise Data Steward would escalate it to the Data Governance Board members. This might work as a separate issue list for the Data Governors, or it might require an email and/or meeting be held, managed by the Data Governance Manager.
5. Once a reasonable solution was found, the solution could be posted to the list for feedback or voting.

The main advantages to managing the appropriate items this way are three-fold. First, the Business Data Stewards are notified automatically of all issues that may require their attention. Second, they are able to do their research and respond at their own convenience, which means that meetings with the entire group don't need to be scheduled. Last, there is a clearly documented trail of discussions that were held and solutions proposed. No one has to keep track of multiple email threads in order to document what was discussed.

> **TIP**
>
> Success with online collaboration also depends on company culture. In some organizations, people interact effectively online. In other organizations, if there has not been a meeting on a topic, then the topic remains open. It takes some prework within an organization to get people adjusted to the approach of online collaboration.

## Using Working Groups

Between full Data Stewardship Council meetings and using the interactive forum(s) is the possibility of forming "working groups." These are committees formed by Business Data Stewards who are responsible for gathering feedback from interested parties to resolve an issue or settle a disagreement. The working groups are needed when a question requires widespread input from the business community. The Business Data Steward schedules and runs the meetings; the participants are business users who are impacted by items such as:

- A proposed change to a business data element definition or derivation.
- Detection and correction of a perceived data quality problem, including revising data quality rules
- Changes to usage and creation business rules.

The organizing Business Data Steward is accountable for getting the issue resolved and for bringing back a consensus to the Data Stewardship Council to propose adoption and sign-off where appropriate.

> **IN REAL LIFE**
>
> An example from the Insurance world illustrates how an interactive forum (called a "discussion board" at this company) and a set of working group meetings helped to resolve an issue around a key term: *Close Ratio*. The process for resolving this issue also closely followed the process flow illustrated in Fig. 6.2.
>
> The term (BDE) *Close Ratio* had been defined, approved, and entered in the Business Glossary by the owning business function (Sales). However, during a project, the term came up in internal discussions, and business people were confused by the usage and name. They therefore "decided" to change the definition. Fortunately, one of the team was aware of the Data Governance Program Office, and advised the project team that they did not have the
>
> *(Continued)*

**(CONTINUED)**

authority to make the change. Data Governance was then engaged in the process (see the step "Identify Data Element" in Fig. 6.2).

The Sales Business Data Steward got a working group of the concerned participants together who voiced their concerns and the confusion around what the term meant. The steward then created an issue on the Discussion Board, listing those concerns, and subscribed everyone in the working group to the issue. People individually stated what they thought the definition should be, as well as identifying variations on the term which could be considered as additional terms. The steward then proposed the names and definitions on the Discussion Board (Rationalize). The Assignment (to Sales) did not change. The Discussion Board entries fleshed out the full definition of the renamed term (*Unique Quote to Close Ratio*), the additional identified terms, and how the term was derived (Provide metadata). In the end, the revised definition was entered into the Business Glossary (Document) and the Sales Business Data Steward approved it.

If you are interested in seeing the very complete definition and derivation associated with this business term, please see Appendix A.

## How Project Data Stewards work with Business Data Stewards

Project Data Stewards represent Data Stewardship on projects. The challenge of being a Project Data Steward is that you need to balance the needs of the project (which are likely to be immediate and time-constrained) with the needs of the Data Stewardship Program (which necessarily has to have the bigger picture in mind). This is made more difficult because the Project Data Steward does not have the authority to make decisions, and must consult with the responsible Business Data Steward (who may be the data domain Lead Data Steward). Use the following guidelines for the Project Data Stewards to work with the Business Data Stewards:

- *First and foremost, it is important not to overwhelm the Business Data Stewards.* Make sure that the Business Data Stewards are aware that the Project Data Stewards will be working with them. In addition, the Business Data Stewards need to include the interaction with the Project Data Stewards in their time estimates (and time limits).
- *The Project Data Steward should attempt to collect as much of a definition, derivation, and data quality rule(s) from the project business analysts and subject matter experts.* This information is then brought to the Business Data Steward. If (as often happens) the BDE is the subject of a debate within the project team, the Project Data Steward should

collect all the opinions presented so the Business Data Steward has as much information as possible. In other words, the Project Data Stewards should do their homework on any questions or concerns that they may need to bring to the Business Data Stewards.

- *For data quality questions, data profiling should be performed and the results reviewed with the project team before bringing the information to the Business Data Steward.* The data profiling shows what is actually in the database (rather than guessing at that information) and the project participants may decide that the condition of the data does not represent an issue for the project after viewing those results. In that circumstance the Business Data Steward may not need to provide input. Nonetheless it is still usually a good idea to share the results with the Business Data Steward who may see something that the project members do not.
- *The Project Data Stewards should compare their project BDE lists* to cull duplicates so that different Project Data Stewards don't end up asking the Business Data Steward about the same BDE.
- *If a Business Data Steward has not yet been identified for the project BDEs, the question should come to the Enterprise Data Steward to identify a potential Business Data Steward or data domain using the Assignment process.*

## USING AN ISSUE LOG TO GET THE DAY-TO-DAY WORK DONE

Data which is considered to be under Data Governance has issues worked through an Issue Log. By using a centralized Issue Log and working on the issues using a set of well-defined processes, a clear picture of the status of issues can be provided to stakeholders. In addition, priorities can be established and resources allocated to getting the work done.

### What is the Issue Log?

Not too surprisingly, the Issue Log is where issues and questions about governed data are documented, worked on, and resolved. That is, the Issue Log is about tracking and knowing what the issues are, what their status is, and what impact they have. Resolving an issue may take the form of reaching a simple agreement or agreeing to a proposal to remediate the issue. Agreeing to a proposal is necessary when technical changes (which may require a project) are needed to remediate the issue. Understand also that resolving an issue may end with a proposal that additional data be governed, perhaps because the data has become important (as described earlier in this chapter in the "Choosing Key Business Data Elements" section).

## Managing the Issue Log

The Issue Log is usually managed by someone from the Data Governance Program Office, often the Enterprise Data Steward. That doesn't mean, however, that the Program Office staff is responsible for doing all the input. Depending on how permissions are set up, issues and questions can be entered by Business Data Stewards, Data Governors, Stakeholders, and others. However, the Data Governance Program Office staff *is* responsible for ensuring that all the pertinent information is entered for each issue or question. This is an important responsibility: if issues are poorly defined, it is really hard to resolve them. In addition, if someone is not actively managing the log, then there is a risk of duplicate entries, erroneous entries, or issues which are never addressed.

A number of types of items tend cause issues, such as a change request or onboarding new data. On the other hand, the presence of issues may drive other kinds of work, such as onboarding new data or data quality improvement. These are summarized in Fig. 6.6.

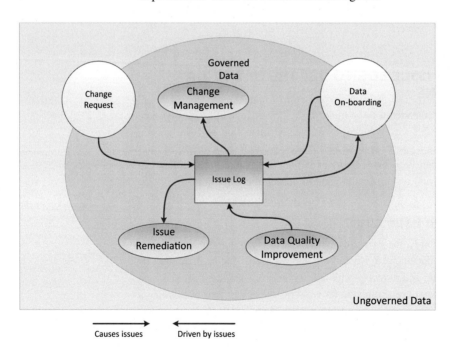

■ **FIGURE 6.6** Certain items cause new issues to be opened, while others are the result of resolving issues. Some items (such as a Change Request) may also cause more data to become governed.

**ISSUE LOG FIELDS**

To properly record issues and questions in the Issue Log, you need the right set of fields. Although you will need to tune this list for your own requirements, here is a starting list of fields that should help you get going. These fields are adopted from the Collibra's *Data Governance Center* tool, and are used with permission:

- Issue Description: A description of the issue and why it is important that the issue be dealt with. For example, it is not good enough to simply state that the meaning of a location code changed; the description must also state that the change could lead to staffing errors and how that might happen.
- Analysis: Records the results of analyzing the issue, ideas on root causes, potential solutions, and impacts to the Information Chain and processes. Analysis should include as much as possible quantification of the issue (number of records impacted, timeframes impacted, and number of customers or business areas impacted).
- Resolution: The chosen solution and reasons for that choice. Note that the solution may be to do nothing and accept the risks associated with that choice. Those risks should be listed in this field as well.
- Priority: The importance of the issue, chosen from an agreed-upon set of priorities (properly documented, of course!).
- Related to: This documents any connection from the issue to any other type of enterprise asset. For example, if the issue is poor data quality, the "related to" could be the BDE and the physical data element (and the system it is in). The data quality rule that is being violated is documented in the "Violates" field (below).
- Impacted by: This documents any connection from the issue to any other type of enterprise asset that impacts the issue. For example, another issue could impact this issue.
- Requestor: The person that submitted the issue.
- Reviewer: The person that reviews the issue, reviews the resolution, assigns priority, or in some way needs to provide input. Multiple persons can be listed.
- Assignee: The person responsible for handling and resolving the issue.
- Violates: Governance assets (such as a data quality rule) that the issue is violating.
- Resolved by: Governance assets (such as a new procedure, policy, or rule) that are put in place to prevent the issue from reoccurring.
- Business Function Domain: The business function and/or data domain that owns the issue.
- Date the issue was identified.

## Understanding the Issue Log processes

Working on the issues and questions in the Issue Log requires executing on a well-defined set of processes to drive to a solution or remediation. The tasks involved are listed and defined in Table 6.1 and a simplified process flow is shown in Fig. 6.7.

**Table 6.1** Issue Log Processes, Descriptions, and Who Is Responsible

| Task | Description | Responsible |
|---|---|---|
| Log | This task involves logging a description of the issue, including what the issue is, who noticed it, the extent of the issue (how many records, over what time period, etc.) and a statement as to the possible negative impacts to the company. It is important to fill in as many of the fields noted in the last section as possible—the better the information logged, the easier it will be to find a solution. | The issue should be logged by a member of the Data Governance Program Office staff and possibly Business Data Stewards. However, *anyone* can report an issue to have it logged. |
| Research | This task largely consists of validating that the reported issue actually *is* an issue, and if it is, locating the root cause of the issue. The research should be carried out by either the Business Data Steward responsible for the data, or by a team led by that individual (possibly including Operational Data Stewards). | Business Data Steward(s) |
| Propose solution | Once the root cause is identified, the people most knowledgeable about the affected data can propose a solution to alleviate the issue. Potential solutions could be making a simple workaround, making system changes, or even instituting a major project. The proposed solution should also include the impacts to the information chain, including systems, reports, data stores, ETL, and Data Governance tools such as the metadata repository. It is likely that IT support will be needed to identify the impacts. | Business Data Stewards Technical Data Stewards |
| Escalate | Since many issues cannot be solved at the Data Stewardship Council level, the next step may be to escalate to the Data Governance Board for prioritization and approval. For large issues, or where board members cannot agree upon proposed solutions, it may be necessary to escalate to the Executive Steering Committee. | Business Data Stewards Data Governors Executive Steering Committee member(s) |

*Continued*

**Table 6.1** (Continued)

| Task | Description | Responsible |
| --- | --- | --- |
| Prioritize | When multiple issues must be dealt with (the normal case), prioritization is necessary. This consists of establishing the order in which issues will be worked, as well as the resources (both people and funding) that will work the issue. At this stage it will be necessary to get cost estimates from IT as part of the input to the decision. In addition, other efforts (such as major implementations) can have significant effect on the priority of an issue. | Data Governor(s), Executive Steering Committee member(s), Technical Data Steward(s) |
| Approve | This step is where people with sufficient authority approve the plan and resource allocation, or, alternatively, choose to reject remediation of the issue and accept the impacts and risks associated with doing so. | Data Governor(s) Executive Steering Committee members(s) |
| Communicate | This task involves making all impacted parties aware of how the issue is going to be resolved (or not resolved). It is a parallel task to all the others. That is, interested parties should be able to track the issue through the process and provide input as necessary. | Data Governance Program Office |

## DOCUMENTING AND COMMUNICATING: THE COMMUNICATION PLAN

One imperative of a successful Data Stewardship (and Data Governance) effort is a set of communications to both the direct participants in the effort as well as those who are affected by the effort—in other words, all users of the data and all of those who depend on the processes that depend on the data. As you can see, almost everyone is a stakeholder and thus must be included in the communications.

### What Must be Communicated?

The communications should inform the stakeholders of decisions made, general information and developments, a complete awareness of what Data Governance and Data Stewardship are working on, as well as the goals achieved. This awareness can include success stories, mandatory training, metrics, and "branding" of the Data Governance organization.

Business Data Stewards make decisions and provide metadata that can affect a wide audience. Even if the detailed results of such decisions are

**NOTE**

Just like with products you buy, "branding" is important in keeping the enterprise aware of the goals and achievements of the Data Governance organization, but also what is currently being worked on and the value that the Data Governance effort delivers. Many organizations have found that a well-designed logo, applied to all the work that Data Governance is involved in, goes a long way toward achieving branding.

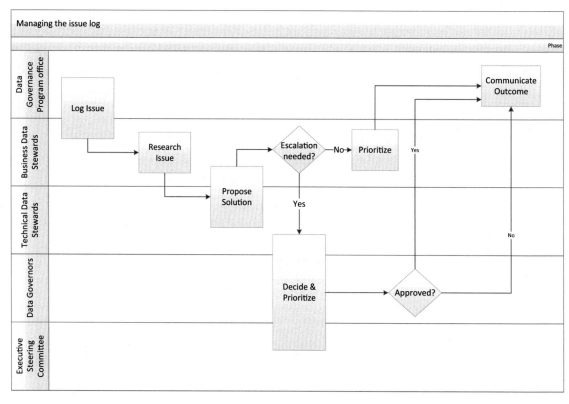

■ **FIGURE 6.7** A simplified process flow for managing the issue log.

documented in other places (such as a business glossary), it is extremely important to let all the interested parties know that decisions have been made and where to find the pertinent information. For example, anyone who wonders how a particular business data element is defined or derived should be able to easily find that business data element in the business glossary. But they have to know that the business glossary exists, how to get access to it, and the basics of how to use it. That is, sharing this information obviously requires that the interested parties are aware that definitions are being created, and that they are being stored in something called the business glossary.

## What Must be Included in a Communications Plan?

The good news is that since Data Stewardship is part of Data Governance, a Communications Plan should have been built early in the

**NOTE**

Many tools may include publish and subscribe mechanisms so people can get periodic notifications about issues and decisions. Summary reports are also useful, especially for executives and Data Governors.

implementation of Data Governance. This plan (see Table 6.2 for an example) should, at a minimum, include:

- The purpose that the communication serves.
- The title of the communication output.

**Table 6.2** Data Stewardship Communications Plan Sample

| Purpose | Output | Audience | Medium | Frequency | Presenter |
|---|---|---|---|---|---|
| Update Executive Steering Committee about Data Governance and review changes to Policies, Procedures, Process, Org and Roles and Responsibilities documents | Data Governance Overview Deck | Executive Steering Committee | Meeting | Semiannually | Business Sponsor, IT Sponsor, Data Governance Manager |
| Update Data Stewardship Council about Data Governance and decide on changes to Policies, Procedures, Process, Org and Roles and Responsibilities documents | Data Governance Overview Deck | Data Stewardship Council | Meeting | Semiannually or as needed | Data Governance Manager |
| Provide periodic updates regarding project profiling results to project managers | Project Data Profiling Report | Project Managers | Email | As Needed | Data Governance Manager |
| Provide periodic updates regarding ongoing enterprise data profiling results | Enterprise Data Profiling Report | Employees, Data Analysts | Email | Monthly | Data Governance Manager |
| Provide periodic updates regarding ongoing enterprise data profiling results | Executive Summary of Enterprise Data Profiling Report | Executive Steering Committee, cc. Data Stewardship Council | Meeting | Semiannually | Data Governance Manager |
| Introduce practitioners to Data Governance to highlight goals, org, supporting documents (e.g., roles/resp/org, policy, procedure, processes), and project phase review process | Introduction to Data Governance Deck | Project Managers, Project personnel | Meeting | Start of project | Enterprise Data Steward |
| Introduce Project Managers to the Data Governance Phase Review process, including review of project planning and review of existing business glossary | Introduction to Data Governance Deck; Business Glossary; Data Governance Phase Review Process | Project Managers, Project Personnel | Meeting | Start of Project, Major Project Milestones | Enterprise Data Steward |
| Present overview of Data Governance activity and highlight sample projects with successful Data Governance involvement | Data Governance Status Deck | Business Owners | Meeting | Quarterly | Business Sponsor |

*Continued*

**Table 6.2** (Continued)

| Purpose | Output | Audience | Medium | Frequency | Presenter |
|---|---|---|---|---|---|
| Newsletter from the Data Governance Manager that includes key highlights from Data Governance including recent project profiling results, new members, news from the Board or Steering Committee, and success stories from data governance projects | Data Governance Newsletter | Data Stewardship Council, Project Managers, Executive Steering Committee, Data Analysts, employees | Email | Quarterly | Data Governance Manager |
| Issue Log updates | Status updates | Data Stewardship Council | Email | As needed | Enterprise Data Steward |
| Introduction to Data Governance, including organization, goals, responsibilities, value to the enterprise, and how the audience can contribute to the success of the program | Introduction to Data Governance Deck | Data Analysts, developers, business people | Meeting, webinar | As needed | Data Governance Manager |

- The audience for the communication. This normally consists of various groups within the enterprise who will benefit from this information, including Project Managers, Developers, Data Governors, and Data Stewards.
- The communication medium. Information can be communicated in various ways, such as meetings, emails, pushed via subscriptions, and so on.
- The frequency in which the communication is issued.
- What role is responsible for "presenting" the communication to the audience.

Data Stewardship progress should also be included in normal company publications, so that the "general public" is made aware (and kept aware) of the efforts going on in Data Stewardship. Table 6.3 shows how a schedule of company publications might look. The Content column is a general classification of the type of content included in the article. The Article Title/Heading column is the name of the column or article in the publication.

## The Importance of Targeted Communications

In addition to general communications, it may be necessary to use "targeted communications" to notify interested parties about the sources and

| **Table 6.3** Company Publication Schedule for Data Stewardship | | |
|---|---|---|
| **Content** | **Article Title/Heading** | **Frequency** |
| What's going on/what are we up to? | Newsletter Column: Passport | Every other month |
| Information just in time | Newsletter Column: What you need to know | Every other month |
| Data Stewardship Milestones | Web Column: Company Achievements | Quarterly |

uses of data. These can include data changes, data source system changes, and metadata changes (such a change in definition or derivation). While all of this is important, these communications must be targeted to the appropriate audience. The "appropriate audience" includes those that consider this information newsworthy. In other words, those that consider it "news" and not "noise."

When using data domain–based Data Stewardship (see Chapter 11: Governing and Stewarding Your Data Using Data Domains) this work has largely already been done because the BDEs are grouped into data domains, and decisions are made by the Data Domain Council that represents the owner(s) and stakeholders. They should also get notifications about changes to these BDEs. There are however, other ways of looking at the BDEs besides how they are grouped into data domains (or owned by business functions). Several important additional ways of grouping content—and thus of targeting communications—include the following:

- *Privacy/Information Security Class.* Known by various names, this category refers to how sensitive the information is to being shared. For example, the full name of a customer may be considered "highly sensitive" and thus how that data is used and shared is restricted both by company policy and by regulations such as the European Union's Global Data Protection Rules. The value of the Security Class assigned to the data can change due to new policies and regulations, as well as changes to existing policies and regulations. Further, something as simple as relocating the data from one country to another can *also* change the Security Class. The stakeholders of this information are rarely limited to a single business function or data domain, so it is important to understand who needs to be notified (or to have input) into this metadata.
- *Source system.* The business functions that use data will do their best to find the best (most trustworthy and up-to-date) sources of that data. But as Data Governance progresses and the enterprise gains a better understanding of its data, it may be that the "best" source changes, either because another source is found to be better suited, or because

a better and more trustworthy source is created. This often occurs as part of the creation of a data lake or "approved provisioning point" for a data domain. Notifications to the users of the previous "best source" need to be made to ensure that the most trustworthy data is being used.

- *Business Process.* Business processes both use and create data, usually with support from various technical applications as well as procedures followed by personnel belonging to the business function that owns the process. For example, an insurance agent performs a business process each time a new policy is written, using an Underwriting application. Grouping data by the business processes that generate it or depend on it is critical to ensuring that the process is using the best source (see previous bullet point) *and* that all procedures are followed when creating data. If a definition of a BDE changes, or the rule by which the quality of the data is judged changes, this can have a significant effect on business processes—and thus, the link between data and the business processes is an important one to know and understand.

## ADDING DATA GOVERNANCE TO THE PROJECT METHODOLOGY

A prime tenet of practical Data Governance is integrating the processes and deliverables associated with governing the data into your organization's project methodology. The reasons for doing so are many, starting with the fact that most projects use or create data, and thus *need* the participation of Business Data Stewards.

### The Benefits of Adding Data Stewardship Tasks to a Project

In addition, Data Stewardship tasks benefit from being included in a project for the following reasons:

- The scope of a project is limited. The project is going to focus on a limited block of data and a limited number of source systems. Because of this limited view, people working on the project can focus on getting the necessary information, rather than spreading their efforts across a wide swath of data.
- A project has a professional (the project manager) who is specifically trained and charged with ensuring that the project stays on schedule, adequate resources are assigned, and that the progress on deliverables associated with the project is tracked. If the project's "work

breakdown structure" (WBS) includes Data Stewardship tasks, then those tasks will be included in the project schedule and resources allocated to those tasks.

- A project has the business' attention. Projects go through a rigorous process to justify the value to the business and justify the expenditure of funds and resources to accomplish the project's goals. Subject matter experts—often including Business Data Stewards—are assigned to work on the project and held accountable for completion of their tasks.
- A project has business requirements. These requirements will include data requirements, and as new BDEs are identified, they can feed directly into the business glossary during the delivery phase. In fact, the project should not be considered complete until the business glossary has been updated with the BDEs and other metadata related to the project.

## Data Stewardship Roles to Support the Project

On some projects, the Business Data Stewards and even the Data Governors may work directly on the project, playing a dual role. For example, the Data Governors can contribute to evaluating data issues as they come up and helping to determine how best to address them. Business Data Stewards can work directly with business analysts to draft data definitions and define other metadata, such as data quality rules. They would then work with the data quality analysts to review and validate the data profiling results. See Chapter 7, The Important Roles of Data Stewards, for more about how Business Data Stewards contribute to the data quality efforts.

One issue that often comes up, however, is that the Business Data Steward who would be appropriate for owning and defining a project's data is not assigned to that project. We've all seen the result—metadata is guessed at, or a committee is assigned to identify the stakeholders and try to come to a consensus on what the data means, how it is derived, what the "best" source is, and so on. As anyone who has been through this can tell you, this is inefficient and can delay the project. A much better answer is for Data Stewardship to be represented on each project, even if the appropriate Business Data Stewards are not available. But how do you do this?

As you may have guessed from reading Chapter 2, Understanding the Types of Data Stewardship, the answer is the "Project Data Steward." This is an individual assigned to the project to represent Data Stewardship. The

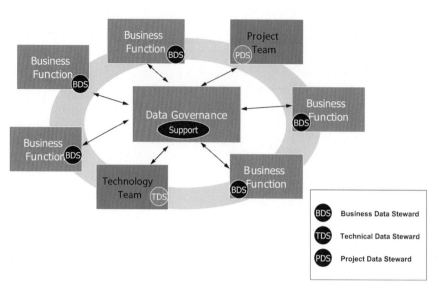

**■ FIGURE 6.8** The hybrid model of data stewardship on a project.

role of the Project Data Steward is initially to collect the best available name, definition, data quality rules, physical location, and other metadata about the BDEs from the subject matter experts as well as business analysts assigned to the project. The Project Data Steward then provides that information during the assignment meeting, where the appropriate Business Data Steward or data domain is selected. From there, it is up to the Business Data Steward or Data Domain Council to validate this information, document it, and provide any corrections back to the Project Data Steward for communication to the project. This "hybrid" model of Data Stewardship because work is done both by the Project Data Steward and the Business Data Steward(s), is shown in Fig. 6.8.

**IN THE REAL WORLD**

Of course, Project Data Stewards are not free; someone has to pay for these extra personnel to represent Data Stewardship on projects. On large projects such as new applications or a data warehouse, the project should be funded to include this resource. During the early planning stages, the Data Governance Program Office (DGPO) must work with the Project Management Office (PMO) to understand the scope and estimate what resourcing (and cost) must be included in the project funding. Unfortunately until this becomes a standardized step in the planning process, it is all too easy for the PMO to "forget" to do this. In addition, it is

*(Continued)*

**(CONTINUED)**

usually not until the Business Requirements Document (BRD) is at least in draft form that the scope is really well defined. Of course, by *that* time the funding may be set, so it is important to include enough in the early estimates to cover a reasonable scope.

Finally, very small projects may not have enough funding to cover the extra cost of a Project Data Steward. The ideal solution is to have a Project Data Steward that is part of the DGPO who can be assigned to many small projects to cover this contingency.

## Data Stewardship Tasks and Templates

As you work with the PMO to add Data Stewardship tasks to the work breakdown structure (WBS) used to lay out projects, you are going to need some idea of the Data Stewardship tasks that need to be added, as well as the information (metadata) about the tasks. While every project management methodology is different, Table 6.4 can give you a good idea of those tasks and how

**Table 6.4** Data Stewardship Tasks for the Software Development Lifecycle

| Requirements | Analysis | Design | Development and Testing | Change Management |
|---|---|---|---|---|
| Identify business terms | Conceptual analysis and diagrams | Alignment of Use Cases to data and business metadata | Alignment of requirement and specification changes to business metadata (see Fig. 6.9) | Defect review drives updates to business glossary |
| Begin approval process for business glossary | Completion and updating of business metadata | Alignment of user interface design to data elements and business metadata | Participate in development issues resolution | Data quality issue tracking |
| Scope project and assign resource | DQ rules and profiling of candidate data | Alignment of data model to data elements and business metadata | DQ test cases and defect review | Data Profiling (ongoing) |
| Review and revise project plan deliverables | Generate DQ issues and remediation plan | Reference data design, values, and participate in ETL mapping | Data quality issue tracking | |
| | Identification of data requiring test cases and criteria | Validate technical metadata | Choose suite of final data sources | |
| | Identification of candidate data sources | Review solution for data integrity | Ensure source to target mapping addresses the requirements | |

they line up with a simple software development lifecycle (SDLC). These tasks are a great place to start integrating with the project methodology.

As you develop the tasks listed in Table 6.4 (or whatever variation you choose for your organization), there are key pieces of metadata that should be captured for each task, a sample of which is shown in Fig. 6.9. These should include:

- The stage of the project in which the task is executed. Some may span multiple stages.
- Background and Objective: The purpose of this task as well as what should have been achieved when the task is complete.
- Benefits of executing the task
- Reference document(s): The details of the task and how to perform it are often laid out in great detail in a policy, standard, or guide.

## Alignment of requirement/specification changes to business metadata

| Requirements | Analysis | Design | Development and Test | Production Change Management |
|---|---|---|---|---|

### Foundation

**Background/Objective:**
- This task is required for a new system development or where an existing system is modified for source data systems.
- This task is required for Critical Business Data Elements and Terms.
- Ensure access to Business Glossary is available to perform this task.
- Access Business Glossary platform in order to validate the definition, business owner, data stewards, and other business metadata of the critical data elements within the scope of the project. If metadata does not already exist, the Data Analyst should work with business to define new terms and metadata.

**Benefits:**
- Drives standardization of business terms and definitions to allow consistent use of terms and reduce errors resulting from mismatched definition.
- Implementing the Metadata management framework for both Business and Technical Metadata and utilizing the Enterprise Metadata Repository will enable and ensure consistency across the enterprise and the ability to leverage and reuse content.

**Reference:**
- Data Lifecycle Management Guide

### Artifacts

**Required Document:**
- Data Requirements Excel Template

**Document Location:** SharePoint Project link

**Instructions:**
- Please utilize the completed Data Requirements excel document embedded in the Functional Specifications document.
- Go to the Basic Properties section in Data Elements tab.
- Search for the identified critical data elements in the Business Glossary. Update Data Ownership and Business Glossary section on the Data Elements tab for the findings and decision.
- Once all of the information has been completed, the Data Analyst must:
  1. Review the information with the designated "Reviewers"
  2. Obtain approvals from the designated "Approvers"

### Responsibility

**Role responsible for completing the overall task:** Data Analyst
**Reviewer:** Business Data Steward
**Approver:** Business Data Steward

### Task Participants

Project Manager (I)    Business Data Steward (A)
Business Analyst (C)    Data Governor (C)
Enterprise Data Steward (I)    Project Data Steward (R)
Business Data Owner (C)

R = Responsible, A = Accountable, C = Consulted, I = Informed

■ **FIGURE 6.9** A sample of the detailed information about a project task.

- Artifacts: Many tasks use one or more templates, this section states which templates need to be used, where those templates are located, and the instructions for filling out the template(s).
- Responsibilities: Lists the role responsible for completing the task, as well as reviewing the work and approving the work.
- Task participants: This section states the RACI (Responsible, Accountable, Consulted, and Informed) roles for the task.

## Training Project Managers

Once the Data Governance tasks are integrated into the WBS and included in the project plan, it is very important to work closely with the project managers to ensure that they have all the information they need, as well as being comfortable understanding what the tasks are, how to know when they're done, and how long they take. This almost always involves providing some training to the project managers. General topics should include what Data Governance is and what value the project gains from your involvement, what resources are needed and where they come from, and information on what may be unfamiliar processes such as data profiling.

Probably the most important topic to address is how to manage the impacts of these "extra" tasks to schedule and cost. The main point is that although there is a cost to the Data Governance tasks, there are also some serious benefits. These can include:

- Avoiding arguments or endless meetings about what the data means or what is the proper way to derive it. The Project Data Steward will take such things as a "to do" and bring back an answer.
- More quickly identifying the right data to use and understanding what that data looks like before conversion.
- A better-quality result that meets business needs better.

## BUILDING AND FOLLOWING A DATA GOVERNANCE OR DATA STEWARDSHIP ROADMAP

As with any other major organization-wide effort, Data Governance and Data Stewardship don't happen all at once. Various stages take place over time, and just like a project, there are milestones that must be achieved before you can move on to the next phase. The Data Governance "roadmap" lays out the tasks, milestones, and dependencies

**NOTE**

A highly detailed training plan (including answers to questions such as what value Data Governance brings to a project) is included in Appendix B. This plan also includes understanding tasks around data quality, writing Quality Assurance test cases related to data, and evaluating the solution for troublesome areas (such as overloading data elements).

of the effort. There may be several different roadmaps, covering different portions of the implementation:

- An overall roadmap that covers an agreed-upon length of time, such as 18 months.
- A roadmap for various tool implementations.
- A roadmap for the cycle to onboard new BDEs and related metadata.

Key items in the roadmap may be explained in more detail, including a description, assumptions, deliverables, dependencies, duration, necessary resources, rationale, and activities.

Fig. 6.10 shows an 18-month roadmap for implementing Data Governance. In the upper left corner is a task to hire the Data Governance Manager. Table 6.5 provides an example of the details for the hiring task.

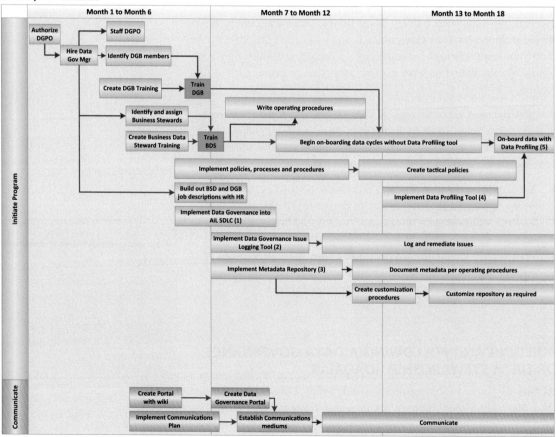

■ **FIGURE 6.10** A sample 18-month roadmap for Data Governance.

**Table 6.5** Details for a Roadmap Task

| Detail | Detail Description |
|---|---|
| Description | Recruit, hire, and train the role to run the Data Governance Program Office (DGPO). |
| Assumptions | Organization has the willingness to staff and fund the DGPO including the open headcount. |
| Deliverables | • Job description for the Data Governance Manager<br>• Individual hired into the role<br>• Organization structure into which the DGPO will fit<br>• Agreed-upon responsibilities for the role |
| Duration | 8 weeks |
| Resources | • Hiring manager<br>• Recruiter<br>• Executives (to interview) |
| Rationale | Hiring a Data Governance Program manager is a necessary early step in setting up Data Governance, and also a prerequisite to a successful program. Failure to hire someone dedicated to this position is highly likely to lead to early failures. |
| Activities | • Create reporting structure for DGPO<br>• Hire Data Governance Manager<br>  • Coordinate with recruiting/HR to create job requisition with associated hiring manager.<br>  • Post job requisition and compile candidate list<br>  • Interview candidates<br>  • Consult with hiring manager and make decision/offer.<br>  • Hire and onboard new employee |

It can also be advantageous to break down certain sections of the overall roadmap into more detailed pieces. For example, you'll notice that there are tasks to integrate Data Governance into the SDLC (1), implement the Data Governance issue logging tool (2), the Metadata Repository (3), and the data profiling tool (4). The more detailed versions of these tasks are shown in Fig. 6.11.

The last detailed roadmap (Fig. 6.12) is a bit different. It shows the duration of a large effort (such as onboarding a specific batch of BDEs) and the detailed steps. However, the detailed steps do not represent the elapsed time for each BDE, but only the steps themselves and how they depend on each other. Different BDEs can take vastly different amounts of time to onboard (as is noted in the roadmap) and hundreds (or more) of them may be onboarded during this phase. Thus it is not practical to try and show each BDE onboarding cycle.

## SPECIFYING THE DATA STEWARDSHIP TOOLS

There are four important tools that can help document the Data Stewardship effort and communicate the results of these efforts. The four tools are the

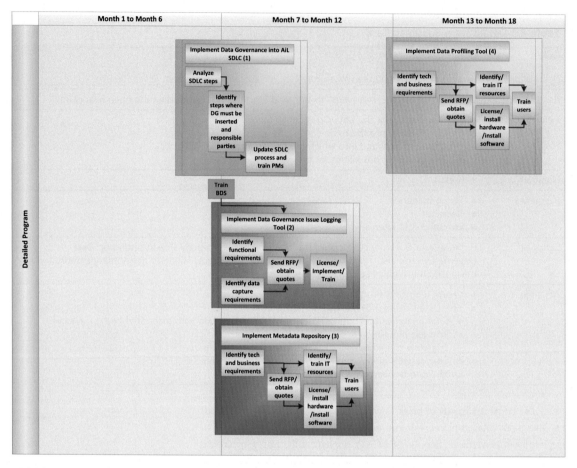

■ **FIGURE 6.11** The detailed roadmaps show the same timing and duration as the overall roadmap, but with more detailed steps.

Data Stewardship Portal, the Data Stewardship Wiki, the Business Glossary, and a Metadata Repository (MDR). Note that the Data Stewardship Portal should include links to the other tools, and usually displays the contents of the Wiki and possibly the Business Glossary and Issue Log as well.

## Data Stewardship Portal

It is imperative that Data Stewardship efforts be transparent. People directly involved with Data Governance and Data Stewardship (e.g., members of the DGPO, Business Data Stewards, Data Governance Board members, etc.) and people who need and use the information provided by the Data Stewardship effort (which should be pretty much everyone else)

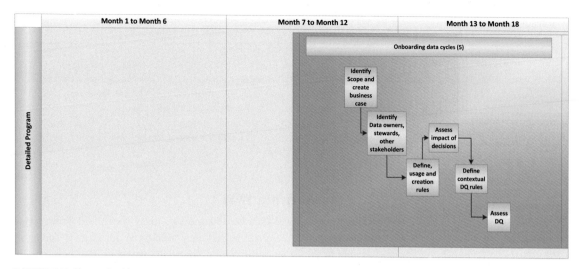

**■ FIGURE 6.12** The overall onboarding elapsed time cycle. The steps shown are repeated each time a new data element is onboarded, and are not meant to show the actual elapsed time for the BDE.

should have a web portal where they can find what they need. The web portal should provide staffing information, links to other tools (such as the Business Glossary), FAQs, and links to status reports, policies, procedures, issues, and contact information.

In addition, the web portal home page should provide a brief description of "who we are" and "what we do." Think of these sections as the "1-minute elevator speech" version of Data Stewardship. Fig. 6.13 shows a sample of what a web portal home page might look like.

**PRACTICAL ADVICE**

The FAQs on the Data Governance Portal should not assume that viewers have much (if any) knowledge of Data Governance and Data Stewardship. Some typical questions that can be answered are:

- What is Data Governance?
- What does the Data Governance Program Office (DGPO) do?
- What are the goals of Data Governance?
- What is the purpose of the Data Governance Council?
- What is the purpose of the Data Stewardship Committee?
- What are the responsibilities of a Business Data Steward?
- How does Data Governance and Data Stewardship impact the data strategy of the organization?

*(Continued)*

> **(CONTINUED)**
> The status reports should include a monthly version and an annual version. The monthly version should be short—just a few slides—that lists the top issues addressed, current Data Governance metrics and work being done, and contact information. The annual version can be longer, and include a reminder of what Data Governance is and the benefits of the Data Governance program. Additionally, it can display a timeline with the major accomplishments for the year and a list of the positive impacts to various business areas.

## Data Stewardship Wiki

Data Stewardship and Data Governance uses many specialized terms, forms, and processes. As these are defined, they need to be documented and easily available to the target audience. Documenting everything also improves the

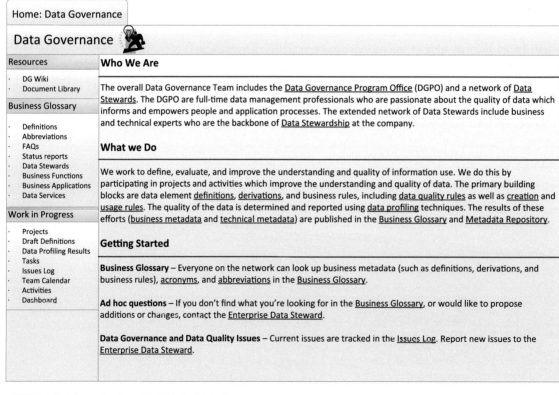

**Home: Data Governance**

### Data Governance

**Resources**
- DG Wiki
- Document Library

**Business Glossary**
- Definitions
- Abbreviations
- FAQs
- Status reports
- Data Stewards
- Business Functions
- Business Applications
- Data Services

**Work in Progress**
- Projects
- Draft Definitions
- Data Profiling Results
- Tasks
- Issues Log
- Team Calendar
- Activities
- Dashboard

**Who We Are**

The overall Data Governance Team includes the <u>Data Governance Program Office</u> (DGPO) and a network of <u>Data Stewards</u>. The DGPO are full-time data management professionals who are passionate about the quality of data which informs and empowers people and application processes. The extended network of Data Stewards include business and technical experts who are the backbone of <u>Data Stewardship</u> at the company.

**What we Do**

We work to define, evaluate, and improve the understanding and quality of information use. We do this by participating in projects and activities which improve the understanding and quality of data. The primary building blocks are data element <u>definitions</u>, <u>derivations</u>, and business rules, including <u>data quality rules</u> as well as <u>creation</u> and <u>usage rules</u>. The quality of the data is determined and reported using <u>data profiling</u> techniques. The results of these efforts (<u>business metadata</u> and <u>technical metadata</u>) are published in the <u>Business Glossary</u> and <u>Metadata Repository</u>.

**Getting Started**

**Business Glossary** – Everyone on the network can look up business metadata (such as definitions, derivations, and business rules), <u>acronyms</u>, and <u>abbreviations</u> in the <u>Business Glossary</u>.

**Ad hoc questions** – If you don't find what you're looking for in the <u>Business Glossary</u>, or would like to propose additions or changes, contact the <u>Enterprise Data Steward</u>.

**Data Governance and Data Quality Issues** – Current issues are tracked in the <u>Issues Log</u>. Report new issues to the <u>Enterprise Data Steward</u>.

■ **FIGURE 6.13** A Sample Data Stewardship Web Portal Home Page.

| Home: Data Governance | | |
|---|---|---|

**DG Wiki**

| Resources | | Name | DG Project Evaluation Form |
|---|---|---|---|
| **DG Wiki** | Chief Data Steward | | |
| Document Library | Data Governance Board | Content | This form requests information about what the project will do and general information about the data impacted by the project. Filling it out and reviewing it with Data Governance Program Office is a milestone for the PM early in the project. |
| | Data Governance Manager | | |
| | Data Governance Sponsor | | |
| **Business Glossary** | Data Stewardship and SDLC | | |
| | Data Stewardship Council | | |
| Definitions | Data Stewardship | | |
| Abbreviations | Defect Review | | The form helps determine whether Data Governance should be considered a stakeholder for the project and what <u>level of data governance involvement</u> and staffing needs to be provided to the project to drive Data Governance activities (such as collecting business metadata). |
| FAQs | **DG Project Evaluation Form** | | |
| Status reports | Domain Data Steward | | |
| Data Stewards | Domain Data | | |
| Business Functions | Enterprise Data Steward | | |
| Business Applications | Exporting results to Excel | | |
| Data Services | IDE Project Naming | | |
| | Information Principle | | |
| **Work in Progress** | Issue Tracking | | Click <u>here</u> to link to the latest version of the form. |
| | IT Champion | | |
| Projects | Level of Data Governance | | |
| Draft Definitions | Involvement in Projects | | |
| Data Profiling Results | Logical Model | | |
| Tasks | Logical Model metadata | | |
| Issues Log | Master Data Management | Modified By | Joe Smith |
| Team Calendar | Metadata analyst | | |
| Activities | Metadata documentation | | |
| Dashboard | Metadata Repository | Modified | 06/16/2013 10:33 am |
| | Metadata Requirements | | |
| | Metadata | | |
| | PMO Tracking Tool | | |
| | Technical Data Steward | | |

■ **FIGURE 6.14** A Sample Data Stewardship Wiki Page.

standardizing of terms, forms, and processes. Fig. 6.14 shows a sample of what a Data Stewardship Wiki might look like, and a sample of the terms that could be present and available.

## A Critical Artifact: The Business Glossary

To manage data as an asset, the data must be inventoried. And, since data doesn't define itself, the BDEs that you need to track must also be defined. A Business Glossary is a tool that records and helps to manage business metadata. According to DAMA, a business glossary is a tool that is used to document and store an organization's business concepts and terminology, definitions, and the relationships between those terms. Put in perhaps more simple terms, the Business Glossary is where the business metadata is published and used.

### Why do You Need a Business Glossary?

There are a number of goals that a business glossary can fulfill, including:

- Help to establish and document the organization's common vocabulary—BDEs (terms) and definitions that are understood and used across the enterprise. A related capability to having an easily-usable set of terms is a robust search function. This function should be able to search on all text fields, be able to be limited to specified domains of data, and have modifiable search parameters (using standard *and* and *or* searches). The search functionality helps to locate potential duplicate BDEs even when the names don't match exactly.
- Establish and document the ownership and decision rights for BDEs and other metadata stored in the business glossary.
- Ensure timely access to the business metadata. By having a central store of business metadata that is easily available to everyone who needs it, business metadata can be found and used quickly.
- Enable documenting important relationships between business metadata assets. For example, BDEs may be produced by certain business units; the business glossary should allow the creation and navigation of this link within the tool. Additionally, you may have business data quality rules that are associated with BDEs. For more suggestions on what might be stored in a business glossary, see the sidebar "What Should You Keep in a Business Glossary?" later in this chapter.
- Allow defining not only general terms but also driving them down to more specific terms where those are necessary to distinguish different uses (or more specialized versions) of the BDE. For example, the term illustrated in Appendix A (*Unique quote to close ratio*) started out as *Close Ratio*—but that term was so general that there were many different definitions because stakeholders were thinking of different specific terms.
- Automate common Data Stewardship processes (such as creating and approving BDEs with their definitions) using workflows.

### The Importance of Properly Naming Business Data Elements

The Business Glossary also helps to enable the Business Data Stewards to rationalize the BDEs, picking out the unique BDEs from those that are actually the same but with variations in business names (or the same names but a different definition).

Some data analysts are not as careful as they should be when naming BDEs and don't recognize that the naming that works for them may not

**Table 6.6** Rationalizing the Data Elements

| Data Element | Different Names or Different Data? | Total Data Points |
|---|---|---|
| Entry time | Ticket issue time, time of entry, transaction start time | 1 or 4? |
| Prepayment time | Ticket paid time, payment time | 1 or 3? |
| Amount due | Transaction total, transaction amount | 1 or 3? |
| Payment method | Payment type | 1 or 2? |
| Amount tendered | Amount paid, collected amount | 1 or 3? |
| Change issued | Overpayment amount, refund amount, amount due to client | 1 or 4? |
| Receipt issued | Receipt requested, receipt printed | 1 or 3? |
| Actual exit time | Exit time, departure time | 1 or 3? |
| Total | | 8 or 25? |

work for everyone else. As a result, data analysts often don't provide BDE names which are specific enough. The Business Data Stewards have to deal with these naming inconsistencies and must ensure that an agreed-upon and rigorous naming standard is followed when creating BDE names. For example, Table 6.6 shows how much of a difference proper naming can make in the inventory of the BDEs.

The Business Glossary is where the business metadata is published. This metadata should include attribution that is important to the business. This could include the Business Name, Definition, Derivation, Valid Values (where appropriate), any Usage Notes, Data Security Classification, the stewarding business function or link to the data domain, Approval Status, any related projects, who proposed, reviewed, and approved the metadata, applications known to use this data, and reference documents. The key deliverable is a set of business names with business function or data domain (as shown in Table 6.7). Fig. 6.15 shows a sample of how an element in the Business Glossary might look.

**BUILDING A HIERARCHY OF TERMS**

One capability of a robust Business Glossary is the ability to define a semantic hierarchy of BDEs. A hierarchy enables the Business Data Stewards to classify their BDEs and show the relationships between them. It also helps to sort out a multitude of BDEs that seem to overlap or

*(Continued)*

**(CONTINUED)**

conflict in meaning. By building a hierarchy and defining each node, a clear picture of the meaning and relationships between BDEs can be derived.

A good example was the large number of BDEs used in referring to a *driver* in an automobile insurance policy. These BDEs included *Excluded driver, Non-ratable driver, Non-rated driver,* and *primary driver.* By building the hierarchy shown in Fig. 6.16 and defining each node it was possible to create a coherent picture of these related BDEs.

## Customizable and Configurable Business Glossary

One of the sad truths about commercially licensed tools is that, no matter how smart and dedicated the vendor is, there are going to be certain things you will need to change about how the tool works. A business glossary

**Table 6.7** Business Names, Definitions, and Owner/Stewards

| BDE Name | Definition | Function/ Data Domain |
| --- | --- | --- |
| Location | Any place where customers do business with the company. Includes all types of locations, such as a *branch, express outlet, contact center, main office,* and *Internet.* | Sales |
| Location ID | A unique identifier for a *Location.* a.k.a. company location ID, office number, Branch ID. | Sales |
| Policyholder tenure | The number of years a member has owned a policy with the company, including affiliated companies in other states. | Sales |
| Collection posting date | The date on which the collection amount was recovered by the company. | Financial operations |
| Retired employee indicator | Identifies whether or not a person is a retired employee of the company. | HR |
| Accident surcharge waiver indicator | Identifies whether the surcharge for an *Accident* was waived during the rating process based on certain business rules. a.k.a. Accident Forgiveness Indicator. | Underwriting |
| Accounting state | *Residential Address State* where the policyholder resided at the time a new business transaction took place. | Financial reporting |
| Assumed earned premium | *Earned Premium* assumed from another insurer, when the company is the *Reinsurer.* As a reinsurer assuming risk from another insurer, we effectively assume part of the risk and part of the premium originally taken by the *Primary Insurer.* | Financial reporting |

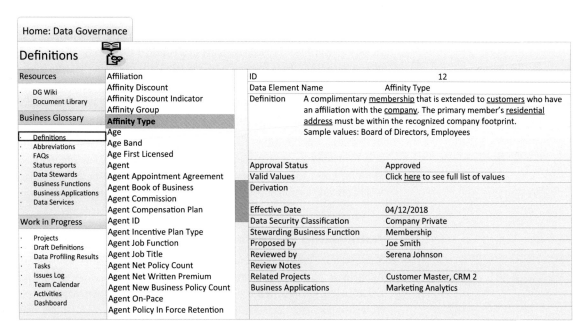

**FIGURE 6.15** A sample screen from a Data Stewardship Business Glossary.

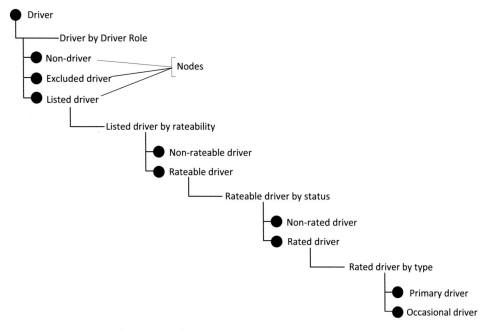

**FIGURE 6.16** A hierarchical description of the terms related to *driver*.

tool dictates how you are able to capture your metadata, and the underlying model (metamodel) limits what you can do. Perhaps you want to have a set of BDEs with links to business units that consider them to be key business elements (KBEs). However, the metamodel probably doesn't include a relationship from the BDE to business units, so you'd need to add one. Of course, it might also be missing all the other links that might make sense, such as to policies, business data quality rules, and so on.

In this case—and probably hundreds of others—it becomes important to be able to modify the metamodel so that you can configure how the business glossary works to meet your business needs. Ideally, the business glossary would provide a straightforward way of creating these configurations.

## Automating Processes with Workflows

Some vendor-provided business glossaries integrate a workflow engine. A business glossary workflow enables governance processes to execute according to a specified set of steps. This automated set of tasks can request inputs and decisions from people in designated roles. It can handle branching based on conditions, enforce business rules, and send notifications to achieve a desired result.

### Advantages of Using Workflows

Although a workflow almost always requires writing code, there are key advantages to using them that make it worth the effort. These include:

- Automating repetitive tasks and sending out notifications to the people assigned to roles that participate in the workflow. The workflow steps contain information on what occurs if the person does not execute on the task within the specified time (the "service level agreement," or SLA).
- Ensuring that all necessary steps are followed to reach a result. As you are likely aware, creating a manual "workflow" via emails and/or a shared document makes it easy to skip steps that should be executed.
- Recording an audit trail of changes, decisions made, and the people who made the decisions. This is extremely important when the workflow includes creating or modifying regulatory-related metadata.
- Enforcing business rules. While business glossaries can usually enforce simple rules, a workflow is much more capable in this regard. For example, if a field/attribute of a metadata asset is required only when certain values are used in another field/attribute, a workflow

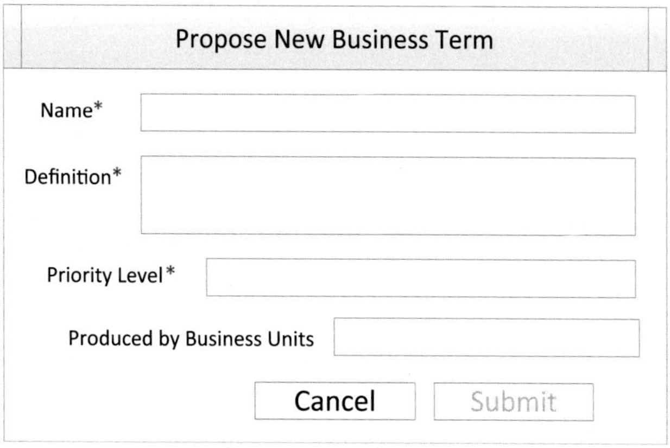

| Propose New Business Term |
| Name* |
| Definition* |
| Priority Level* |
| Produced by Business Units |
| Cancel     Submit |

■ **FIGURE 6.17** A sample workflow form for inputting and viewing a metadata asset. Note that the "Submit" button does not become available until all the business rules have been fulfilled.

can enforce this complex rule, while (on their own) most business glossaries cannot.

- Enabling the presentation of metadata in a custom form and format. Many commercial business glossaries—especially those based on a web-based interface—are quite limited in how the details of a metadata asset are presented on the screen. They often require considerable scrolling because the screen space is inefficiently used. Workflows can use "workflow forms" (similar to Windows dialog boxes) that present the information and input fields in a more compact and understandable format. These forms help to enforce business rules as well. For example, unless the mandatory information is supplied (indicated by the red asterisks in Fig. 6.17), the form cannot be submitted to move to the next step in the workflow.

## Gathering the Workflow Design Information

A workflow requires that you actually design it and capture the business requirements needed in order to get to the proper end result in the manner that is needed. To design a workflow, you need to know the following items:

- What do you want to achieve? In other words, if the workflow executes successfully, what is the end result? For example, if you are creating a BDE, then the end result (assuming the request is approved) will be a new BDE in the location specified.
- What roles are allowed to start the workflow? It is usually *not* wise to allow just anyone to start a workflow, as not everyone will have been trained on how to put good quality metadata into the workflow form.

For example, you may wish to allow only Business Data Stewards and members of the DGPO to start a workflow.

- What must be true in order to start the workflow? You'll probably want to specify which screen you need to be on in order to start a workflow. For example, if you want to propose an edit to an existing BDE, you'll probably want to require that the proposer is viewing it on the screen. You may also want to check that the BDE is in a particular state. For example, you probably don't want to allow the edit workflow to be started if one is already running.

---

**PRACTICAL ADVICE**

Assigning a status to metadata is a useful way for the workflow to figure out what is going on. For example, a BDE could be in "Accepted" status when it is created and approved, and must be in that status in order for the Edit workflow to begin. Once the Edit workflow begins, the asset could be moved into a status of "In Review." This status would inform the workflow that another Edit workflow is not allowed. Once the workflow finishes (either because the change is approved or rejected by the decision maker), the asset would move back into the "Accepted" status after the changes are rolled back.

Another common occurrence is that the role charged with making a decision does not have anyone assigned to it, perhaps because the previous occupant of the role has left the company. One common "fix" for this is to have the workflow detect this condition and have another role (sometimes called the "Role Manager") assign a new person to the role so the workflow can continue.

---

- What decisions must be made and what role must make each decision.
- For each decision, what branches are possible based on the decision. In addition, how long do you wait for the decisions to be made (the SLA), and what is the result if the decision is not made (times out).

Fig. 6.18 shows an example of detailed table that records the workflow design. In addition to the items listed above, it also shows which workflow form is used to capture the metadata. Fig. 6.19 shows the actual workflow in a swimlane diagram, showing each role and decision points/branches.

### Specifying the Workflow Forms and Rules Applied

A workflow form specification (as shown in Fig. 6.20) are used to collect the information to define the metadata and (where appropriate) enforce

| Process Step | Process Step Description | Business Rule | Roles Involved | Asset Status | User Input Required | Form Name | SLA | Notification Required? | Notification Name |
|---|---|---|---|---|---|---|---|---|---|
| Initiate Workflow | Asset Proposer initiates the workflow from within a domain. | N/A | Asset Proposer | N/A | N | N/A | N/A | N | N/A |
| Display Input Form | System displays the Propose Business Term input form. | N/A | N/A | N/A | N | Propose Business Term | N/A | N | N/A |
| Populate Input Form | Asset Proposer populates the Propose Business Term input form. | N/A | Asset Proposer | N/A | Y | Propose Business Term | N/A | N | N/A |
| Submit for Approval? | Asset Proposer submits the proposal for approval. All required fields/relationships must be populated before the "Submit" button is enabled. | N/A | Asset Proposer | N/A | Y | Propose Business Term | N/A | N | N/A |
| Create Asset | System creates an asset of type "Business Term" within the current domain. | BR-N-BT-001 | N/A | In-Review | N | N/A | N/A | N | N/A |
| Create Relationship to Identified Assets | System creates the relationship identified in the Propose Business Term input form. | BR-N-BT-002 | N/A | In-Review | N | N/A | N/A | N | N/A |
| Asset Approver Exists? | System determines if Asset Approver role player exists. See "Role Determination" tab. | N/A | N/A | In-Review | N | N/A | N/A | N | N/A |
| Create Role Assignment Task | If No (Asset Approver does not exist) -> System generates a task assigned to the Role Manager. See "Role Determination" tab. | N/A | N/A | In-Review | N | N/A | N/A | N | N/A |
| Notify Role Manager | If No (Asset Approver does not exist) -> System generated a task notification addressed to the Role Manager | N/A | Role Manager | In-Review | N | N/A | N/A | Y | Task Notification |
| Assign Asset Approver | If No (Asset Approver does not exist) -> Role Manager assigns Asset Approver | BR-N-BT-004 | Role Manager | In-Review | Y | Task | 15 days | N | N/A |
| Create Approval Task | System generates a task assigned the Asset Approver. | N/A | N/A | In-Review | N | N/A | N/A | N | N/A |
| Notify Asset Approver | System generates a task notification addressed to the Asset Approver. | N/A | Asset Approver | In-Review | N | N/A | N/A | Y | Task Notification |
| Approve Asset? | Asset Approver approves or rejects proposed asset. | BR-N-BT-004 | Asset Approver | If Yes -> Accepted If No -> In-Review | Y | Task Vote | 15 days | N | N/A |
| Display Comment Form | If No (Asset Approver rejects) -> System displays the Comment form. | N/A | N/A | In-Review | N | Comment | N/A | N | N/A |
| Input Comment | If No (Asset Approver rejects) -> Asset Approver populates the Comment form and submits | BR-N-BT-003 | Asset Approver | In-Review | Y | Comment | N/A | N | N/A |
| Delete Asset | If No (Asset Approver rejects) -> System deletes the asset. Any relationship to the asset is also deleted. | N/A | N/A | In-Review | | N/A | N/A | N | N/A |
| Notify Asset Proposer | If Yes (Asset Approver approves) -> System generates an Approval Notification. If No (Asset Approver rejects) -> System generates a Rejection Notification. | N/A | Asset Proposer | Accepted | N | N/A | N/A | Y | Acceptance or Rejection |

■ **FIGURE 6.18** A sample workflow form for inputting and viewing a metadata asset.

business rules. Each form needs to be defined, with the following information:

- Field Name
- Data type. This is not necessarily the physical data type (as stored in the database) but rather the data type recognized by the business glossary or other tool in which the workflow is running.
- Whether the field is required or optional (Required?)
- Whether the field can accept data (Enabled?). Some fields are just shown but cannot be changed. This occurs frequently during an "edit" workflow in which there are fields which are not allowed to be changed once they were specified in the workflow that created the metadata
- Applicable business rules. Business rules play a very important part in workflows. Many tools (including business glossary tools)

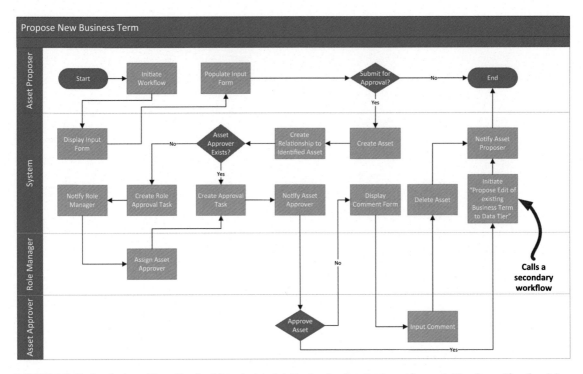

■ **FIGURE 6.19** The flow for the workflow, with a "lane" for each role and decision branches. Note that the workflow can "call" another workflow if needed.

| Propose Business Term | | | | | | |
|---|---|---|---|---|---|---|
| **Element** | **Data Type** | **Multi Valued** | **Allowed Values** | **Required?** | **Enabled?** | **Business Rule** |
| Name | Text | N | N/A | Y | Y | N/A |
| Usage Notes | Text | N | N/A | N | Y | N/A |
| Example | Text | N | N/A | N | Y | N/A |
| Note | Text | N | N/A | N | Y | N/A |
| Alias | Text | N | N/A | N | Y | N/A |
| KDE Flag | True/False | Y | True or False | Y | Y | N/A |
| KDE ID | Text | N | N/A | N | Y | N/A |
| KDE Priority Level | Selection | N | 1<br>2<br>3<br>4 | N | Y | N/A |
| Reference Data Indicator | True/False | N | True or False | Y | Y | N/A |
| Acronym | Text | Y | N/A | N | Y | N/A |
| Managed By Business Unit | Selection | Y | Business Unit | N | Y | BR-N-BT-006 |
| Consumed By Business Unit | Selection | Y | Business Unit | N | Y | N/A |
| Golden Source (System) | Selection | Y | System | N | Y | BR-N-BT-007 |
| Is Applicable to Geography | Selection | Y | Geography | N | Y | N/A |
| Comment (i.e. Reason for proposal) | Text | N | N/A | Y | Y | BR-N-BT-005 |

■ **FIGURE 6.20** Details of requirements for a workflow form.

| Rule ID | Rule Statement |
|---|---|
| BR-N-BT-001 | The Business Data Element name must meet the Business Data Element Name standard |
| BR-N-BT-003 | A Reason for Rejection must be added if the proposal is rejected |
| BR-N-BT-004 | The Status of a Business Data Element must be set to "Rejected" if the SLA of the approval task is exceeded |
| BR-N-BT-005 | The Comment text must be captured |
| BR-N-BT-006 | The Business Unit must belong to same legal entity as the business data element glossary. |
| BR-N-BT-007 | The relationship to a system should be limited to the systems available within the same legal entity as the one that contains the Business Term |

■ **FIGURE 6.21** Specifying the business rules that apply to the workflow.

| Notification Name | Subject | Sent To: | cc | Salutation | Body |
|---|---|---|---|---|---|
| Task Notification | Workflow Notification | <Asset Approver> | <Asset Proposer> | <Asset Approver> | A new Business Term approval task has been assigned to you. Please complete the task within fifteen (15) business days |
| Approval Notification | Workflow Notification | <Asset Proposer> | <Asset Approver> | <Asset Proposer> | Your request for the creation of the Business Term <business term name> has been approved. |
| Rejection Notification | Workflow Notification | <Asset Proposer> | <Asset Approver> | <Asset Proposer> | Your request for the creation of the Business Term <business term name> has been rejected for the following reason: <Comment.Reason for Rejection> |

■ **FIGURE 6.22** Specifying the notifications that the workflow sends out.

are not able to enforce more complex business rules. Good examples include when a set of optional fields become mandatory if a certain value is provided in another field, or when a set of valid values changes based on other information. Fig. 6.21 illustrates a set of business rules.

## Specifying the Notifications to the Roles

An important aspect of workflows is that they can limit which roles can start the workflow as well as route approvals to the right roles. Notifications are an important part of this functionality. The approving roles (called "Asset Approver" in Fig. 6.22) must get a notification that they have an approval task, and a variety of roles may need to be informed that a workflow has been approved or rejected. Fig. 6.22 shows some common specifications (including the subject line, who the notification is sent to and copied, and the body of the text) associated with these notifications.

**WHAT SHOULD YOU KEEP IN A BUSINESS GLOSSARY?**

As has been made clear in this book, the business glossary should include BDEs. However, a lot of other information is related (either directly or indirectly) to the BDE. These other metadata assets are not only useful in and of themselves, but also provide context to the BDEs. Fig. 6.23 shows a simple Metamodel of some useful metadata that you can store and maintain in the business glossary. In this sample, you can see the physical version of the BDE, the business data quality rule for the BDE as well as the more technical "Data Quality Rule Specification" (see Chapter 7: The Important Roles of Data Stewards) that is tested against the physical data element and gives you the profiling results (Data Quality Results) and any issues that are raised as a result of those results. If your enterprise has a need to file regulatory reports, this model also shows the structure of those reports as well as where the data to populate the reports comes from (and the data quality of that data).

Extending this model to gain a more complete picture of related metadata is something that will occur over time. Just don't fall into the trap of adding content to the business glossary (or any other tool, for that matter) just because you can. Some key points to remember as you determine what to put into the business glossary are:

- Information must be maintained—stale/out-of-date metadata is misleading. Thus if you don't have any idea how you'll input the changes and maintain the content, think hard before you put it in.
- Just because something is in the business glossary, does not mean it should be maintained there. As mentioned, the system of record (where the metadata is actually maintained) is often another tool, such as the Metadata Repository (MDR) for physical data elements or the data profiling tool for data quality results and issues. Those tools have the ability to automate a lot of the maintenance, after which the results can be shown (but not changed) in the business glossary.

Note that while the business glossary is the system of record for almost all of these assets, the Physical Data Element is specified and updated in the Metadata Repository (MDR) and should be view-only in the Business Glossary. Other assets that do not have the business glossary as the system of record are the Data Quality Results and Data Quality Issues, both of which usually come from the data profiling tool.

## A Metadata Repository

At its most basic level, a Metadata Repository (MDR) is a tool for storing metadata. In some cases, the MDR is largely focused on recording physical and technical metadata, such as data models, database structures, metadata associated with Business Intelligence tools (e.g., Business

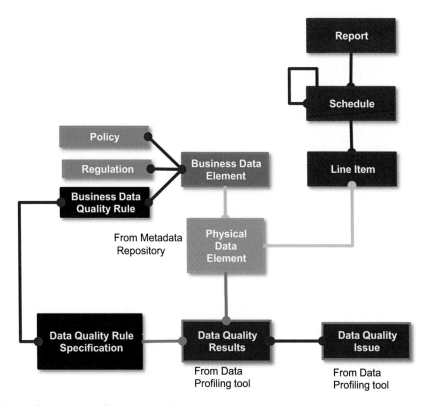

■ **FIGURE 6.23** Some useful metadata assets for storage in your business glossary.

Objects universes), ETL, Copylibs, file structures, and so on. Business metadata (such as BDEs, definitions, business rules, etc.) is often thought of as being stored in a Business Glossary, but there are many times when some business metadata may also be shown in the MDR, and some physical metadata may be shown in the business glossary so as to present a more complete picture of the metadata. The MDR can provide impact analysis for proposed changes, and lineage (where data came from and how it was manipulated). The MDR should also provide the link between the BDE (in the Business Glossary) and the physical implementation of that BDE. Finally, rules (such as the list of valid values for a physical data element) should be documented, and in sophisticated MDRs, even managed from the repository.

An MDR is critical to Data Stewardship because of the ability to link the BDE to its (potentially) many physical implementations. This is crucial for:

- Impact analysis (or forward dependency). When changes are proposed, it is very important to know everywhere the data exists

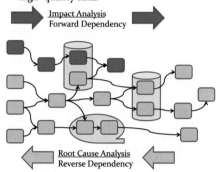

- Analyzing Data Dependencies
  - Unsuspected data dependencies introduce risks in ensuring high -quality data.

Impact Analysis
Forward Dependency

Root Cause Analysis
Reverse Dependency

■ **FIGURE 6.24** Impact analysis traces the dependency of the data forward in the data flow. Root cause analysis traces the dependency of the data backwards in the data flow.

downstream of the change—or everywhere there is data that depends on the data that was changed. Having this information enables the impact (a key deliverable from the Data Stewards) to be assessed and the proposed change to be propagated everywhere the data element exists. Fig. 6.24 illustrates a simple view of impact analysis as well as root cause analysis.

- Root cause analysis (or reverse dependency). When something goes wrong with the data (often identified as a data quality problem), it is important to trace the data back to where the problem occurred, thus identifying the root cause of the problem.
- Data quality improvement. In order to assess the quality of data (and potentially improve that quality), the data must profiled so that the actual quality can be compared against the stated quality needed for business purposes. This process usually starts by identifying a BDE; however, the profiling assesses the physical data in the database. Thus it is necessary to establish a link from the BDE to the physical data element. This link is sometimes called "logical/physical lineage." The link is built using the tools in an MDR.

## SUMMARY

Practical Data Stewardship includes choosing key BDEs based on their value, and then assigning responsibility and determining and documenting the business metadata (definition, derivation, and creation and usage business rules) for those business data elements.

In order to execute on Data Stewardship, issues must be recorded and worked on in an Issue Log, using repeatable processes driven by workflows. These processes include rules for the interactions between the Business Data Stewards and between the stewards and the Data Governance Program Office.

A robust set of tools—including a portal, wiki, business glossary (with workflows), and MDR—are also instrumental in documenting and publishing the progress of the stewardship effort as well. More importantly, these tools enable the effort to have the desired impact and be easily accessible to those who need the output from the Data Stewardship program. On top of the tools, a communications plan must be designed and used to let everyone know what Data Stewardship is, and what it is accomplishing.

# Chapter 7

# The Important Roles of Data Stewards

## INTRODUCTION

Business Data Stewards play an extremely important role in many enterprise processes and initiatives that work with data. These roles include inspecting and improving data quality, managing reference data, many of the aspects of master data management (MDM), specifying how data elements should be classified for security and privacy purposes, supporting Quality Assurance (QA), lineage, calculations of process risks, and compliance with privacy regulations. Without the involvement of Business Data Stewards, these efforts can make incorrect decisions, go down blind alleys, and even implement "solutions" that don't meet the needs of the data users in the company. Failure to enforce the privacy regulations will almost certainly result in punishment, including large fines.

In this chapter, we will discuss how Business Data Stewards contribute and guide these processes and play a key role in these initiatives.

## THE ROLE OF DATA STEWARDSHIP IN IMPROVING DATA QUALITY

Even if you start out with perfect data (which no one does), data quality can deteriorate over time without rigorous monitoring and input from Business Data Stewards. In many cases, no one is even sure what the quality of the data is because the data quality has not been measured and compared against a defined set of data quality rules.

### Measuring and Improving Data Quality

Stating a set of requirements (rules) for quality data is a crucial part of establishing the quality of the data. That's because regardless of who you listen to (including the ISO 9001 standard), quality is measured against a set of requirements. The requirements are driven by how the business will use the data—or how the business *wants* to use the data. As Jack Olson says in his book *Data Profiling, the Accuracy Dimension*: "You cannot tell if something is wrong unless you can define what being right is."

**Data Stewardship. DOI: https://doi.org/10.1016/B978-0-12-822132-7.00007-3**

The basic tenets of enforcing data quality—and the stewardship role in that endeavor—are illustrated by a story from my career as a Data Quality Manager at a large bank. A while back, a friend of mine (a technical manager in IT) was in charge of the enterprise data warehouse at the bank. One day at a meeting, one of the business leads asked her why the data warehouse couldn't deliver good-quality data. She responded that she would love to, but in order to do so, she needed to know three things:

- *What the business meant by good data quality.* That is, she needed rules to apply to tell her when the data did not meet the business requirements.
- *What to do with the data that did not meet the data quality rules.* Did she continue to load the data? Stop the load? Do something else?
- *Who to tell about the data quality issues discovered.* She needed to know who was responsible for dealing with what was discovered. She realized that just "knowing" of a failure didn't actually accomplish anything—someone had to do something with that information.

The answer to the first and third question is that the Business Data Steward is responsible for the data in question. And the Business Data Steward has to provide input into the second question, deciding what failures were important enough to disrupt the load.

There are three key points to this story. The first is that in order to measure data quality, you need to define what you mean by quality. The second is that to determine data quality, you must measure it. As the British physicist Lord Kelvin said, "If you cannot measure it, you cannot improve it." The third is that you need accountable decision-makers to respond to violations of the data quality rules. Just knowing isn't enough—you need to make corrections.

## Preventing the Deterioration of Data Quality

**NOTE**

The quality of data is often stated in terms of *data quality dimensions*. For example, the first bullet in the "Preventing the deterioration of data quality" section discusses two of these dimensions, namely *accuracy* and *completeness*. Table 7.1 defines a common set of dimensions of data quality.

There are many reasons why data quality deteriorates or is unknown. Among these are:

- *In many cases, data producers are incented to be fast, but not necessarily accurate.* Any time a data producer is paid solely based on how many new customers, new policies, new accounts, and so forth, can be entered, they will figure out how to "game" the system (you get what you pay for). Fields that can be left blank will be left blank, default values will be left unchanged, and so on. There are few cases in which data producers have an incentive to produce better data for downstream users. To change this behavior, Business Data Stewards must champion changing the business priorities, and having

**Table 7.1** Data Quality Dimensions.

| Data Quality Dimension | Description |
| --- | --- |
| Completeness | The degree to which data is populated based on the business rules that state when data is required to be populated with a value. For example, every account must have an Account ID. A more complex rule might state that a collateral record is required *if* (and only if) a Loan record is present and the Loan type requires collateral (such as a mortgage). |
| Uniqueness | The degree to which data is allowed to have duplicate values. For example, the Tax ID of each customer must be unique, no two customers can have the same Tax ID. |
| Validity | The degree to which data conforms to the business rules for acceptable content. This can include:<br>• Format<br>• Pattern<br>• Data Type<br>• Valid value list<br>• Domain<br>• Range |
| Reasonableness | The degree to which data conforms to rules about reasonable values when compared to real-world scenarios or in comparison to other data. For example, the Prescription Fill Date must be later than or equal to the Prescription Written Date. |
| Integrity | The degree to which data elements contain consistent content across multiple databases. For example, a Prescribed Drug is the same in the transaction database and in the Pharmacy Data Warehouse. |
| Timeliness | The degree to which changes to the data are available within the timeframe required by the business. For example, a change to an assigned airline seat must be reflected on the website in real time. |
| Coverage | The degree to which data supports all business functions that need the data to perform their specific business purpose. For example, data collected for homeowner's insurance must include a birth date to support master customer. |
| Accuracy | The degree to which the data corresponds to known correct values in the real world, as provided by a recognized or established "source of truth." For example, the address of a customer matches the address provided by the postal service. Many "sources of truth" are external like the postal service. Others may be internal such as survey data of company locations. What makes a source of truth is that people agree that it is a source of truth. |

data producers incented to be accurate and complete as well as fast. *Completeness* (one of the data quality dimensions) needs to be defined by the stewards so that data is filled in that serves the needs of all the data users, and not just the direct benefactors of the data entry effort. *Accuracy* (another of the data quality dimensions) can be helped in a variety of ways such as eliminating default values; thus, it takes just as much time to put in the accurate value as any other.

• *Individual data users may make their own "corrections."* If data consumers perceive that the data quality is insufficient for their needs, they may extract data and apply their own changes, thinking that those changes improve the quality. They may then pass that data along to coworkers, propagating their errors. The problem is that the changes may not improve the quality at all because the data still does not meet the needs of the downstream users. The data consumer may not understand what constitutes good quality, or even what the data actually is. Of course, if they have the meaning of the data wrong (poor metadata quality), then anything they surmise or change will be incorrect. To change this situation, Business Data Stewards need to make sure that the data is defined and that data quality rules are defined as well. If the data quality is insufficient for a data consumer, there needs to be a way for the consumer to engage with the Business Data Steward to raise an issue and have the quality improved.

- *Poor-quality data is not detected proactively.* Without Data Stewardship, poor-quality data is often discovered only at the point where someone wants to use the data and finds that it won't meet their needs. There generally follows a mad scramble to "fix" the data (often without fixing the root cause of the poor quality) or to find other data to use. Meanwhile, a business opportunity may be evaporating due to data that is of insufficient quality to take advantage of the opportunity. Business Data Stewards can make the business case (and provide the impetus) to enforce data quality rules at the point of origin and during data loads as well as to put in place a process for remediating the quality issues that come to light when the data does not conform to the defined rules (Data Quality rule enforcement).

- *Data Quality rules are not defined.* It is pretty hard to determine the quality of data if the rules that define that quality have never been defined. Without rigorous, measurable rules, data quality is largely anecdotal with varying opinions on the level of quality. The Business Data Stewards can define the data quality rules, and work with the stakeholders to ascertain the level of quality needed for various purposes (in context).

## What is Data Quality Improvement in Context?

Most people talk about improving the quality of data as an absolute—the data starts out with bad quality, and you improve the quality to have good-quality data. But it is not quite that simple. This approach raises two critical questions:

- *How do you allocate scarce resources to improve data quality?* As data quality issues arise, you may find that you don't have the resources to fix them all, so you will need to prioritize them. A business case (including cost/benefit analysis and return on the investment) needs to be made to establish those priorities and correct data quality issues. The most compelling case is usually to correct regulatory or compliance issues, followed by gaining competitive advantage by being able to use data that was not usable prior to the quality improvement effort. Similar to the guidelines for choosing key business data elements (discussed in Chapter 6: Practical Data Stewardship), other priorities include issues raised by company executives and issues that need resolution for use in high-profile projects.

- *How do you know when you're done?* That is, at what point has the data quality been improved enough that the data becomes usable for the intended purpose? This threshold will vary for different purposes. For example, cleaning up addresses for the purpose of sending out marketing fliers probably has a lower quality threshold than if the clean addresses were used to correctly identify patients for medical purposes. Thus setting the level of quality *in context* (for the intended purpose) is crucial. Obviously, spending time and money to improve the quality beyond what is needed is not an intelligent use of scarce resources. By having the Business Data Stewards (in concert with the stakeholders) establish the level of quality needed, you can tell when you're done and should move on to the next task.

To define the data quality rules and establish the thresholds in context, the Business Data Stewards need to work with data stakeholders. It is the stakeholders who care about the quality and who are impacted by poor quality. It is also the stakeholders who can establish the value to the company of improving the quality, and how that value is realized. For example, improving the quality for the country of residence for accountholders at a bank could reduce or eliminate anti-money laundering fines.

## The Importance of Improving Data Quality to the Overall Data Stewardship Effort

Improved data quality is one of the most visible and impactful results of a Data Stewardship effort—in fact, many feel it is the fundamental purpose of Data Stewardship. Whereas deliverables like repeatable processes, logistics, and workflows mainly benefit the efficiency of Data Stewards (which is important, make no mistake), improved data quality (and improved metadata quality) enables a company to operate more efficiently and take advantage of opportunities to get more value out of their data. In fact, much of the return on investment (ROI) for Data Stewardship and Data Governance revolves around improvement in data quality.

## Understanding the Dimensions of Data Quality

As the Business Data Stewards move forward to define the data quality rules, it is helpful to understand the *dimensions* of data quality. Data Quality

**NOTE**

It is often the case that the Business Data Stewards are themselves stakeholders. In fact, choosing a Business Data Steward who is a major stakeholder in the data they steward is a good idea.

dimensions are ways to categorize types of data quality measurements. In general, different dimensions require different measurements. For example, measuring *completeness* requires analyzing whether there is a value (*any* value) in a field, whereas measuring *validity* requires comparing existing data formats, patterns, data types, ranges, values, and more to a defined set of what is allowable.

While many dimensions have been listed and defined in various texts on data quality, there are key dimensions for which the Business Data Stewards can relatively easily define data quality rules. Once the conformance to those rules has been measured by a data profiling tool, the data quality can be assessed by Business Data Stewards. As mentioned previously, the data quality necessary for business purposes can be defined, and data profiling will tell you when you've achieved that goal.

The data quality dimensions that are often used when defining data quality rules are listed in Table 7.1.

## Specifying the Data Quality Rules

Data quality rules serve as the starting point for inspecting what is actually in the database (data profiling). A Data Quality Rule consists of two parts:

- *The business statement of the rule ("Business Data Quality Rule").* The business statement explains what quality means in business terms (see example). It may also state the business process to which the rule is applied and why the rule is important to the organization.
- *The "Data Quality Rule Specification".* The Data Quality Rule Specification explains what is considered "good quality" at the *physical database level.* That is, it explains at the physical datastore level, how to check the quality of the data. This is because data profiling examines the data in the database. The analysis portion of the data profiling effort then compares the database contents to the Data Quality Rule Specification.

For example, a rule for valid values of Marital Status Code for Customers might look like:

> *Business Data Quality Rule*: The Marital Status Code may have values of Single, Married, Widowed, and Divorced. It may not be left blank. A value must be picked when entering a new customer. The values for *Widowed* and *Divorced* are tracked separately from *Single* because risk factors are sensitive to whether the customer was previously married and is not married anymore.
>
> *Data Quality Rule Specification*: Customer.Mar_Stat_Cd may be "S," "M," "W," or "D." Blank is considered an invalid value.

The Data Quality Rule has to be highly specific as to what data element it applies to. In the previous example, it would have been necessary for the Data Quality Rule Specification to specify in which system (and possibly in which database) the table and column existed that were being tested. In a different system (with a different business process), the Data Quality Rule may look quite different, as in this example for Employees:

---

*Business Data Quality Rule*: The Marital Status Code may have values of Single and Married. It may not be left blank. A value must be picked when entering a new employee. Only *Single* and *Married* are needed as a check for benefits selected.

*Data Quality Rule Specification*: EmployeeDemographics.Marital_Cd may be "Sng," or "Mrd." Blank is considered an invalid value.

---

Another key point when specifying data quality rules is to specify all the rules that should exist. At the physical level, data quality rules break down into three main types, all of which can be important in evaluating the data quality:

- *Simple Column Content Rules.* These are considered "simple" because you only need to inspect the contents of a single column and check to see if the contents meet the rules. Samples of this type of rule include:
  - Valid values, ranges, data types, patterns, and domains.
  - Optional versus Mandatory (evaluates completeness).
  - Reasonable distribution of values. For example, in a customer database, you would expect a fairly even distribution of birthdays; a much larger number of birthdays on a given day of the year probably indicates a problem.
- *Cross-column Validation Rules.* The rules require inspecting values in multiple columns (typically in a single row of a single table) to determine whether the data meets the quality rules. Samples of this type of rule include:
  - *Valid values that depend on other column values.* An overall list of location codes might pass the Simple Column Content Rules, but only a smaller list of locations is valid if the *Region Code* is set to "West."
  - *Optional becomes mandatory when other columns contain certain data.* The *Value of Collateral* field may be optional, but if the *loan type* is "Mortgage," a positive value must be filled into the *Value of Collateral* field.

- *Mandatory becomes null when other columns contain certain data.* The *Writing Insurance Agent Name* field might normally be mandatory, but if the *Origination Point* is "web" (indicating the customer applied for the policy online), the *Writing Insurance Agent Name* must then be blank.
- *Cross-validation of content.* Detects inconsistencies between values in different columns. One example cross validates the name of a city with the name of a state in an Address table. That is, Minneapolis is *not* in Wisconsin. Another example is that the "Maiden Name" column must be blank if the Gender is "Male."
- *Cross-table validation Rules (see* Fig. 7.1*):* As the name suggests, these data quality rules check columns (and combinations of columns) across tables. Samples of this type of rule include:

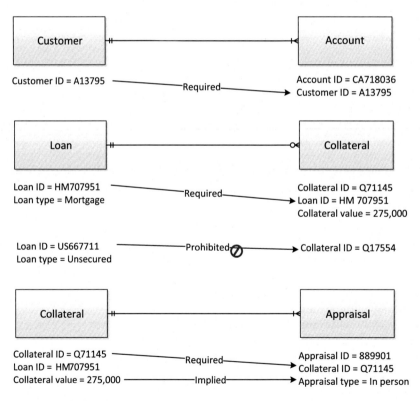

■ **FIGURE 7.1** Cross-table validation rule relationships.

- *Mandatory presence of foreign key relationships.* For example, if an Account must have a Customer, then the Account table must have a value in the *Customer ID* column that matches a value in the *Customer ID* column of the Customer table.
- *Optional presence of foreign key relationships depending on other data.* For example, if the *Loan_Type* is "Mortgage" in the Loan table, there must be a matching value for *Loan_ID* in the Collateral table. On the other hand, if the *Loan_Type* is "Unsecured," then there must *not* be a matching value for *Loan_ID* in the Collateral table because "unsecured" means there is no collateral for the loan.
- *Columns in different tables are consistent.* For example, if the *Collateral_Value* column contains a value above a certain level, the *Appraisal_Type* must be "in person" because of the high value of the property.

## Supporting Improvements in Data Quality and Data Profiling

To understand how Business Data Stewards participate in data profiling, it is helpful to understand the overall data profiling workflow, as shown in Fig. 7.2. The Business Data Stewards get heavily involved (as will be

> **NOTE**
> The categories of these physical data quality rules look much like the data quality dimensions discussed previously in this chapter because those are the very dimensions being tested.

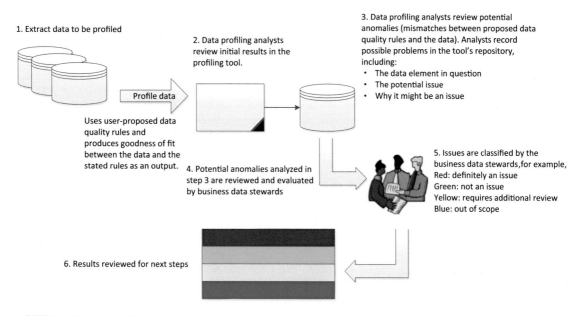

1. Extract data to be profiled

Profile data

Uses user-proposed data quality rules and produces goodness of fit between the data and the stated rules as an output.

2. Data profiling analysts review initial results in the profiling tool.

3. Data profiling analysts review potential anomalies (mismatches between proposed data quality rules and the data). Analysts record possible problems in the tool's repository, including:
   - The data element in question
   - The potential issue
   - Why it might be an issue

4. Potential anomalies analyzed in step 3 are reviewed and evaluated by business data stewards

5. Issues are classified by the business data stewards, for example,
   Red: definitely an issue
   Green: not an issue
   Yellow: requires additional review
   Blue: out of scope

6. Results reviewed for next steps

■ **FIGURE 7.2** The value gained from data profiling depends on the input and decisions from the Business Data Stewards.

discussed in this chapter) beginning in step 4, reviewing the potential issues, evaluating and classifying them to make decisions, and determining the next steps. These steps are the real "heart" of data profiling (the rest is largely extracting data and running the tool) and produce the true value that comes out of the data profiling effort.

Data quality rules come from two main sources. First of all, the data quality rules may be documented prior to beginning the data profiling effort and can be specified as an input into the tool. The data profiling tool then reports how well the data matches the rule (called *goodness of fit*). The second possible source of data quality rules can come from the tool itself. Many profiling tools are capable of suggesting *possible* data quality rules based on the data—what Jack Olson calls *Discovery*. For example, the tool may detect that a particular column in a large table virtually always contains a unique value. The tool would then propose (through the output) that this column should have a uniqueness data quality rule. However, there may be a few rows that are *not* unique; these would be flagged as outliers (violations of the proposed rule). In the case of tool-proposed data quality rules, the Business Data Stewards must make two decisions:

- *Is this really a rule?* Sometimes, the proposed rule is simply a coincidence, and is not a valid rule at all. In that case, the outliers may not be a problem. One example of this is when a column contains customers' phone numbers. The phone numbers may be largely unique, but occasionally two customers have the same phone number. Since there is no requirement for the phone number to be unique, the duplicates are not an issue.
- *If the rule is valid, what action should be taken about the outliers?* If there is a small number of outliers in old records (which can happen with systems that have gone through many revisions), the Business Data Stewards may choose to do nothing, especially if these are not active records any more. But the Business Data Stewards need to make this decision.

The second major role played by the Business Data Stewards is in reviewing the results of the data profiling against the stated business rules; what Jack Olson calls *Assertion Testing*. If the data does not conform well to the rule, (poor *goodness of fit*) it may mean that the rule has been misstated—often because of some special condition being left out. For example, in one company where I worked, a data quality rule stated that the credit score for a customer should be an integer between 300 and 850. This was generally true, but about 5% of the values were 999,

**NOTE**

In some organizations, the role of the Data Profiling Analyst (steps 2 and 3) may be handled by the Business Data Stewards.

**NOTE**

Even when the choice is to "do nothing," the issue and decision to not correct the data should be recorded along with the data profiling results for future reference.

clearly violating the rule. Upon being notified of data quality rule violation on a significant number of records, the Business Data Steward recalled that the value 999 meant that the score was unknown. These "special values" have to be stated as part of the rule or the fit of the data to the rule will be less than perfect.

The Business Data Stewards provide input and decisions when there are potential detected data quality problems. They must address these items:

- *Rule Violation.* Is a rule being violated? As discussed previously, unexpected values, patterns, data types, and ranges may indicate that either the data quality is poor, the rule is invalid or incomplete, or both! On the other hand, if the data profiling tool suggested the rule, it may not be a rule at all.
- *When a rule is violated, whether the violation is worth remediating.* For example, at a company I worked for, an auto insurance policy system showed over 13,000 unique values for the auto body type (4-door sedan, pickup truck, etc.). The expected number of valid values (according to the data quality rule) was only about 25. Analysis showed that the root cause was that the Auto Body Type Code field was free-form text, allowing any value to be entered. Upon examining the business process for writing a new policy, however, it was discovered that the field was not used even though auto body type is a key component of establishing the price of the policy. Instead, the auto body type was specified by the vehicle's VIN (Vehicle Identification Number), which has the body type built into the value of the VIN. Since the auto body type code field was not ever used, the decision was made that it wasn't worth correcting the values in the field.
- *Where the data comes from and how it originates.* This is important information in figuring out what is going wrong because (as noted previously) data production is often not focused on the downstream uses of the data. Of course, in an environment with a metadata repository, you may be able to inspect the lineage of the data to find out where it came from.
- *Characteristics of the data that may impact whether the quality is a concern.* These characteristics may include:
  - *The age of the data.* For example, often outliers (or rule violations) are from old records and it isn't worth correcting the data.
  - *Whether the data describes an active record.* If the data quality issue is in an inactive record such as an insurance policy that expired many years ago, it may not be worth correcting.

- *The threshold for data quality below which the issue doesn't matter.* As mentioned previously, the threshold for quality will depend on what the data will be used for ("in context").
- *Workarounds to get good-quality data.* A *workaround* is a method to obtain good-quality data without correcting the poor-quality data. The workaround itself may require spending money and effort, however, and as such, it must be evaluated and prioritized. In one example, an invalid timestamp was present on data coming from an outside vendor. It was possible to correct the timestamp with a simple calculation. In another case, a set of birthdates was known to be incorrect, and we were able to get the birthdates from another system. However, it was necessary to create an extract, transform, and load (ETL) job to access the high-quality birthdates.
- *Evaluation of the impacts to the business if the data issue is not addressed.* The business impact is a crucial ingredient in all of these decisions. If the field in question has little business impact, (or no business impact as in the example of the Auto Body Type Code) it shouldn't have a high priority for resources to correct the data quality. On the other hand, if the quality of data in a particular field is keeping an enterprise-critical system from going into production or causing a regulatory report to have inaccurate results, it may need to be fixed right away.
- *Evaluation of whether the data quality rule is valuable enough to set up automated enforcement and notification.* For important data quality rules on key data elements, it may be important to use automated methods to protect the quality of the data and keep it from deteriorating in the future. This decision should not be made lightly, as will be discussed here.

**NOTE**

Ignoring data issues that impact the business builds up "data debt." Like real debt, there may be ongoing costs to dealing with the data issues (interest) and a time may come when the data issue must be corrected, often at a higher cost than when it was originally discovered (balloon payment). The larger the business impact of the data issue, the larger the data debt.

## Enforcing Data Quality During a Load

The enforcement of important data quality rules requires defining the rules, managing any necessary reference data (as will be discussed in this chapter), and programming those rules into some sort of a Rule Engine (see Fig. 7.3).

Normally, IT has to be involved in the programming of data quality rules as well as the handling of data that violates the data quality rules (the invalid records). Handling violations includes:

- *Recognizing violations and "splitting" the stream of data into valid records and invalid records.* Note that this does not mean that invalid

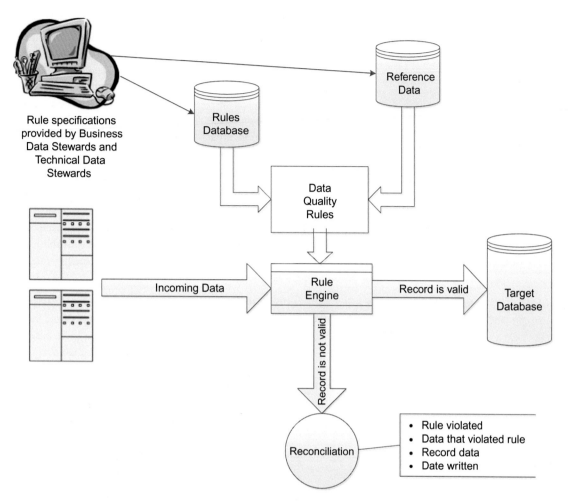

■ **FIGURE 7.3** Enforcement of data quality during a load requires specification of the rules by Data Stewards and the development of the enforcement mechanism (Rule Engine and error-handling) by IT development resources or through licensed applications.

records won't be loaded, but whether they are loaded or not, records that are not valid must be recognized.

- *Handling data that violates the data quality rules.* A number of options are available such as not loading invalid records, loading the records but keeping track of them for remediation, or even stopping the load.
- *Writing out information for invalid records and routing that information to the appropriate decision-makers.* Some data needs to be written out to help with reconciling the data with the data quality

rules that the data violates (see Fig. 7.4). The reconciliation process requires that the Business Data Stewards (and possibly Technical Data Stewards) perform an analysis and prioritization of the errors, determine which of these require a project to fix, and which of these can be immediately corrected (though "immediately" may actually take a while if resources are limited). In some cases, the correction may merely require an update to the rule (perhaps allowing for a wider range or a different data type) or an adjustment to the reference data (such as adding a new valid value).

Finally, it is necessary to execute an action to take if there is invalid data. Although IT is responsible for the development effort to accomplish the intended action, the Business Data Stewards and Technical Data Stewards need to provide input on what action(s) should be taken. There are essentially four possible things that can happen when invalid records (records containing data that violates one or more data quality rules) are detected during a data load:

- *Stop the load.* This is the most drastic action as it leaves the target database either unusable or populated with the contents of the last load (depending on how the load works). However, in some cases—such as a requirement for uniqueness that is tied to the table's primary key—there is no other choice. The load may also be stopped if less drastic errors occur more than a specified number of times— that is, the errors exceed the threshold for a data quality rule.

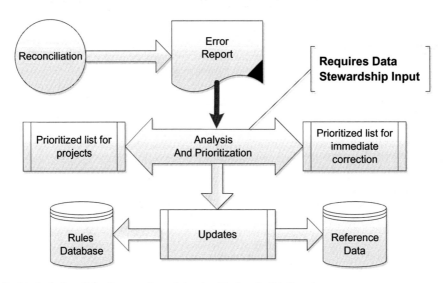

■ **FIGURE 7.4** The Data Quality Reconciliation Process requires analysis and updates from the Data Stewards.

- *Skip the invalid records and write them out to error tables.* In this scenario, the invalid records are not loaded into the database. Instead, they are loaded into a set of tables specifically designed for error analysis. After correction of the data (or determination that correction is not needed), the data is then loaded into the database, filling in the "holes" in the data. Unfortunately, this can be a complex process, especially if delaying the load of invalid records triggers other rules (e.g., if a missing parent record means that dependent child records also cannot be loaded). Further, if the errors are not addressed right away (which can certainly happen), the holes in the database grow with each new load, which may make the target database unusable.
- *Load the invalid records into the database, but also keep a log of the invalid records.* In this scenario the invalid records are loaded into the database but also into a set of error tables. This error log is the simplest solution, in that the target database is fully loaded, and a record of the data that failed the data quality rules is kept track of, perhaps as in Table 7.2. Once the corrections are made, however, the target database must be updated, either via direct edits or by reloading the corrected data from the source. Further, if you *are* going to load records that are known or suspected to violate data quality rules, some sort of warning to the users of the data should be provided.
- If your database structure supports it, you can flag the invalid records inline (right in the database), then find them later via a query/report. This satisfies the need (noted in the previously) of warning users that errors have been detected. However, your target database must have a column to hold the rule violation (which serves as a flag as well). This approach only works well if you are recording a single rule violation (a given record can violate more than one rule) or have a way to insert multiple rule violations into a single column—and parse the multiple rule violations during the query/report.

In any of these cases, a necessary additional action is to notify the responsible Business Data Steward and send an email notification (or create a

**Table 7.2** A Sample Invalid Records Table Structure.

| Date | ID | Table | Column | Value | Rule ID |
|------|-----|-------------|---------------|-------|---------|
| 2/13/2019 | 101 | Account | Account_Id | Null | NoNull1 |
| 2/14/2019 | 102 | Credit_Check | FICO_Score | 200 | Rng350 |
| 2/14/2019 | 103 | Person_demo | Marital_Status | Q | VValMS |

*In this table, the identifier for the invalid record is recorded, as well as the invalid data and the data quality rule violated.*

task in the workflow engine) to the responsible steward as well as the Enterprise Data Steward. Ideally, both the notifications and creation of the tasks in the workflow engine are fully automated.

**NOTE**

Identifying the appropriate Business Data Steward may involve consulting the Technical Data Steward, who should know who that is.

## THE ROLE OF DATA STEWARDSHIP IN METADATA QUALITY

Although what we do is termed "Data Governance" and "Data Stewardship," much of what the Business Data Stewards work with is actually metadata. Definitions, relationships between business data elements and their physical instantiations, lineage (as will be described in this chapter) and much more are metadata.

As a result, creating high-quality metadata—and measuring the quality of the metadata—is yet another responsibility of Business Data Stewards. As discussed in Chapter 6, Practical Data Stewardship, one of the most important pieces of metadata is a robust definition for a business data element. If there are similar terms—which might be mistaken for the defined term—it is important to ensure that these similar terms are clearly delineated and that users of the defined terms understand the difference.

Creating high-quality metadata and measuring that quality are especially important as it relates to measuring and improving data quality. That is because data quality rules are metadata, and the results of profiling data against those rules are also metadata. When you profile data, it results in a determination that:

- The interpretation of the data given by the metadata (data quality rules) is correct and the data is of good quality, or
- The interpretation of the data given by the metadata (data quality rules) is correct and the data is of poor quality, or
- The data quality is good, but the metadata quality (data quality rules and definitions) is poor, or
- Both the data quality is poor and the metadata quality is poor.

Fig. 7.5 summarizes these results, with the ideal outcome being that we get good metadata (correct data quality rules and definitions) and understand where our data quality is not sufficient. Fig. 7.6 shows an example of how the Data Quality Rule statement might need to be adjusted when the results of the profiling indicate a poor fit to the rule.

### "Profiling" Metadata

If the quality of metadata is so important, then it should be measured. In data quality this analysis includes data profiling as discussed previously

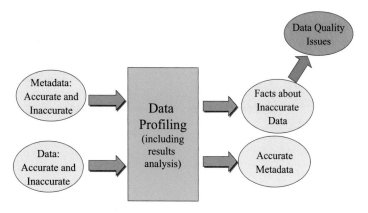

■ **FIGURE 7.5** How data profiling affects data and metadata.

- Data quality rules are metadata
- There can be errors in the statement of these rules, which become apparent when analyzing the results of data profiling – usually when the data quality has a poor match to the rules that define what good quality is.

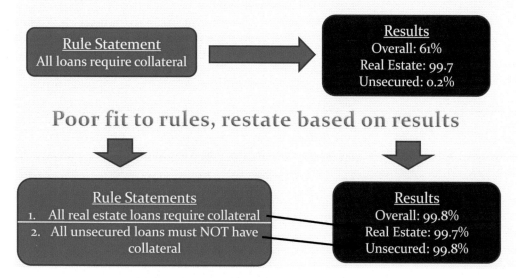

■ **FIGURE 7.6** If the fit to the data quality rule is poor, it may be the rule that is the problem.

in this chapter. You can profile metadata too, though the process is somewhat different. Fig. 7.7 summarizes this process, and should look similar to the process for data profiling.

There are some key differences, however. The first is that the "source system" on the left side of the figure is a system that stores metadata

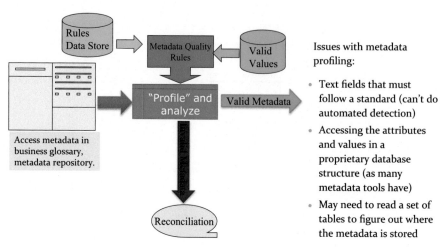

Issues with metadata profiling:

- Text fields that must follow a standard (can't do automated detection)
- Accessing the attributes and values in a proprietary database structure (as many metadata tools have)
- May need to read a set of tables to figure out where the metadata is stored

■ **FIGURE 7.7** The process for profiling metadata.

such as a business glossary or metadata repository. Next, some of the "profiling" needs to be carried out against text fields (such as definitions) and it is difficult to automate the determination as to whether the definition is a "good" definition—that is, it meets the standards of a good definition. As with the reconciliation of invalid data, the reconciliation of invalid/incorrect metadata is also carried out by Business Data Stewards, but typically the key is to correct the metadata, rather than focusing on the root cause. However, that is not always true, the root cause of a set of poor definitions may be an incompletely trained Business Data Steward, and that is something that should be addressed.

As with data quality rules, metadata quality rules come in several types. The rules can depend on other relationships or attribute values, much as with data quality rules. Table 7.3 explains the types of metadata quality rules.

## Dimensions of Metadata Quality

We are used to talking about dimensions of data quality (as described previously in this chapter) as a way of grouping similar types of quality rules and measurements together. Many similar dimensions can help to gauge the quality of metadata. These often have the same name as a data quality dimension, but may mean something different when referring to metadata quality. Table 7.4 details a set of metadata quality dimensions. These dimensions represent different potentially measurable aspects of

**Table 7.3** Types of metadata quality rules and related business rules.

| Type | Description | Related Business Rule(s) |
|------|-------------|--------------------------|
| Textual | Definitions and other text. | Standards must be followed to create a clear and unambiguous definition so the meaning is not open to interpretation. |
| Structural | Entity connections/relationships. These specify how metadata assets are related to other metadata assets as well as how many instances of the connection are permitted (cardinality) and whether the relationships are allowed, required, or prohibited. | Interactions between relationships that state how the presence or absence of a relationship affects the presence or absence of another relationship. Also, interactions between values of attributes that affect whether relationships are optional, mandatory, or prohibited. |
| Attribute | Properties of the asset. These state how limits of attributes are determined (including whether optional or mandatory). | Interactions between the values of attributes that affect whether the attributes can be populated, must be populated, and what values are valid. |

metadata quality. Once a method for measuring is established, the results of the measurements can be used to review metadata quality. You must be able to determine what is most critical to measure in terms of the processes supported (such as regulatory governance processes).

## METADATA IN QUALITATIVE DIMENSIONS OF DATA QUALITY

As described by David Loshin (*The Practitioner's Guide to Data Quality Improvement*), *Qualitative dimensions* of data quality show a higher level of oversight by listing and defining assets of the enterprise that help to evaluate data quality at a higher level. This metadata must be of high quality as well. These dimensions include:

1. Authoritative Sources. Check whether trusted data sources are specified. That is, each physical instantiation of a business data element contains a reference to a trusted authoritative source. An incorrect authoritative source means that you may focus on the wrong data to profile.
2. Agreements. Service Level Agreements (SLAs) governing data supplier and governance performance are defined. Conformance to the SLAs is measured. Incorrect SLAs mean you are measuring performance against an incorrect baseline.
3. Identity protection. Unique identifiers that are subject to privacy policies do not contain data that can be used to identify an individual. That is, decomposing or combining data elements with unique identifiers cannot be used to identify an individual.
4. Standards/Policies. Enterprise data standards are specified. Conformance to these standard and policies will be measured. Poorly understood policies and standards means that evaluation of data processes against these policies and standards will be incorrect as well.

**Table 7.4** Dimensions of Metadata Quality.

| Dimension | Description | Examples | Effort/Value |
|---|---|---|---|
| Completeness | Measures whether all required metadata fields and relationships have been populated. | 1. Every Business Term must have a Definition.<br>2. If a Business Term has the *Derived Flag* set to "true," it must have a Derivation. | Effort: Low (can be automated)<br>Value: High |
| Validity | Measures whether the content meets the requirements of a particular type of metadata. Metadata must meet the requirements of the standards, policies, and rules. | 1. Business Data Element definition and entity creation rules must meet the requirements of the published standards.<br>2. Metadata attributes have a value that falls within the stated set of valid values or range. | Effort: High (little automation possible)<br>Value: High |
| Accessibility | Measures whether:<br>• The metadata can be easily found.<br>• The tools available make it easy to search for/filter the metadata you are looking for.<br>• The people who need to access the metadata actually know how to do that.<br>• The value of the metadata is understood. | | Effort: Medium (survey)<br>Value: Medium |
| Timeliness | Measures whether the metadata is available and up to date at the time authorized users are attempting to use it. | 1. Input processes (including bulk import) achieved according to the agreed-upon service level agreement (SLA) for getting metadata into an environment where it can be used, searched, and filtered.<br>2. Approvals and other governance processes executed within the stated SLAs and the state of the metadata at any time is shown and understood. | Effort: Medium (automation and surveys)<br>Value: High (reflects on effective use and user satisfaction) |
| Consistency | Measures whether the various metadata is consistent or whether it conflicts with other metadata. | 1. Business Data Element: The Key Data Element Flag is not set, but the Key Data Element Priority field has a value.<br>2. The usage rule requires that certain pieces of data be used, but the Creation rule does not require that the data be captured. | Effort: Low (automation possible)<br>Value: High (Minimize confusion, support business processes) |
| Usefulness | Measures whether:<br>• The metadata provided actually enables the data managers and data users to understand their data and use it for the purposes needed.<br>• The metadata enables the Business Data Stewards to govern their data effectively. | | Effort: High (automation difficult, may use survey)<br>Value: High (understanding of data for effective use) |

*Continued*

**Table 7.4** Dimensions of Metadata Quality. *Continued*

| Dimension | Description | Examples | Effort/Value |
|---|---|---|---|
| Uniqueness | Measures whether a particular value can occur only once. | 1. Each business data element must have a unique name.<br>2. One asset can be linked to many others, but a rule states that only one of these types of links is allowed at a time.<br>3. A value/description pair in a list of valid values overlaps or means the same thing as another pair.<br>4. A set of fields overlap or represent the same information so they may conflict. | Effort: Medium (documented/ enforced in tool, but may need inspection)<br>Value: Medium |
| Accuracy | • Measures whether the attributes of the metadata:<br>  • Are from a verifiable source.<br>  • Describe the metadata correctly. | Part 1: A business data element has a definition that meets the standard for a good definition: Valid.<br>Part 2: The business data element definition actually describes a different business data element: *Not* Accurate.<br>Part 1: The Report Type is designated as "Regulatory": Valid.<br>Part 2: The report is actually a Risk report: *Not* Accurate. | Effort: High (automation difficult or impossible; needs source of truth)<br>Value: High (builds trust) |
| Integrity | Refers to structural integrity as specified at the model (entity) level. | 1. Relationship existence: Whether two entities can be related. If the model does not show a relationship between the entities, but the data shows a connection, that is a problem.<br>2. Relationship mandatory/Optional: Whether two entities *must* be connected or whether that connection is optional. Can be influenced by other conditions such as the value of an attribute.<br>3. Relationship cardinality: Whether an entity can be connected to just one instance of another entity or to multiple instances. | Effort: Medium (check actual data relationships against metamodel)<br>Value: Medium |

## THE ROLE OF DATA STEWARDSHIP IN MANAGING REFERENCE DATA

According to Danette McGilvray in *Executing Data Quality Projects*, Reference Data are sets of values or classification schemas that are referred to by systems, applications, data stores, processes, and reports as well as by transactional and master records. Examples include lists of valid values, code lists, status codes, state abbreviations, demographic fields, product types, gender, chart of accounts, and product hierarchy.

Organizations often create internal reference data to characterize or standardize their own information. Reference data sets are also defined by external groups such as government or regulatory bodies, to be used by multiple organizations. For example, currency codes are defined and maintained by the International Standards Organization (ISO).

The simplest case of reference data is "enumerated attributes," which refer to data that is limited to specific valid values. For example, the Marital_Status_Code might be limited to the value of "M" (for "Married") and "S" (for "Single"). To manage this type of reference data properly, the code value ("M" or "S") and the description that goes with each code ("Married" or "Single") must be defined and documented. Each code/description pair should have a business definition, though in practice this is rarely done, especially for the simpler values. For more complex values, however—such as the status of an account or insurance policy—it is important to have a definition for when (for example) the status is "active" or "inactive." This is particularly important when the code must be derived. For example, the status might be derived as "active" only when the Account_Start_Date is less than the system date, and the Account_End_Date is null (or some date in the future).

Reference data can be thought of as composed of two parts, namely a business description and a code value associated with that business description. The business description concerns itself only with the description and definition of that description, and doesn't worry about the code value that goes with it. The code value can vary from one system to another *even when the business description is identical between systems.* For example, one system may record the *gender code* as "M" and "F," while another system may record it as "1" and "2." The fact that both "M" and "1" have the description of "Male" is simply a difference in how the systems are implemented. Business Data Stewards must focus on ensuring that the list of descriptions meets their business needs, while the Technical Data Stewards can provide insight into the code values.

Business Data Stewards have an important role in specifying the descriptions, which are, in effect, definitions of the associated codes. If the description is insufficiently rigorous, the wrong code may be used during data input and data users will often misinterpret what the code means and use the data incorrectly. In addition, inadequate descriptions of codes make it difficult to map equivalent codes between systems.

In many companies, there is no "system of record" for much of their reference data. This is often the case with the enumerated attributes with a small list of values such as Marital Status Code or Gender. In that case, the Business Glossary/Metadata Repository can serve to hold this information. However, it is often not appropriate to store reference data in the Glossary or Repository. For example, the Chart of Accounts would have the Accounting system as its system of record, since that is where the list must be maintained for the system to operate correctly and where the validation rules are in place to prevent creating invalid accounts. There are also extremely large standardized lists (such as the ICD10 codes for medical diagnoses) that need to be stored and managed in a central area where systems that use that information can access it easily. In cases such as the Chart of Accounts or ICD10 codes, the Business Glossary should state where the reference data is stored (such as a table that contains ICD10 codes), rather than storing the reference data.

## General Maintenance of Reference Data

Business Data Stewards play a key role in the maintenance of reference data in critical systems. They need to:

- *Document and record the existing valid values to ensure that the values are well understood.* Data profiling can help with this process, and assistance from the Technical Data Steward may be required to access the data. However, the biggest challenge in understanding some sets of values is getting information from the business SMEs who produce the data.
- *Evaluate the need for a proposed new valid value to ensure that the value*:
  - *Does not overlap an existing value.* For example, the value of "widowed" for the marital status code overlaps the value "single." The Business Data Steward may choose to allow this overlap, but it should be done knowingly, rather than accidentally. Also realize that if the marital status is "Widowed" and the person remarries, a rule has to be in place to determine whether to change the marital status to "Married," losing the fact that the person was once widowed.
  - *Does not duplicate information that is recorded elsewhere.* For example, the value of *deceased* for the Person Status overlaps the *Deceased Flag* (a check box) recorded elsewhere. Again, this may be allowed, but any time you record information multiple times, the possibility exists for the data to conflict.
  - *Is consistent with the meaning of the field.* All too often, a new value is added to an existing valid value set to avoid adding a new field, a practice referred to as "overloading." For example, a new insurance policy status was added (to the existing values of "in

**NOTE**

Different systems may have different sets of reference codes (and descriptions) even for data elements that appear to be the same. Differences in the reference data occur due to differences in the data element definitions between the two systems. For example, one insurance system had a *policy status code* with values of "A" (active) and "I" (inactive). A second insurance system had a *policy status code* that used the codes "A" (active), "I" (inactive), and "M" (make renewal call). The definition of the *policy status code* in the second system has to include the fact that the status code was also a trigger for the business process of calling the customer to renew.

force" and "inactive") of "make renewal call." This new status is supposed to tell the agent that the policy is within 30 days of expiring, and that they should contact the customer. But it is *not* a status; the policy is still "in force." This information should be recorded in its own field or derived and presented on a report.

- *Evaluate the impact of the new value and ensure that the stakeholders are informed and consulted about these impacts.* For example, a transformation may fail because it does not handle a newly added value. Again, assistance may be needed from the Technical Data Steward to perform this evaluation.
- *Approve and document the addition of a new value.*
- *Detect the unauthorized use of new values.* It is important to detect when new values have been added to the list of "valid" values without going through the proper processes. Ideally, the time to detect unauthorized values is before they are used. Detecting these values may be possible if the source systems maintain their own list of values, which can be queried on a regular basis and compared to the authorized list. Another way to detect unauthorized values is to perform data validation during data movement (ETL) such as when loading a Data Warehouse.

## Aligning Reference Data Values Across Systems

Physical codes in reference data are often more complex than the business descriptions. Even when equivalent data elements in different systems have the same description, the code values are often different. For example, a system may use "Ma" and "Si" (rather than "M" and "S") for the marital status codes. However, comparing reference data from different systems is often far more complex than just converting equivalent values (such as "M" to "Ma") because there is not always a direct correspondence between the data elements. To use the marital status code as an example, one system might simply have a *Married Indicator* (with values of "Y" or "N") showing that you are either married or you are not. All the codes that indicate married would map to "Y," and all those that indicate not married would map to "N." The granularity of *Divorced* and *Widowed* would be lost unless you have a method to preserve that information, as will be discussed.

> **NOTE**
> The set of mappings between the values in a source data element code set and the set of values in a target data element code set is often called a "crosswalk." The crosswalk contains the set of "code mappings." Each code mapping specifies the source code set and value, the target code set and value, and the transformation logic.

During the mapping process, you are mapping values from various source systems to create an "enterprise aligned" data element with "enterprise aligned" values, as illustrated in Fig. 7.8. Fig. 7.8 shows the source system data model down the left side with the source element and its multiple values. The right side shows the shared (or "aligned") elements with their values. In the center are the mapping rules that show how the value of an element in a source system is mapped to the value in an aligned element.

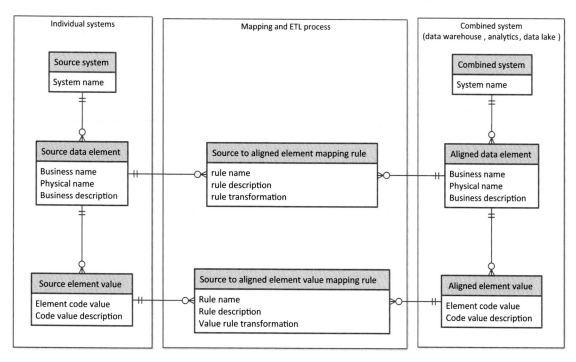

■ **FIGURE 7.8** Mapping source system data elements (and their values) to aligned elements and aligned values.

It is always advisable to profile the reference data to determine what actual values exist in the database as well as the distribution of those values. The Business Data Steward can then make decisions about what values must be converted (also called "harmonized") as well as what to do with values that are not converted.

In addition to mapping equivalent values directly, several different mapping cases need to be dealt with:

- *Data elements with the same name that mean something entirely different.* Column names tend to get specified by a developer, DBA, or modeler—and two different systems may use the same terminology for different purposes. For example, in one automobile insurance system, Sex_code referred to the gender of the primary policy holder. In the equivalent Homeowner's policy system, Sex_code referred to the gender of the oldest person in the household (used for discounting purposes). Thus despite being named the same and even seeming to contain the same format of data, these fields did not represent the same thing.
- *Data elements with different names that have the same meaning.* This case is common for the same reasons as the previous one. Older systems tend

to use short names, while newer systems may use a longer, more descriptive field name. For example, one system may call the Marital Status Code MS_CD, while another might call it Marital_Status_Code.

- *Data elements that mix several different elements together.* Fig. 7.9 illustrates this case. In Source System 1, some of the valid values (Widowed, Divorced) are not marital status codes at all; instead these values describe *why* someone's marital status is "Single." Thus in the Enterprise-Aligned view, those values should be mapped to a Marital Status Reason Code, and they should also set the value of Marital Status to "Single." Source System 3 shows the case where a new valid value for "Registered Domestic Partner" was simply added to the Marital Status Code when the company decided to record this information and provide the same benefits to registered domestic partners as they did to married couples. However, "Registered

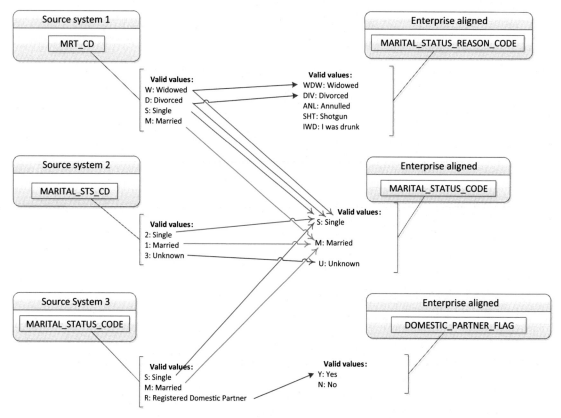

■ **FIGURE 7.9** Mapping mixed sets of valid values to the enterprise-aligned view. Each system calls the column something different. In addition, the valid values are different from one system to another, and there are differences in the granularity and meaning of the columns.

Domestic Partner" is *not* technically a marital status; it describes an entirely different situation. Thus in the Enterprise-Aligned view, it is mapped to an entirely different data element (Domestic_Partner_Flag), which has values of "Yes" and "No."

The process of bringing reference data together from multiple systems (and dealing with the issues discussed) is called "harmonizing values." This is necessary any time you need to combine data such as when building a data warehouse across multiple business functions or to use reference data as one of the determining attributes for performing identity resolution as part of MDM. A simple example involves creating a "central patient" record for a healthcare company. The gender of the patient is often a determining attribute in resolving multiple patient records. But the gender code might be recorded as "M" and "F" in one system, and "1" and "2" in another. These values have to be understood and mapped together to match up the patient records. The role of Business Data Stewards in Identity Resolution in MDM is discussed in more detail in the next section.

Business Data Stewards play an important role in managing reference data when harmonizing values, as shown in Fig. 7.10. The Business Data Stewards must:

- Review and understand the source system reference data element and each of the valid values associated with the element.
- Determine what reference data is needed in the enterprise-aligned view, and what those values should be.
- Map and approve the source value to the enterprise-aligned (harmonized) values.
- Manage the harmonized values and mappings.

> **NOTE**
>
> A case could be made that *registered domestic partner* actually does represent a marital status because, at least for the purposes of this company, the business processes and benefits afforded to married couples were being extended to registered domestic partners. Again, it would be up to the Business Data Steward to make a recommendation on how to handle this new business case.

## THE ROLE OF DATA STEWARDSHIP IN IDENTITY RESOLUTION FOR MASTER DATA MANAGEMENT

> **WHAT IS MASTER DATA?**
>
> In any organization, there are going to be commonly recognized "business entities" that are the subject of key business processes and represent real "things" in the world. Examples include customers, products, vendors, and employees. That is, the data that represents a customer in an application actually corresponds to a real person or organization. Those business entities that matter the most to the organization are considered core
>
> (*Continued*)

**(CONTINUED)**

(master) business objects and together with their associated metadata are thus called "master data."

Master data entities usually exist in multiple business functions and applications, though the set of data captured and available in each may be different based on the needs of that business function or application. According to David Loshin (*Master Data Management*, Elsevier, 2009) the goal of master data management is to "support an organization's needs by providing access to consistent views of the uniquely identifiable master data entities across the operational infrastructure." In other words, with successful master data management, any time you look at data that describes a master data entity (such as an actual customer), you know *which one it is, and which ones it is not.*

David Loshin also goes on to state that master data management supports business needs in many key ways, and among these are:

- Identify core information objects relevant to business success that are used in different application data sets that would benefit from centralization. *In other words, choose which core business entities are worth "mastering."*
- Manage collected and discovered metadata in an accessible, browsable resource, and use the metadata to facilitate consolidation.
- Collect data from candidate data sources, evaluate how different data instances refer to the same real-world entities, and create a unique, consolidated view of each one.
- Institute the proper Data Stewardship and management policies and procedures at corporate and line-of-business levels to ensure a high-quality master data asset.

These business needs all require involvement from Business Data Stewards (as well as other types of data stewards) to be successful and not only make it possible to create the master data entities, but enable people across the organization to benefit from this effort.

One of the most important parts of an MDM effort is resolving multiple instances of data that represent the same entity into a single record for that entity. This is called "identity resolution." For example, an insurance company has separate systems for selling automobile insurance, home-owner's insurance, and personal liability insurance. A customer might own all three types of insurance, but unless the insurance company has a way to resolve the identities of the customers in all three systems, they would never know that the same person was a customer for all three types of insurance. This could lead to missed multipolicy discounts and effort wasted trying to sell a person insurance they already had (which

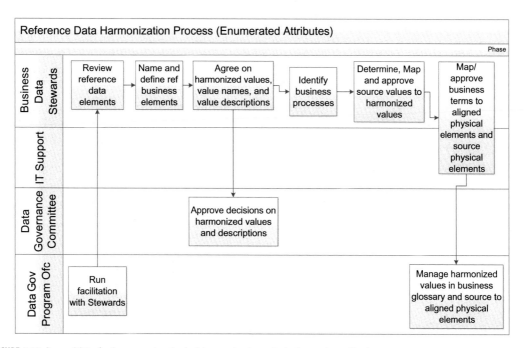

■ **FIGURE 7.10** Responsibilities for the process steps involved in managing harmonized reference data valid values.

certainly would not help the credibility of the company either). Another example is a chain drug store where the same person might have prescriptions filled at multiple different stores. Without being able to tell that it is the same person, there is a danger of failing to catch potentially harmful drug–drug interactions and fraud.

Business Data Stewards have a number of important decision-making responsibilities during the identity resolution process.

Fig. 7.11 shows the overall workflow for identity resolution, and as you can see (and as we will discuss), the Business Data Stewards (as well as IT support, which may include Technical Data Stewards) have many roles to play and many decisions to make in arriving at the "golden copy"—the single record that represents a real-world entity.

## Identifying the Identifying Attributes

*Identifying attributes* are those fields that, when used in combination, uniquely identify records as describing the same "real-world" instance of

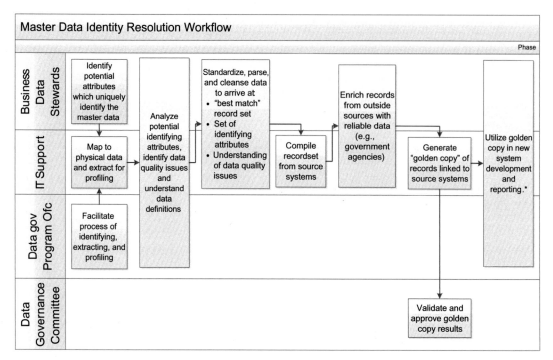

■ **FIGURE 7.11** The workflow for identity resolution. Processes that include the Business Data Steward "swim lane" require input and decisions from the Business Data Stewards.

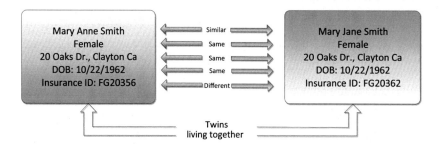

■ **FIGURE 7.12** Compare the values in the identifying attributes of two records to discern whether they represent two different entities.

a master entity. For example, the identifying attributes for a customer might be a combination of first name, last name, gender, birth date, address, and email address. That is, if two people had the same values for all these attributes, they would be considered to be the same person. Fig. 7.12 shows how you might use identifying attributes to distinguish between two very similar records. The identifying attributes are compared across the two records and differences between the two records help to make the decision.

It can be tricky to figure out the identifying attributes. On the one hand, you want the minimum set of attributes as they must exist in all the systems from which you want to aggregate records to create the golden copy. Balancing that, however, is the need to have a high degree of confidence that you are indeed compiling a set of records that represent the same entity. On top of these needs is the requirement to have good-quality data in the identifying attribute fields. For example, you might have a field for the Social Security Number for your customers (a great unique identifier), but if the field is mostly empty, it is not a good identifying attribute.

The Business Data Stewards should have knowledge of what data exists, what issues there are with the data, and how to find the data. Gathering the set of identifying attributes can become an iterative process as you map the fields between systems, examine the completeness and other quality dimensions of the data, and attempt to create the golden copy. And even though there are software tools that can catalog potential identifying attributes and propose a set of candidates to use, the Business Data Stewards are your best decision-makers on the final set of identifying attributes.

Another important decision that must be made is the sensitivity of the golden copy to false negatives and false positives. A *false negative* is when two instances of the same entity are classified as being different entities. For example, if the marketing system has two records for a customer and one has the wrong birth date, it might be concluded that these are really different people. The end result might be that the customer gets two copies of a catalog, or fails to get a volume discount because purchases are not aggregated to the same customer. The example of the missed drug—drug interaction (which can potentially be fatal) is another consequence of a false negative. A *false positive* is when instances of different entities are incorrectly merged to be the same entity. For example, two patients in a hospital system are determined to be the same patient when they are not. The end result could be incorrect dispensing of medications, improper surgeries, and misdiagnoses of diseases. Clearly, the consequences of a false positive in the case of a hospital patient are far greater than for a marketing customer, and, thus, the confidence level at which the merging of hospital records can take place must be far higher than that for a marketing customer. The Business Data Stewards have important input in determining this sensitivity. A high required confidence level usually leads to a larger number of high-quality identifying attributes being required before a golden copy is created. It also leads to more effort being required to cleanse and standardize the data to enable it to be used for identity resolution.

**NOTE**

In the ideal case, the data might contain a field that is unique to an individual such as a tax id (examples include Social Security Number or Social Insurance Number). That single attribute would then be the only needed identifying attribute. Another example might be a company-issued identifier for registered members such as a user ID. However, keep in mind that there need to be checks, even in the case of a unique identifier. The checks are needed because numbers can be miskeyed or otherwise mistakenly entered. In the case of a person, for example, it would be good to do a check on name and birth date. Such a check would also pick up "normal" occurrences such as when a woman changes her name after marriage.

There are software tools that can assist with identity resolution. Many of these tools use a score to indicate how closely two records (when compared to each other) match. The higher the score, the higher the probability that the records represent the same entity (based on the tool's algorithms). Fig. 7.13 shows what the output from such a tool might look like. In this example, the tool is comparing records from two systems (System 1 and System 2).

The Business Data Stewards must provide input to:

- *Set the score above which two records are considered to be an automatic match.* This score is sometimes called the *Upper Trust Limit*. Pairs of records with scores above the Upper Trust Limit are considered automatic matches. If there are too many false positives, the Business Data Stewards may recommend raising this limit. In Fig. 7.13, the record pairs above the Upper Trust Limit bar would automatically be considered to represent the same entity (matches).
- *Set the score below which two records are considered to be an automatic nonmatch.* This score is sometimes called the *Lower Trust*

| System 1 | System 2 | |
|---|---|---|
| John J. Jones, 03/12/1954, M, 123 Main St., Nashville, TN | J.J. Jones, 03/12/1954, M, 123 Main St., Nashville, TN. | |
| Mary Ann Smith, F, 10/10/1960, 426 Gulf Road, Teaneck, NJ | Mary A. Smith, F, 10/10/1960, 426 Gulf Road, Teaneck, N.J. | |
| Achmed Matsoumis, M, 04/06/1971, 202 West St., New York, N.Y. | Achmed Matsoumes, M, 04/06/1971, 202 West St., New York, NY | Upper trust limit |
| Billy Bob Yahoo, M, 04/12/2000, 1414 14th St., Louisville, KN | William Robert Yahoo, M, 04/12/2000, 1414 14th St., Louisville, KN | |
| Abigail J. Worster, F, 03/04/1987, 2020 Moon St., Portland, OR | Abigail Jay Worster, F, 04/03/1987, 2020 Moon St., Portland, OR | |
| Martin Robert Piers, M, 05/22/1061, 155 Kirkwood Ave., SF, CA | Martin R. Piers, M, 05/22/1961, 155 Kirkwood Ave., SF, CO | Lower trust limit |
| Larry R. Matheson, M, 12/12/1988, 44 15th Ave., Seattle, WA | Lorens R. Matheson, F, 10/14/1988, 45 15th Ave., Seattle, WA | |
| Bobby Kinnison, F, 09/06/1977, 125 Memson Ct., Los Angeles, CA | Robert Kinnison, M, 09/10/1978, 125 Momson Ct., Torrance, CA | |
| Laura M. Garcia, F, 07/05/1988, 202 Broadway, Abilene, TX | Laura A. Garcia, 07/10/1990, 313 Broadway, Apt. A, Abilene, TX | |

■ **FIGURE 7.13** The Upper and Lower Trust Limits specify the records that are considered to be automatic matches (Upper) and automatic nonmatches (Lower). Records that fall between these limits require further analysis to determine whether they represent the same entity.

*Limit.* Pairs of records with scores below the Lower Trust Limit are considered automatic nonmatches. If there are too many false negatives, the Business Data Stewards may recommend lowering this limit. In Fig. 7.13, the record pairs below the Lower Trust Limit would be considered to represent different entities (nonmatches).

Pairs of records that fall between the Upper Trust Limit and the Lower Trust Limit are candidates for further analysis. Oftentimes a human being (perhaps an Operational Data Steward) can examine these records and make a match/no match decision. However, if there are too many of these records, it can be difficult and time-consuming to get through them all. Adjusting the Trust Limit scores can reduce the number of these candidates, but the tradeoff is that it may also increase false positives or false negatives.

## Finding the Records and Mapping the Fields

The Business Data Stewards and Technical Data Stewards need to work together to:

- *Figure out what systems contain records that must be integrated into the golden copy.* If you are going to have a master record (golden copy) then all the systems that contain records corresponding to the entity must be mapped so they can be used properly.
- *Figure out the metadata that describes the fields in each system.* Field names may give a clue, but they are usually not the whole story. For example, the "Birth date" field in a homeowner's insurance policy system actually contained the date of birth of the oldest person living in the home, and *not* necessarily the policy holder's birth date. Assuming that the field contained the Policy holder's birth date would have led to a false negative and would have missed the fact that the customer had a homeowner's policy. This effort exposes a lot of information about the contents of identifying attributes, as illustrated in Fig. 7.14.
- *Profile and examine the data in the identifying attributes.* Analyzing what is stored in the fields can help to understand what the field means as well as how the field is being used in a particular system. It is also crucial in understanding what data is stored and in what format. For example, a full name field might contain multiple full names (which would need to be parsed), in which case a matching algorithm would not match the full name in that system's field with the full name stored in another system. The problem here is that in order to match records, you need to be able to clearly define the

**NOTE**

In addition to adjusting the scores that represent the Upper and Lower Trust Limits, the Business Data Stewards may recommend additional (or different) identifying attributes. They may also recommend additional data cleansing, standardization, or enrichment (as will be discussed in this chapter).

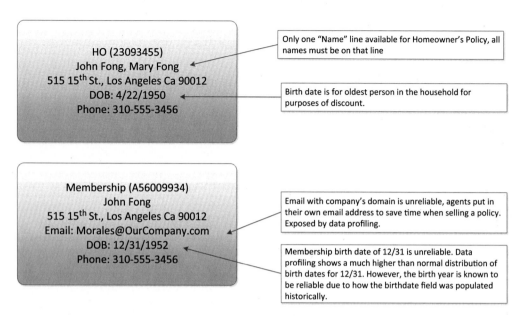

HO (23093455)
John Fong, Mary Fong
515 15th St., Los Angeles Ca 90012
DOB: 4/22/1950
Phone: 310-555-3456

Only one "Name" line available for Homeowner's Policy, all names must be on that line

Birth date is for oldest person in the household for purposes of discount.

Membership (A56009934)
John Fong
515 15th St., Los Angeles Ca 90012
Email: Morales@OurCompany.com
DOB: 12/31/1952
Phone: 310-555-3456

Email with company's domain is unreliable, agents put in their own email address to save time when selling a policy. Exposed by data profiling.

Membership birth date of 12/31 is unreliable. Data profiling shows a much higher than normal distribution of birth dates for 12/31. However, the birth year is known to be reliable due to how the birthdate field was populated historically.

■ **FIGURE 7.14** Understanding the metadata and field contents of potential identifying attributes.

content and structure of each field in the record. Another example is addresses. Profiling the address fields exposed numerous misspellings and "impossible" addresses (Detroit is not in Illinois). But by knowing about these errors (which would not have been matched to the addresses stored in other systems), we were able to apply an address standardization algorithm and obtain matches. As you can see from the address example, it is critical to clean up data before attempting to match data between systems.

## Standardizing the Values

Since MDM depends so much on matching values to determine where various records indicate (or don't indicate) the same real-world entity, a step in which the data is standardized for matching is important. For example, in many systems, addresses are free-form fields, which allows for spelling mistakes to occur (especially in street and city names), variations in abbreviations (Street, Str., St.), and "extra data" entered on address lines when no other field is available (Trustee for John Smith). Name fields may have the same problem if no field is provided for a "generation code" (Jr., III, etc.) or for an honorific (Mr., Dr., Professor, etc.). Phone number formats vary widely, using spaces, dashes, parens, and other symbols. Fig. 7.15 shows some of the steps that a name/address associated with various accounts in different systems may go through in order to facilitate matching.

## Enriching the Data From Outside Sources

It is often possible to enrich the data (and identifying attributes) you have by using outside sources (see Fig. 7.16). For example, an automobile insurance policy system may have unreliable addresses, but highly accurate driver license numbers for the policyholders. The DMV, on the other hand, has reliable addresses linked to the driver license numbers because the registration and other paperwork must be mailed to the driver. By retrieving the addresses from the DMV using the driver license number, it is possible to enrich the addresses with accurate information. The Business Data Stewards will usually know where this is being done or is possible, and may even be able to suggest what outside sources will work best. The Business Data Stewards may also know where there are issues with the quality of the data such that enrichment may be impractical or unreliable. In one case, for example, fake driver license numbers were being filled in by the agents to get policies written without needing to force the policyholders to provide their driver licenses. In cases where the fake driver license numbers corresponded to real ones (for someone else), the enriched data that came back from the DMV was inaccurate (did not represent data for that individual) and represented a significant data quality problem, as well as insurance fraud on the part of the agent!

> **NOTE**
>
> As difficult as it is to perform identity resolution for individual human beings, it can be even more difficult when dealing with customers that are not human beings—such as corporations, charities, wholly-owned subsidiaries, etc.

| System/Record Id | Field | Change to | Note |
|---|---|---|---|
| Auto (XG12590) HO (23093445) PrsLiab (PL33490) Mbrship (A5609934) | Address | Standardize to 515 15th St., Los Angeles, CA 90012 | Correct zip, remove any line with "*Trustee*" use standard abbreviations of St., Ln., Ave. |
| HO (23093445) | Name | Parse name field to extract individual names | Names are separated by "/" or "*" |
| Auto (XG12590) | Name | Extract "Jr", "III" to suffix field | Auto system has generation code in last name field |
| HO (23093445) PrsLiab (PL33490) Mbrship (A5609934) | Phone | Fully format phone field to add area code  310-556-3456 | Phone numbers formatted differently in different systems |

- If possible, additional data should be captured to fill in data "gaps"
- Where appropriate, enhance systems to make data capture easier
- Discovered major data quality issues may lead to change in incentives

■ **FIGURE 7.15** Standardizing the data in multiple records helps matching occur.

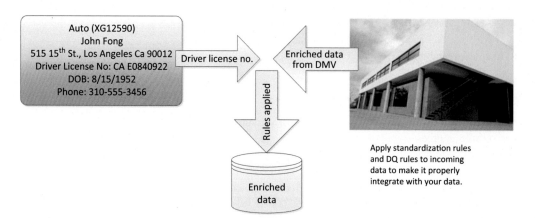

■ **FIGURE 7.16** Enriching and enhancing data.

## THE ROLE OF DATA STEWARDSHIP IN MASTER DATA MANAGEMENT SURVIVORSHIP

Another key aspect of MDM is called *survivorship*. David Loshin defines this concept in his book *Master Data Management* (Elsevier, 2009, page 193) as "the process applied when two (or more) records representing the same entity contain conflicting information to determine which record's value survives in the resulting merged record." To determine the values that survive in the golden copy record requires a set of business rules to resolve the conflicting values and choose one. Loshin describes it this way, "The master data attribute's value is populated as directed by a source-to-target mapping based on the quality and suitability of every candidate source. *Business rules delineate valid source systems, their corresponding priority, qualifying conditions, transformations, and the circumstances under which these rules are applied.*" The Business Rules must be determined by the Business Data Stewards for the mastered data based on the variety of considerations that Loshin discusses.

Fig. 7.17 illustrates a simplified view of the Survivorship process. The Business Data Stewards and Technical Data Stewards (as well as other contributors) identify the various sources of each master data attribute. This is typically done in the early stages of the MDM effort, alongside the effort to locate the identifying attributes. Once the sources of each attribute are documented, the survivorship business rules need to be specified. The business rules establish the priorities of the available

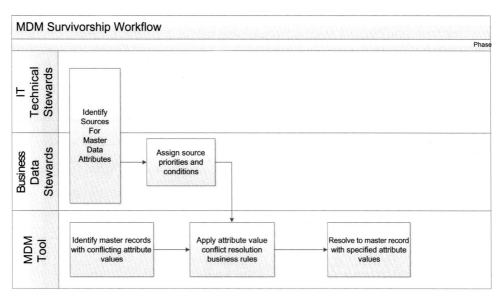

■ **FIGURE 7.17** Business and Technical Data Stewards set the survivorship rules that are then applied by the MDM tool.

values—that is, what value should be chosen to populate into the golden copy. Examples of establishing priorities include:

- *Value missing or blank.* Clearly, if a value is missing or blank, it can't be used, and the value must be found elsewhere. This can occur when a system has the attribute, but the attribute is not always populated.
- *By date.* If multiple systems have an available value for an attribute, a possible rule would be to choose the value with the most recent date. This is not always a good choice, especially if the most-recently populated attribute value is incomplete or violates other data quality rules such as being invalid, of the wrong format, or with a suspect value distribution. For example, one system had a more recent birth date than any other available source, but the distribution of the birthdates indicated that at least one of the dates (12/31) wasn't reliable.
- *By data quality.* The values in some systems may be chosen (even over more-recently entered data) if they meet the specific data quality rules, as noted previously.

Once the business rules are established, they are used by the MDM tool to resolve attribute values in the survivorship process. The tool identifies the master records from multiple sources that have conflicting attribute values, applies the resolution rules, and creates (or updates) the golden copy with the selected value. An example of this process is shown in Fig. 7.18.

**NOTE**

Keep in mind that it may be possible to keep multiple values in some cases such as addresses. This reflects the real world, where people can have multiple valid addresses. However, even with multiple values (or value sets, as in addresses), a rule is needed to select the value/value set to use in circumstances where only a single value is allowed (e.g., a system that can store only a single address).

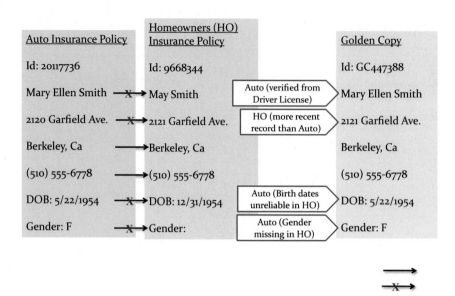

■ **FIGURE 7.18** An example of the results of survivorship and the value that make it into the final MDM record ("golden copy").

## THE ROLE OF DATA STEWARDSHIP IN MASTER DATA MANAGEMENT EXCEPTION HANDLING

An MDM engine (or *hub*) takes in records and performs a large number of processes, including cleansing, matching to existing records, inserting new records, updating existing records, merging records that represent the same entity, unmerging records that were merged in error, and deleting obsolete records. The processes follow a set of rules that have been carefully established and tested to handle the incoming data with known data quality (established by profiling the data) and data quality issues. However, data (and data quality) changes over time, and the rules may fail under these circumstances. Examples of source data changes that can cause rule failure include:

- *Invalid Lookup.* Often an incoming code or data value in the MDM data will trigger a lookup to translate the code or value into either a *harmonized* code (a code that has been standardized across systems), a different (standardized) data value, or a description. An invalid lookup can occur when the incoming code or data value is not found in the lookup table, resulting in an error because the lookup transformation cannot take place.
- *Data quality exception.* The MDM processing engine expects data to have certain traits such as a given length, data type (e.g., numeric or

string), format, range, or pattern. A data quality exception can occur when the arriving data is not as expected. For example, if the data type is different from what was anticipated (e.g., numeric is expected, but alphabetic characters are presented), this can cause a data quality exception that must be remediated. Another example is when the value falls outside the expected range, causing a conversion to fail or create a result that violates the allowed result.

- *Missing parent exception.* Records in the MDM hub may have a hierarchy, a missing parent exception occurs when a child record occurs without the parent record being present.
- *Invalid Relationship exception.* Records in the MDM hub may have mandatory relationships, which can include hierarchical relationships. If the record from either end of the relationship is missing, this can cause an exception. For example, an individual in the Employee master may have a mandatory relationship to an organization. If the organization record is missing or invalid, an invalid relationship exception occurs.
- *Missing data exception.* If data is missing from a field, this can cause an exception. This can also be thought of as a violation of the data quality Completeness dimension. For example, if an address record is supposed to have all the fields (street, city, state, country, zip, etc.) populated, and one or more fields are empty, a missing data exception occurs.

The Business Data Stewards are heavily involved in analyzing and mitigating exceptions, as shown in Fig. 7.19. Once the MDM tool encounters an exception, the processes involved are:

- *Receive and log exception.* The MDM engine keeps track of all exceptions and produces a report for analysis. At a minimum, the report must include the data that violated the processing rules as well as the rule that was violated. The Business Data Stewards (or designated personnel such as Operational Data Stewards) receive the report and keep track of the exception as an issue.
- *Conduct root cause analysis.* The next step is to figure out what caused the exception. The reason is almost always data that did not have the traits expected. Of course, the important question is *why* the data was not as expected. Assuming that the data was originally profiled and cleansed when the MDM processes were specified, built, and tested, something must have occurred to change the traits of the data. For example, a new code might have been added to the list of valid values for a field, or a change in the source system may have allowed a new data type to be entered. Root cause analysis delves

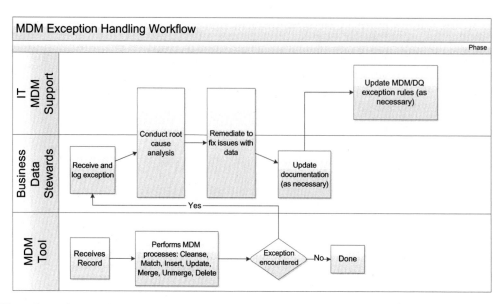

**■ FIGURE 7.19** Business Data Stewards must investigate the causes for MDM exceptions and propose either corrections to the source data or changes to the exception rules.

into the reasons for the violation. Since information about source systems and (possibly) MDM processing may be needed, IT will have to assist with root cause analysis.

- *Remediate to fix problem.* Once the problem has been located, changes need to be made to remediate it. This may involve new instructions to the data producers on how to enter data, adding new constraints in the source system (which will require help from IT), or changing the MDM exception rules to handle the new data traits (which will also require help from IT).
- *Update documentation.* Where necessary, the documentation on how the MDM engine processes data (including conversion and transformation rules) must be updated to reflect any changes.
- *Update MDM/DQ exception rules.* If the exception rules must be updated to handle the new data traits, IT will need to make those changes and test the new exception rules.

## THE ROLE OF DATA STEWARDSHIP IN INFORMATION SECURITY

Protecting the privacy and security of data is another important activity where Business Data Stewards (as well as many others) play an important role. The overall process is illustrated in Fig. 7.20. The process typically starts with a standard or policy that establishes the categories into which the data should be classified, and how each category can be used and must be protected. The categories will have names like Public, Company Private, and Confidential. In many industries (such as healthcare and insurance), the policies are almost always driven by legislation. The legislation often sets how the data must be treated, from which the appropriate Information Security category can be derived. For example, in the automobile insurance business in California (and many other states), the Driver License Number must be encrypted both at rest (in the database) and in motion (ETL). This led the insurance company where I worked to classify the Driver License Number as *Highly Confidential* as that category required these same protections. Legislation—and thus policy—may also specify privacy rules for handling groups of data elements. For example, while a customer's last name *by itself* might be considered Public, the combination of the Last Name, First Name, and Zip Code could well be considered Confidential.

> **NOTE**
> The process of protecting information has gotten much more complicated in the past few years as various governing bodies have passed stringent laws, mostly concerned with protecting personally identifiable information (PII) data and the rights of people whose data is being stored. These considerations are examined later in "The Role of Data Stewardship in Data Privacy Regulations" section.

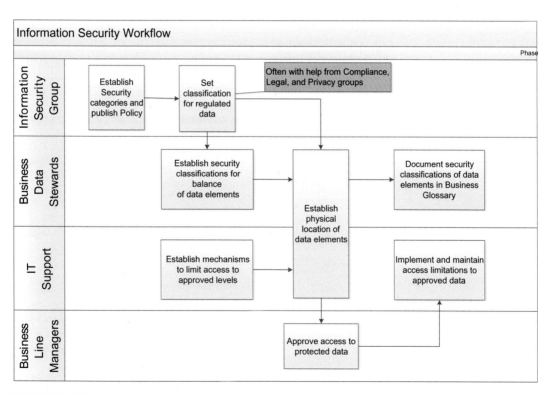

■ **FIGURE 7.20** Establishing and enforcing information security requires participation from many different roles.

It is typical for experts in applying the rules set forth in the regulations to establish the classification for business data elements (BDEs) that are specifically called out in the regulations, as in the example of the Driver License Number already discussed. These experts will usually come from Legal, Compliance, Privacy, or other risk-related groups. To properly establish the correct classification, the experts will depend on the definition for the BDE. Beyond that, though, the Information Security policy often leaves it to "the business" to determine what security classification the data falls into. This breaks down into two steps. In the first step, the Business Data Steward establishes the classification for the BDE or grouping of BDEs, again, often as a result of applying government regulations to the data. In the second step, which includes the BDEs assigned by the previously-mentioned experts, the Business Data Steward works with the Technical Data Stewards (and other IT support) to determine where the data exists physically in the database(s). The Confidential/Sensitive fields are then suitably protected by IT support to ensure that people who do not have a need to know do not have access.

The Data Stewardship Council may also set up (or participate in) the process by which employees receive the necessary permissions (usually by authority from their supervisors or other responsible persons) to have access to Confidential/Sensitive data. This process may be managed by human resources (HR), Data Governance, or some other organization, but the process itself should have the input of the Business Data Stewards.

## NOTE

Human Resources (HR) is often a good choice to manage the process of obtaining permissions for access because they maintain the reporting hierarchy, are responsible for the processes of hiring, transfers, and termination, and maintain job descriptions, which are often referred to when deciding whether access should be granted.

## CLASSIFYING GROUPS OF DATA

One of the more intractable problems related to providing the right security classification to BDEs is what to do with groups of BDEs. That is, a single field (such as a zip code or first name) *by itself* may not be considered sensitive or in need of privacy protection because that field *by itself* does not identify someone or rise to the level of requiring privacy protections. However, that same field when used in combination with other fields *does* require protection and *does* rise to the level of being considered sensitive. That is, the package of data is sensitive, though its individual components may not be. Unfortunately, in the absence of a better solution, many companies simply rate each of the components as "sensitive/confidential," which results in some strange rules like anything with a zip code (including a company address) is considered confidential. The idea of rating various combinations of fields hasn't become popular because even with just 7 or 8 fields, the amount of possible combinations rises to a substantial number, that is, 5040 for 7 fields, and a staggering 40,320 for 8 fields.

*(Continued)*

**(CONTINUED)**

What this approach fails to consider, however, is that in the real world, there are usually certain "packages" of data that are requested by the users. The Business Data Stewards can compile the most popular packages into standardized offerings with a security classification for each of these packages. For example, when HR is approached for employee data, it may offer information about the employee that contains First Name and Last Name, which are considered "Company Private." However, if the Full Address is added to that, the resulting package becomes Confidential. By offering these standardized packages (each with a security classification), the number of combinations and ratings can be reduced to a small number. The standardized packages can be documented in a business glossary by recording the business data elements included in the packages and the information security rating of the overall package.

## THE ROLE OF DATA STEWARDSHIP IN SUPPORTING QUALITY ASSURANCE

The Quality Assurance (QA) phase of a project is where the application or modification is tested to ensure that it meets the business requirements that were laid out. Often, however, no QA test cases are written to test the specified level of data quality or the meaning of the data behind the fields.

Business Data Stewards can help this situation by working with QA to write test cases in these two areas. The test cases are run by the QA analysts, just as any other tests would be, and the results and defects are recorded in the QA tracking system, again, just like any other test cases. They are then prioritized for correction along with any other discovered defects.

Test cases that test for violations of data quality rules look for things like:

- Invalid values that are allowed for fields that have a valid value set.
- Values that are allowed by the application that fall outside of the associated range, pattern, and type.
- Missing relationships (a home equity loan must have a collateral record) based on field values.
- Unpopulated fields are allowed that have been declared to be mandatory.
- Ability to create a record when mandatory data is missing.
- Invalid relationships between fields (Effective Date is later than Expiration Date).

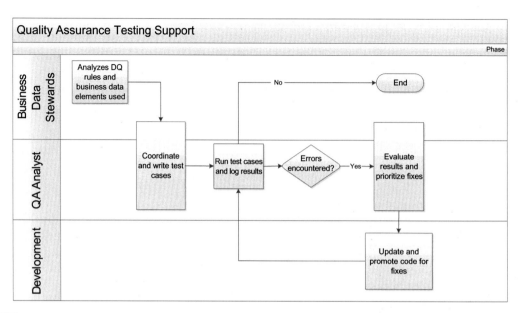

■ **FIGURE 7.21** Business Data Stewards and Quality Assurance analysts can write and run test cases to check data quality.

Test cases that are written using the metadata look for things like:

- Do the fields in the user interface (e.g., screens or reports) show the expected values based on the BDE definitions?
- Do the screens show multiple fields that are actually the same field (due to acronyms)?
- Are calculated fields correctly derived using the derivation rule for the BDE?
- Are field labels correctly named based on the official BDE name?

Fig. 7.21 shows a simplified flow for this process.

## THE ROLE OF DATA STEWARDSHIP IN COMPILING LINEAGE

There are several different types of lineage that are important. Business lineage relates to how business data elements BDEs) are related to each other, and we've discussed how Business Data Stewards build derivation rules to define these dependencies.

Logical/Physical lineage documents how BDEs exist physically in databases. We've discussed how this type of lineage is not only part of what "governed data" requires, but it is also crucial for improving data quality because data profiling tests the physical data quality.

Finally, technical lineage traces the path of the data from source to endpoint through different systems, data stores, and ETL transformations along the way. Technical lineage represents a map and audit trail of how the data travels and changes. Technical lineage is critical to proving the integrity of the data for such purposes as regulatory reporting as well as driving the understanding of business dependencies on the data. As discussed in Chapter 6, Practical Data Stewardship, this technical lineage also makes both Impact Analysis (forward dependency tracing) and Root Cause Analysis (backward dependency tracing) possible.

Business Data Stewards have several roles in tracing technical lineage, as shown in Fig. 7.22. First of all, in the process of identifying the BDEs that are of utmost importance to the enterprise, they are also identifying the data flow (information chain) that must be investigated—that is, the technical lineage that needs to be documented. Once the corresponding physical instantiation of that BDE has been discovered, the metadata repository takes over and does the actual trace, comparing the location of the discovered data elements to the source system (where the data originated) or the "golden source" (system from which the data is expected to be used and for which there are key

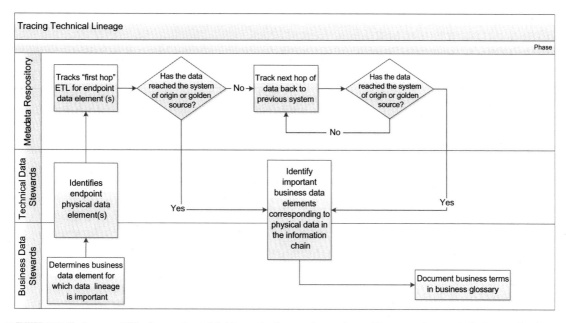

■ **FIGURE 7.22** The key responsibilities for generating technical lineage. A robust metadata repository tool is pretty much a necessity for this type of work.

controls to protect the quality). The results are then presented as a diagram by the metadata repository. The Business Data Steward and the Technical Data Steward inspect this diagram to determine if there are key systems along the information chain for which the physical data should be linked to the BDE (logical/physical lineage created). This is often important if a key data store or data warehouse has a role in many important business processes or is a precursor to complex transformations. If any of these physical data elements do not correspond to an existing BDE, the Business Data Steward may choose to define it if it is important enough.

## THE ROLE OF DATA STEWARDSHIP IN PROCESS RISK MANAGEMENT

Businesses run on their processes. If the processes fail, the business may fail. Risks to business processes come from many places, including the network, code, and servers that the processes run on (if they are automated), poor training of personnel, and the data that the processes use. In a well-run company, these risks are managed by the business (first line of defense) and corporate risk (second line of defense). Part of the responsibility of corporate risk is to ensure that the business is recognizing and addressing risks in a timely manner. And one way that corporate risk can do that is to calculate the level of risk for important business processes.

Not too surprisingly, the quality of the data used in these processes will affect how well the processes run, and the quality of the output. However, not all data is created equal, poor quality in certain key pieces of data can have a disproportionate effect on the output. A number of steps need to be taken to ascertain how sensitive the business processes are to the quality of the data it uses—called the Data Quality Risk Index (DQRI). This is an overall measure of the risk to a business process due to poor data quality, but it depends on the quality of the individual pieces of data the process uses, and how sensitive the process is to the quality of each of those pieces of data.

Fig. 7.23 illustrates these relationships. As noted, the Business Process has an overall DQRI. The data that the process uses is represented by the Physical Data Elements used in the business process. Each of those pieces of data (which are linked to a Business Data Element) has an assigned Business Process Risk Measure (BPRM). The BPRM is the sensitivity of the business process to the quality of the data element. The BPRM is assigned by the Business Process Owner, who is also the person who knows what data the process uses.

Once the data is known, the Business Data Steward and the Technical Data Steward work with the Business Process Owner to map the physical data

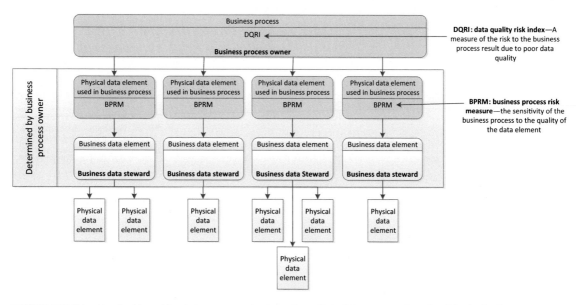

**■ FIGURE 7.23** Determining the data used in a business process and assigning the sensitivity of that process to the quality of the data is a key step.

elements to the business data elements to validate that this is the data that is being used. The data is then profiled, and Corporate Risk calculates the DQRI for that business process. This series of steps is shown in Fig. 7.24.

A sample calculation is shown in Table 7.5. The DQRI Component is calculated by multiplying the value of the BPRM by the Data Profiling Overall Result (expressed as a fraction). In this example, a perfect quality DQRI would be 802, so the process seems to be functioning pretty well with a value of 770.8. The biggest opportunity to raise the DQRI would be to improve the quality of *Number of Delinquent Payments*, since a better score on that data could raise the overall DQRI to 800.

## THE ROLE OF DATA STEWARDSHIP IN DATA PRIVACY REGULATIONS

In the past few years, a set of privacy protection regulations have been passed by various regulators that create protections for specific kinds of data, and grant consumers far more control over their data than was ever possible previously. These are collectively referred to as "data sovereignty regulations." The first major pieces of legislation were the General Data Protection Regulation (GDPR) of the European Union, the Personal Information Protection and Electronic Documents Act (PIPEDA) of Canada, and the California Consumer Privacy Act (CCPA).

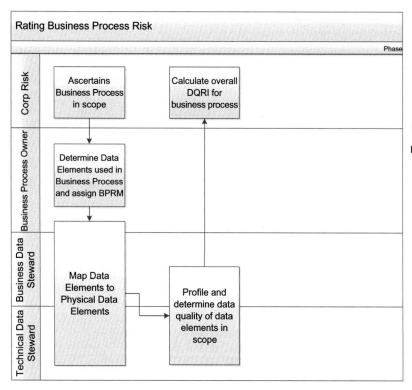

BPRM: Business Process Risk Measure – the sensitivity of the business process to the quality of the data element

■ FIGURE 7.24 The responsibilities and flow for rating business process risk.

**Table 7.5** A Sample Calculation of the Data Quality Risk Index.

| Data Element | BPRI | Data Profiling Overall Result (%) | DQRI Component |
|---|---|---|---|
| Customer ID | 1 (L) | 70 | 0.7 |
| Mortgage Balance Amount | 5 (H) | 99.7 | 498.5 |
| Number of Delinquent Payments | 3 (M) | 90.3 | 270.9 |
| Collateral Value | 1 (L) | 66 | 0.66 |
| Business Process DQRI | | | 770.8 |

## Key Tenets of Data Sovereignty Regulations

While there are certainly differences between these regulations, in general they all require that data subjects have certain rights, including:

- The right to know what information companies have on them.
- The right to have that information deleted under some circumstances.

- The right to opt out of the sale of that data.
- The right to provide or withhold consent for certain data uses.
- The requirement for companies to rectify inaccurate personal information and address incomplete personal data "without undue delay."

## Compliance With the Regulations

Complying with the regulations and providing governance controls requires capturing new kinds of metadata as well as improving the quality of metadata already collected. Table 7.6 details these requirements, the metadata needed, and impacts to Data Governance and Data Stewardship. Many of the types of metadata can be lumped in with topics (like MDM and Lineage) that have already been discussed.

**Table 7.6** Components of Compliance With Data Sovereignty Regulations.

| Components | Metadata/Controls Needed |
|---|---|
| • What information do we capture about individuals?<br>• How do we know that a dataset refers to a particular individual?<br>• How confident are we in this information? | MDM |
| • Where do we capture data about an individual?<br>• How do we move that data between systems and data stores?<br>• What processing was done to the data?<br>• What organizations receive the data (and what is their geographic location)? | Technical Lineage |
| • What personal data is necessary for a process? | • Data collection controls<br>• Capturing the purpose that the data was collected for |
| • Acceptable use governance: Was consent provided and documented to process personal data? | • Consent and collection details captured<br>• How data can or cannot be used, exceptions allowed, limitations<br>• Minimum and maximum retention periods |
| • Right to be forgotten (govern the lifecycle) | • Timing and details of notification, evaluation, and impact<br>• Timing and details of action taken<br>• Operational controls established |
| • Data Sharing Agreements (DSA)<br>• Data Movement Agreements (DMA) | • DSAs in place and approved by compliance and legal<br>• DMAs in place and tied to DSAs with appropriate safeguards |
| • Companies required to rectify inaccurate personal info and address incomplete personal data "without undue delay" | • Timing and details of notification and request for correction captured<br>• Timing and details of correction made captured<br>• Data Governance (controls) to allow data subjects to address any data quality issues relating to their personal data |

## Capturing Additional Metadata for Compliance

In addition to the metadata specific to the new requirements and the establishment and enforcement of controls, some ancillary metadata must be captured to enable the appropriate handling of requests from the data subjects. This additional metadata includes:

- Where the data was generated originally (transaction geographical location)
- Where the data is stored when queried (storage geography)
- What the person's physical geographic location was at the time the data was collected
- To what geographic entity (usually by citizenship) the person belongs

These data elements are crucial because the rules often depend on several types of geography. For example, while it might be permissible for a user in North America (User Geography) to query confidential data about a transaction that occurred in the European Common Union (Transaction Geography) and is stored there, it may well *not* be permissible if the data is moved to another country (the United States) or an international organization for storage. Fig. 7.25 shows how this might look.

In the day-to-day world of Data Stewardship, the Business Data Stewards (with assistance from the Compliance, Legal, and Privacy groups) need

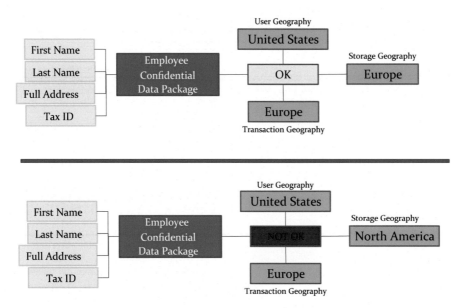

■ **FIGURE 7.25** Various geographies may have an effect on how data is allowed to be handled.

to be aware of the rules and the key pieces of data that must be captured along with sensitive, personally identifiable information (PII). They must help to ensure that the appropriate data is captured, stored, and processed in such a way that the various rights these regulations grant to data subjects can be carried out by the enterprise collecting the data as well as (in many cases) any processors who process data on behalf of the organization.

## A First Look at the Data and Process to Support Data Sovereignty Regulations

As was mentioned previously, new data needs to be captured and new processes built in order to meet the requirements to not only do the work, but track how it was done as well as when it was done. Fig. 7.26 illustrates a simple picture (model) of what data you might need to capture.

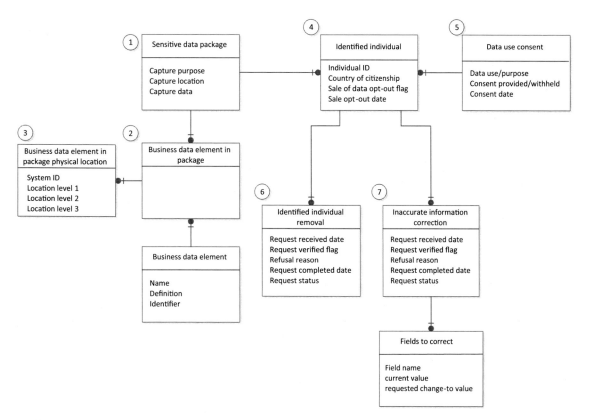

■ **FIGURE 7.26** A simplified model of compliance data that must be captured.

The circled numbers in this model indicate which process in Fig. 7.27 is responsible for handling that data.

In essence, everything starts when a package of sensitive data is captured (1). This data must be used to identify an individual who is the data subject (4), and consent or refusal to use that data for a particular purpose must also be recorded (5).

To govern and understand the data in the sensitive data package, each piece of data must be associated with a business data element that is governed and stewarded. The intersection of the sensitive data in the package to the business data element (2) must be located physically (3) so that should a request be made to delete it (6), the organization can find it. In addition, should the individual notice that any of the sensitive data is incorrect, information about any request to correct it (7) must also be tracked.

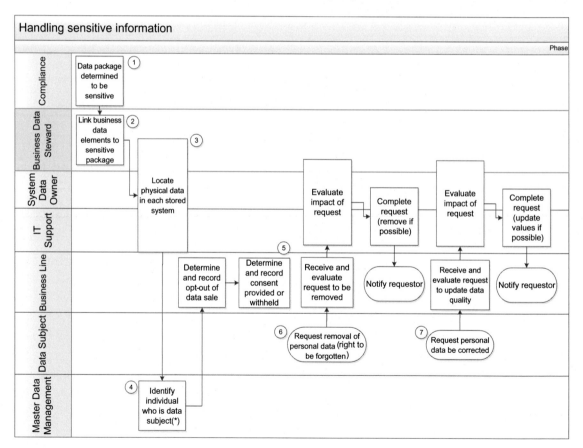

■ **FIGURE 7.27** Roles and process flows for main processes to provide rights to data subjects.

As illustrated in Fig. 7.27, there are a lot of participants involved in ensuring that the data subject has all the rights and capabilities demanded by the regulations. These include:

1. Experts who can determine whether the data being captured is sensitive/ PII, and, thus, must be protected and handled per the regulations.
2. Part of making the determination in (1) involves knowing what the data is—that is, what business data element defines it, which business function or Data Domain Council owns it, and so on.
3. In order to manage the sensitive data—as well as delete or update it at the request of the data subject—you have to know where it is. Understanding where the data is physically stored becomes critical because of this.
4. The sensitive data must be identified with a particular individual, preferably using MDM. It is crucial to know whose data to remove or adjust, and to validate whether the request is coming from the data subject. It is also necessary to record *who* has opted in or out of the sale of their data.
5. The regulations state that the purpose for which the data was recorded must be documented, as well as the consent or refusal to allow the use of the data for specific purposes.
6. The management of the data lifecycle—including the right to be forgotten—requires a multistep process to handle such requests. These steps include:
   a. Receiving and logging the request. This is important to show how long this process took to execute.
   b. Evaluating the impact, especially including how the removal of the data will affect the person's relationship with the organization. For example, you can't own an insurance policy or a brokerage account without that information being recorded, so arrangements would need to be made to terminate those relationships.
   c. Validating that the request came from a person authorized to make it.
   d. Completing the request by either refusing to remove it and providing appropriate reasons or by removing the data from the organization's systems and data stores.
   e. Notifying the requestor of how the request was resolved.
7. The data subject also has the right to request that their data be corrected and the company has a duty to do so within a reasonable period of time. The steps are similar to (6), except that only corrections need to be made. However, it is still necessary to know all the places where the data is stored so that the corrections can be made everywhere.

## SUMMARY

Data Stewards play a pivotal role in many enterprise efforts that involve improving the quality and usability of data assets. While it is not impossible to improve data quality and metadata quality, manage and harmonize reference data, implement and manage MDM, handle information security (including compliance and privacy requirements), determine business process risk, and manage metadata without Data Stewardship, it is more difficult, takes longer, and may require extensive reworking later. You are also less likely to get the results you want. That is because there may be no one responsible and accountable for making decisions about the data, so the results can be suboptimal and may not take into account the needs of all the stakeholders.

Improving data quality involves participation from the Business Data Stewards to understand the uses of the data, establish the data quality rules that define when the data is suitable for those uses, and review the results of data profiling to discern where the quality is not up to the levels needed to run the business. Improving data quality is both one of the main reasons to *have* Data Stewardship and one of the more visible ways that Business Data Stewards show their value to the company.

Improving metadata quality helps to improve data quality because the rules about what determines high data quality as well as the measured results of applying those rules against the data (data profiling) are metadata. Metadata can profiled against a set of rules that determine what we mean by "high quality" when it comes to metadata, though those rules can be harder to use and measure because some of them are hard to automate. The Business Data Stewards must evaluate the metadata quality rules and the metadata quality.

Valid values are established within the source systems based on how the source systems need to transact business. Business Data Stewards are key in not only determining what the valid values should be, but also in managing those values by making decisions about the meaning of each value and adding values when appropriate. Further, anytime reference data from different systems need to be brought together ("harmonized") into a data warehouse or other mechanism for combining data from multiple systems, the Business Data Stewards must map the source values to the aligned values that enable an overall enterprise view of the data.

With the increasing importance of MDM, the need to perform Identity Resolution has become critical. The Business Data Stewards help to identify the Identifying Attributes, locate records that represent instances of the master entity in different systems, examine the contents of the identifying attributes to determine whether they are usable, and map the different attributes from different systems together to enable the creation of a unique "golden copy" of the entity. They must also provide recommendations on the sensitivity of the matches to achieve results consistent with the data usage.

MDM also involves survivorship and exception handling. For survivorship, Business Data Stewards must establish the rules that determine what data to persist in the golden copy when records representing the same entity contain conflicting information. These rules may actually change over time as new systems come online or the trustworthiness of different source systems increases or decreases. For exception handling, Business Data Stewards (with lots of assistance from IT) must analyze new processing exceptions, figure out the root cause, and either fix the data or change the processing rules to handle the new data traits.

Many companies establish an Information Security Policy independently from Data Stewardship and classify certain business data elements specifically called out by the regulations. For the balance of the data, it is the Business Data Stewards who need to assign and document the security classification of the key business data elements as well as help to locate the physical data elements that IT must protect from misuse per the policy.

QA test cases can test for violations of data quality rules and creation rules to ensure that the specified level of quality is being maintained by the application and those records cannot be created if data is missing. Metadata test cases check for correctness of field labels, values in those fields (based on definitions), and other violations of the metadata specified for the data element in question.

In companies that manage their metadata rigorously (especially in a metadata repository), the Business Data Stewards have responsibilities to establish definitions, derivations, and data quality, as well as creation and usage business rules. They must also participate in the effort to relate business data elements to each other and link the business data elements to their physical counterparts. Business Data Stewards work closely with IT to map the lineage of important data where an understanding of the source, target, and transforms is important to prove the integrity of the data.

Calculating the risk to key business processes based on the quality of the data that a process uses can be quite useful. Though it is a multistep process that requires significant knowledge of the process itself and the data that the process uses, this calculation enables the enterprise to spot trouble as well as focus data quality improvement efforts where they are most needed. Business Data Stewards help in many aspects of identifying the data, the rules that determine the quality, and analyzing the results of profiling the data against the rules.

New privacy regulations (with more to come) require companies to track information about the personal data they collect and give the data subject a great deal of control over that data. In order to enable the ability to provide the required controls, Business Data Stewards across the enterprise play key roles in tracking what personal data is collected, the purpose of the collection, what permissions have been given for the use of the data, and the locations where the data is stored. Without all this information, the enterprise may violate the regulations, and be subject to massive fines and risks to their reputation.

# Chapter 8

# Measuring Data Stewardship Progress: The Metrics

## INTRODUCTION

As you have seen previously, a Data Stewardship program requires that resources and effort be expended to improve how an enterprise understands and manages its data. It should come as no surprise, therefore, that you are likely to be called on to measure and report the progress you have made—the return on the investment that has been made in Data Stewardship.

The metrics you can record and report break down broadly into two categories, namely Business Results Metrics and Operational Metrics. Business Results Metrics measure the effectiveness of Data Stewardship in supporting the data program and returning value to the company through better management of the data. Operational Metrics measure the acceptance of the Data Stewardship program and how effectively the Data Stewards are at performing their duties.

---

**IN THE REAL WORLD**

It is all very well to talk about using and reporting metrics, but there are certain critical success factors you need to keep in mind to make metrics effective and relevant. The first (especially for Business Results metrics) is the willingness to consider longer-term value as a result of the Data Stewardship program. A better understanding of data meaning, increasing data quality, and well-understood business rules take a while to make themselves felt in the overall metrics that corporations pay attention to. These overall metrics (as will be discussed in this chapter) include such items as decreasing costs, increasing profits, and shortening time to market.

The second critical success factor is that the company must be willing to attribute the improvements in information-based capabilities to the actions of the Data Governance and Data Stewardship programs. When things improve, there is often a rush to get credit for the improvement.

---

Data Stewardship. DOI: https://doi.org/10.1016/B978-0-12-822132-7.00008-5

> If at least some of the improvement is not credited to the better
> management of data through the efforts of Data Stewardship, it can be
> difficult to show (and quantify) the effect that the program has on the
> company's bottom line.
>
> Finally, you must carefully tailor your metrics to ensure that they are
> meaningful. You should start with the most critical business processes. For
> each of this (hopefully) small number of processes, identify the business
> data elements that are most critical to those processes. Design your
> metrics (such as the overall quality, number of elements with definitions,
> how many elements are owned and stewarded, and so on) around that
> data. Grow your effort as you have the resources to do so. Note that if you
> are performing Business Process Risk Measurement (as described in
> Chapter 7: The Important Roles of Data Stewards), you may already know
> what business processes are most important and what data those
> processes use.

## BUSINESS RESULTS METRICS

Business Results metrics attempt to measure the business value that a
Data Stewardship effort adds. Business value includes such things as:

- Increased Revenues and Profits
- Reduced costs of duplicate data and data storage
- Increased productivity in the use of data
- Reduced application development and system integration costs
- Increased return on investment (ROI) on projects
- Reduced time to market
- Increased adherence to audit and corporate responsibility
- Reduced compliance issues
- Increased knowledge about the customer and customer satisfaction

Many of these items are difficult to measure directly. One technique is to
survey the data users in the company to get their opinions on the business
results of the Data Stewardship effort. That is, find out how they see the
Data Stewardship effort impacting these items:

- Is there better *understanding* of the data?
- Does the data have better *quality*? Note that you can measure directly
  how well the data matches the specified quality rules, but it also helps
  to understand whether the *perceived* data quality has improved.
- Has the enterprise improved its early warning of data quality issues
  through profiling?
- Has the enterprise determined how many customer complaints there have
  been driven by poor quality data? Has this number decreased over time?

- Has the incidence of issues with regulatory and compliance organizations decreased?
- Has the enterprise reduced the amount of time spent cleansing and fixing data?
- Has the enterprise reduced the amount of time spent arguing about what data means or how it is calculated?
- Has the enterprise reduced or eliminated the efforts necessary to reconcile different reports through:
  - Consistent definitions and derivations.
  - Consistent specification of what data is included in reports.
- Have specific costs decreased due to the better management of data (see the sidebar Business Results Metrics Examples)? Can any of these costs be quantified?
- Does the enterprise make *better business decisions*? This one is hard to measure, even as part of a survey. But there is usually some perception about whether the enterprise is getting "smarter" about what it does (or not).
- Has there been a reduction in "data debt?" Mismanagement of data creates data debt, which piles up (just like real debt) the longer data mismanagement goes on.

---

**IN THE REAL WORLD**

According to John Ladley, "data debt" is what an organization "borrows" when it chooses not to pay for something related to data that is (or will be) needed. This debt could typically be avoided by funding and instituting basic Data Governance and data management activities. Like "real" debt, it must eventually be repaid. This can happen slowly over time (with "interest" in the form of higher expenses to build the proper Data Governance and data management later) or in a big chunk ("balloon payment") when a Data Governance and data management program is stood up.

---

**BUSINESS RESULTS METRICS EXAMPLES**

The questions that you ask to try and judge the impact of the Data Stewardship effort will depend on the business you are in. But the more specific you can be, the better your measurements will be. In addition, any claims you make for the positive impact of Data Stewardship on the company will be more defensible. Some sample questions are provided here from an insurance company with a robust Data Stewardship function:

*(Continued)*

**(CONTINUED)**

- *Calling/mailing costs*: How many times did we contact someone who already had a particular type of policy or who was not eligible for that type of policy? How much postage/time was wasted?
- *Loss of productivity/opportunity cost*: How many policies could have been sold if agents had only contacted eligible potential policyholders? How much would those policies have been worth?
- *Loss of business cost*: How many policyholders canceled their policies because we didn't understand their needs or didn't appear to value their business (survey can give you an idea)? What is the lost lifetime value of those customers?
- *Compliance cost*: How much did we spend responding to regulatory or audit requests (demands)? How much of that was attributable to the inability to:
  - Show/prove good data quality?
  - Provide the information to answer their question?
  - Show that the data had integrity from source to target, including all transforms?
  - Show and prove that people are accountable for the data? And yes, regulators are specifically asking about Data Governance! I know because I have had representatives from a variety of US and foreign regulators in my Data Stewardship class.

Note that the business case for establishing Data Stewardship in the first place should already have established some baseline findings for comparison.

## OPERATIONAL METRICS

Operational metrics are a compilation of various measures that indicate:

- The level of participation of the business.
- The level of importance given to the Data Stewardship effort.
- Numerical measures for results achieved.
- How often and how effectively the Data Stewardship deliverables are used.

There are many specific measures that can be tracked and reported on as operational metrics. These include:

- *What changes in maturity measures have occurred for Data Stewardship* (see Chapter 9: Rating Your Data Stewardship Maturity)? There are a variety of ways to measure the maturity level of an effort, and periodic evaluation of these aspects can tell you whether the effort is gaining maturity, starting from sporadic and unmanaged attempts at data management to a well-managed, enterprise-wide, and standardized way of doing business. The *Organizational Awareness* dimension (as discussed in Table 9.1) includes the development of metrics as one of its measurements. In *Level 3 Well-Defined* operational metrics are in place and some participation metrics are included in the evaluation of Data Stewards. In addition, direct impacts to data quality improvements are also measured, and by the time the organization reaches *Level 4 Strategic*, a formalized method for gauging and attributing the value of data quality improvement to Data Stewardship has occurred.

- *How many disparate data sources have been consolidated?* Many companies have a huge number of data sources from "official" systems and data stores to servers hidden under people's desks. Of course, the more data sources that are present, the more likely that the data has different meanings, business rules, and quality. One goal of a Data Stewardship effort is to achieve the standardization of data, identify systems of record, and dispense with redundant data sources and stores. Retiring or shutting down disparate data sources is one measure of the success of a Data Stewardship effort as well as a maturing of the data management culture.
- *How many standardized/owned definitions have been gathered?* Business data elements form the backbone of improvements in understanding and quality. Having a robust definition is the starting point. This is a simple metric as all you need to do is count the number of business data elements with a definition in a "completed" state. An alternative is to count the business data elements that have definitions as well as a set of creation and usage business rules.
- *How many business functions have provided assigned stewards to participate in the Data Stewardship program?* When you are first starting a Data Stewardship program, it is not unusual for some business functions to refuse to provide resources (Business Data Stewards). This is likely to change over time as the results and value of Data Stewardship become apparent, but it will also help to have a scorecard that shows which business functions have provided the required resources.
- *How many business functions have added Data Stewardship performance to their compensation plans?* Although we said earlier that Data Stewardship is the formalizing of responsibility that has likely been in place for a while, rewarding the Business Data Stewards for performing these tasks is a critical success factor. That isn't to say that Data Stewardship is ineffective if it doesn't include a compensation plan, but as with anything else, you'll get a better performance if you compensate people for doing a good job.

- *Which business functions are the most active in meetings, driving definitions, data quality rules, and the like?* Even when people are assigned to perform Data Stewardship functions, not everyone will participate to the same degree. Noting and reporting the level of participation of the most active Business Data Stewards can encourage and reinforce those people as well as encourage nonparticipators to join in as they see the value and rewards of participation. Keep in mind, though, that an increase in the level of participation does not necessary mean that value is being added so use this metric with caution.
- *Who are the most active contributors in each business function?* As discussed previously, a Data Stewardship effort benefits greatly from support and issue reporting from the data analysts in each business function. One of things that occurs as a program matures is that champions (typically, data analysts) appear in the field. These champions help to educate their peers, warn when Data Stewardship tenets are not being followed, and provide valuable input to the Business Data Stewards. Having many of these champions in each business function is a sign that the program is gaining traction, and they should be counted, recognized, and rewarded.
- *How many people have been trained as stewards?* One simple measure of the penetration of Data Stewardship into an enterprise is to count how many people have been trained as Business Data Stewards. As noted previously, this is a rigorous training regimen. And even when Business Data Stewards rotate out of an assignment and new Business Data Stewards replace them, having the previous (trained) Business Data Stewards out in the enterprise is a good thing.
- *How many times has stewardship metadata been accessed?* After doing all the work to gather and document the metadata, you want it to be actively used. A good metric for that usage is to measure how often the metadata is viewed in whatever recording tool (such as a metadata repository or Business Glossary) you are using to store the metadata. You may need to filter the number of views a bit such as to limit the count to unique views by separate individuals, but if the metadata is being viewed often, it is a good sign that it is not only useful, but that the Data Stewardship message is getting out into the enterprise.

Data Stewardship Work Progress is another good set of Operational Metrics. These elements can be tracked in a table (see Table 8.1) or presented graphically in a dashboard (see Fig. 8.1). They may include such things as:

- Business data elements proposed, owned/stewarded, defined, and approved.
- Business rules proposed, owned, and defined (such as data quality, creation, and usage rules).

**Table 8.1** Recording Key Data Stewardship Work Progress Metrics.

| Business Area | Average Time (Days) Owned to Approved | Number of Approved Business Data Elements | Data Elements Linked and Profiled | Data Quality Issues/Resolved |
|---|---|---|---|---|
| Actuarial | 10 | 109 | 22 | 10/6 |
| Underwriting | 12 | 221 | 12 | 5/4 |
| Claims | N/A | 24 | 0 | 4/0 |
| Financial reporting | 16 | 156 | 67 | 14/12 |
| Membership | 15 | 65 | 6 | 8/8 |
| Financial transactions | 8 | 130 | 45 | 9/9 |
| People and performance | 34 | 91 | 21 | 6/4 |
| Marketing | 12 | 57 | 31 | 10/8 |
| Sales | 12 | 156 | 14 | 6/5 |

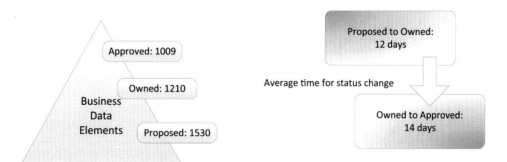

Approved: 1009

Owned: 1210

Business Data Elements

Proposed: 1530

Proposed to Owned: 12 days

Average time for status change

Owned to Approved: 14 days

■ **FIGURE 8.1** Key Data Stewardship work progress in a scorecard.

- Average time elapsed for the change in the state of a business data element from *owned* to *approved*.
- Number of business data elements linked to physical data elements and profiled.

**RUNNING DATA STEWARDSHIP LIKE A PROJECT (THOUGH IT'S NOT)**

It is true that Data Stewardship—and the Data Governance effort it is a part of—is not a project. Instead, it is a program, meaning that although (like a

*(Continued)*

**(CONTINUED)**

project) it has deliverables, requires resources, and must be actively managed at a detailed level, there is no "end date." That is, it continues on, year after year, as an integral part of the overall data management effort.

Just like it is imperative to integrate Data Stewardship tasks into project methodology (as discussed in Chapter 6: Practical Data Stewardship), it is extremely important to *use* project methodology (including the presence of a project/program manager) in the implementation of Data Governance and Data Stewardship. You may have already begun to suspect this, given how much the roadmap (also discussed in Chapter 6: Practical Data Stewardship) looks like a project plan, complete with a timeline, milestones, and implied resources.

First of all, a project manager is needed because the timeline, deliverables, and assigned resources must be actively managed. Business Data Stewards can't do this on their own as they typically lack the skills of a project manager and many don't consider (at least at first) being a Business Data Steward as part of their "main job." Further, Data Governors (who serve as bosses to the Business Data Stewards insofar as the Data Stewardship effort is concerned) often give only sporadic attention to the Data Stewardship effort and usually (at least at first) undermanage the Business Data Stewards. The DGPO *may* be able to fill this role, provided they have the skills—but whether the project manager comes from the DGPO or (more likely) from the PMO, the effect is the same.

And what is that effect? Just like with a project, the project manager ensures that:

- A project/program plan is established, maintained, and updated. This requires that the project manager work with subject matter experts and the Data Governors to:
  - Define clear deliverables that address the established goals for the Data Stewardship program.
  - Establish the phases of delivery for the deliverables identified.
  - Realistically estimate the time required for each phase of deliverables.
  - Gain time commitments for assigned personnel to work on the deliverables.
- A regular cadence of status meetings is established. These meetings provide updates on the deliverables (including the identification of new deliverables), examine the program plan and timeline for any needed adjustments in either timing or assigned resources, and make sure that everyone (including the executive sponsor) is in agreement on the deliverables and the progress toward providing them.

*(Continued)*

**(CONTINUED)**

- A status report is issued and provided to all participants in the Data Stewardship effort (see Fig. 8.2). This is critical so that everyone involved is aware of the overall status of all the efforts. Without such a report, Data Stewards will often manage their efforts individually in a silo just as they are used to doing with their regular business function efforts. It may be necessary (especially in the early stages of Data Stewardship) to review the tasks and efforts as a group, in which case the Data Stewards can be invited to the regular status meetings.

Keep in mind that since a Data Stewardship program has no end date, the program plan should initially cover an agreed-upon time period, and be periodically extended as new goals and deliverables are identified. A reasonable first pass could encompass a 1-year time period.

**NOTE**

While it is typically not necessary for all the Business Data Stewards (and potentially other types of data stewards) to attend these regular status meetings, certain key people may be "invited" to attend if their deliverables show signs of slipping in schedule or are delivered with low quality. As with the "assignment meetings" discussed in Chapter 6, Practical Data Stewardship, only those people needed (and, thus, invited) to the status meetings need to attend.

| Data Stewardship Deliverable | Delivery Date | Data Stewards | Status | Next Steps/Notes |
|---|---|---|---|---|
| Version 1 of Business Glossary | 05/31/20 | All leads | | - Metamodel nearly complete<br>- Complete metamodel<br>- Test workflows<br>- Document and roll-out |
| Establish high-priority Risk & Regulatory reports in business glossary | 06/15/20 | Joseph Smith (Finance) Roberta Bell (Risk) | | - Initial list created and in review<br>- Requires metamodel implemented before input to business glossary |
| Establish naming and definition standards | 02/15/20 | DGPO, All Data Stewards | | - Initial draft in place, under discussion |
| Data Profiling analysis for Insurance data warehouse | 08/30/20 | Alice Chan (Actuarial), Dwayne Black (Underwriting), Kevin Jordan (Claims) | | - Data Profiling underway<br>- See project timeline for detailed deliverables |
| Integration of business glossary with Data Quality tool for results | 03/31/20 | John Vargas (DQ) | | - Waiting for Enterprise Architecture input and plan |

■ **FIGURE 8.2** A sample status report for Data Stewardship.

## SUMMARY

Metrics are important to show the value that Data Stewardship adds to an enterprise, and, therefore, to justify the resources and effort put into a Data Stewardship effort. Business Value Metrics show how a Data

Stewardship program contributes value to a company in terms of increased profits, reduced costs, shortened time to market, fewer compliance and regulatory issues, and other measures that translate into conducting business better and more efficiently. Operational metrics show how much work a Data Stewardship program is performing by counting things like how many business data elements have been defined and owned, how many stewards have been trained, how often the Stewardship metadata are being used, and other measures of the program's efforts.

# Chapter 9

# Rating Your Data Stewardship Maturity

## INTRODUCTION

A Data Stewardship effort matures as you develop it and noting the (hopefully) advancing maturity can be a great way to show progress (in addition to the metrics discussed in Chapter 8: Measuring Data Stewardship Progress: The Metrics). Measuring the maturity of an effort helps to quantify that progress and enables the stakeholders in the Data Stewardship effort to provide their input on the effort.

## DEFINING A DATA STEWARDSHIP MATURITY MODEL: LEVELS AND DIMENSIONS

Maturity can be thought of as occurring in levels, and through several *dimensions*. Each of the dimensions can be rated as having a different maturity level. By laying out the dimensions and levels in a grid (as will be discussed in this chapter) you can show the current maturity as well as the target maturity.

There are many capability and maturity models (CMM) for data quality and given that one of the primary goals of Data Stewardship is to improve data quality, it is no surprise that the maturity model presented bears many similarities to those presented by others. For example, in chapter 3 of *Information Quality Applied* (*Information Quality Applied: Best Practices for Improving Business Information, Processes, and Systems*, Wiley, 2009) Larry English presents the Information Quality Maturity Management Grid. This grid (adapted from P.B. Crosby's Quality Management Maturity Model) shows how a data quality effort progresses from Uncertainty (ad-hoc) to Certainty (optimizing) across six categories. In chapter 3 of David Loshin's book *The Practitioner's Guide to Data Quality Improvement* (*The Practitioner's Guide to Data Quality Improvement*, Elsevier, 2011), Loshin catalogs eight sets of Component Maturity Model Descriptions (including one for Data Governance). Loshin details how each of the eight topics (such as Data Quality Expectations, Data Quality Protocols, Information Policies, etc.,) progresses through five levels of maturity; moving from Initial to

Data Stewardship. DOI: https://doi.org/10.1016/B978-0-12-822132-7.00009-7

**229**

Repeatable, Defined, Managed, and Optimized. This exceptionally detailed set of Component Maturity descriptions is an excellent resource in constructing your own maturity model.

## DATA STEWARDSHIP MATURITY LEVELS

The maturity model presented here has five levels, not including "level zero" where there is no Data Governance or Data Stewardship at all. Each level can be broken down further into four categories. You may want to start from this model and customize it to suit your own needs.

### Maturity Level 1: Initial

- *Response to data issues*: This level is "Reactive"; it shows response to issues as they arise with no attempt to prevent them from happening. Root cause analysis begins as the realization is made that just fixing the data in the target data store doesn't work. Areas to correct become more apparent. Processes form around fixing data issues; those charged with "fixing data" recognize patterns of issues and develop a framework around fixing them. Documenting of resolution processes begins to occur.
- *Attitude of management*: Perception that poor data quality is an IT issue and not a business issue. There is little encouragement to form an organization to manage data and metadata.
- *Handling of Metadata*: Attempts at cataloging and managing data definitions and other metadata are scattered and there is no centralized effort to gather and document metadata.
- *Development of formal organization and structure*: Small teams form to recommend changes.

### Maturity Level 2: Tactical

- *Response to data issues*: Data issues are starting to be responded to using repeatable processes that are becoming more formalized. Individuals charged with "fixing data" may begin to see stewardship duties in job descriptions and objectives that reflect those duties.
- *Attitude of management*: Data quality is still seen as an IT issue, though there is more involvement from business areas that are affected by poor quality data. There is recognition that business areas are responsible for their metadata, data, and data quality.
- *Handling of Metadata*: There is a recognized need to gather metadata around systems and applications and to store that metadata in a central location such as a Metadata Repository.

- *Development of formal organization and structure*: Business Data Stewardship is beginning to appear, as are some Data Governance standards. These are limited to a few business functions that are most affected by data issues. Data ownership is beginning to be recognized as well.

## Maturity Level 3: Well-defined

- *Response to data issues*: Data quality issues are being rigorously tracked. The organization includes risk assessment for data quality in project processes. Data integration efforts begin and include Data Stewardship as a crucial participant. Data quality metrics are beginning to be measured.
- *Attitude of management*: Business areas are stepping up to own their data. The importance of data and data quality is communicated across the enterprise. Business and IT partner to support Data Governance and data quality.
- *Handling of Metadata*: The need for robust business metadata is recognized and it is stored in a central location such as a Business Glossary.
- *Development of formal organization and structure*: Standards are developed, documented, and communicated. The change process now includes data quality and Data Governance as the corporate culture changes to embrace these disciplines. Performance metrics for Data Governance and Data Stewardship are beginning to be measured. A formal Data Stewardship Council and Data Governance Board have been instituted, however, not all business functions are represented. The beginnings of a Data Governance Program Office are in place.

## Maturity Level 4: Strategic

- *Response to data issues*: Tools are added for data quality and profiling with ongoing improvement efforts. Data Stewards are always involved in data quality improvement efforts. Risk assessments for data around projects are done early. Data quality issues and resolutions are measured, monitored, and communicated.
- *Attitude of management*: Data Governance and Data Stewardship metrics have become a primary corporate measurement of success in managing data across the enterprise. Senior management drives Data Governance strategy. Data is seen as a valuable corporate asset. Accountability for quality and understanding of data is practiced across the enterprise. Data quality is a corporate objective, not a business or IT problem. Ongoing investments in managing data and

Metadata are supported and championed. Stewardship metrics are included in assessments of projects and employee performance.

- *Handling of Metadata*: Expertise increases in metadata management and Master Data Management. Single sources of the truth for both metadata and data are identified and documented. All key business data elements have full metadata collected quickly and efficiently.
- *Development of formal organization and structure*: All business functions are represented in Data Governance and Data Stewardship, and participation is mandatory. The executive leadership team gets regular updates and handles escalated issues quickly and efficiently. The Data Governance Program office is fully staffed and funded, and reports progress, metrics, and issues to senior leadership on a regular basis.

## Maturity Level 5: Optimized

- *Response to data issues*: Innovation becomes key in maintaining the vision of improving data quality and remediating data issues. Requirements are in place to safeguard data quality from outside business partners.
- *Attitude of management*: The Corporation is ready to innovate where Data Governance/Data Stewardship and data quality are concerned. Innovation drives the vision of Data Governance. Management and the Data Governance staff keep abreast of important emerging trends in data management and adapt accordingly. Creativity and competitive advantage in using high-quality data is encouraged. Staff is freed up to explore new ideas and new technologies.
- *Handling of Metadata*: All metadata is collected and stored in a central repository. Data profiling results are used to automatically open and remediate issues on an ongoing basis.
- *Development of formal organization and structure*: Data Governance and Stewardship expand to incorporate outside business partners. Standards and controls are in place and have become the corporate culture. The company is considered an example of good Data Governance and Data Stewardship in the global business community.

## DATA STEWARDSHIP MATURITY DIMENSIONS BY LEVEL

The dimensions of Data Stewardship maturity establish the measurement criteria for evaluating each of the five maturity levels. For example, the Value Creation dimension starts in *Level 1: Initial* with no stewardship value recognized and unknown values of the data. In *Level 5: Optimized* Data Stewardship has a proven track record of driving value. *Level 3: Well-defined* is where the value of data is becoming well recognized. As stated previously, in this model there are four of these dimensions, namely Organizational Awareness; Roles and Structures; Standards, Policies, and Processes; and Value Creation.

## Organizational Awareness

The Organizational Awareness dimension rates how well Data Stewardship is integrated into the organization, sponsorship, and the development of the metrics. Table 9.1 shows the various levels of maturity for Organizational Awareness.

| Level | Description |
|-------|-------------|
| | **Table 9.1** Organizational Awareness Dimension by Maturity Level |
| Initial | • *Data Stewardship integrated into the organization*: Business areas look to IT to manage data.<br>• *Sponsorship*: *Data Stewardship* may be defined for some business applications. Some local subject matter experts are promoting the value of Business Data Stewardship for data quality, but are gaining little support.<br>• *Development of the metrics*: There are no Data Stewardship metrics (and probably few data management metrics). |
| Tactical | • *Data Stewardship integrated into the organization*: The need for both business and IT roles in the management of data is emerging. Localized teams or individuals are becoming champions of Data Stewardship and data management practices within the organization. Efforts to educate and raise awareness of the value of Data Stewardship are occurring in isolation.<br>• *Sponsorship*: Some business areas are demonstrating success in adopting a Data Stewardship approach and gaining executive-level visibility and support.<br>• *Development of the metrics*: Some metrics for Data Stewardship participation are being proposed. "Anecdotal metrics" around data quality are being communicated. |
| Well-Defined | • *Data Stewardship integrated into the organization*: Efforts are underway to raise awareness of the value of data management and the need for Data Stewardship across the organization. There is recognized (and endorsed) need for both business and IT accountabilities for data management.<br>• *Sponsorship*: A corporate executive sponsor has emerged. A push for a corporate-level Data Stewardship program has also begun.<br>• *Development of the metrics*: Metrics for operational/participation Data Stewardship are in place and being measured. Some participation metrics are being built into evaluations of the Business Data Stewards. Business results metrics (how Data Stewardship supports the data program) are being proposed. Direct impacts to improvements in data quality are being measured and published, however, there is a lack of acceptance that Data Stewardship is responsible for better data quality. |
| Strategic | • *Data Stewardship integrated into the organization*: Data Stewardship has become part of an enterprise-wide Data Management/Data Governance framework. Data Stewardship has been integrated into the IT development processes. Education about Data Stewardship is being provided to all employees. |

*Continued*

## Roles and Structures

The Roles and Structures dimension rates how well-defined the Data Stewardship roles are as well as how effectively those roles are being staffed and executed. In addition, this dimension rates the completeness and integration of the supporting structures. Table 9.2 shows the various levels of maturity for Roles and Structures.

**Table 9.1** Organizational Awareness Dimension by Maturity Level *Continued*

| Level | Description |
|---|---|
|  | • *Sponsorship*: There is broad executive understanding and support of the need for Data Stewardship across functional areas and business processes.<br>• *Development of the metrics*: Participation metrics and business results metrics are in place and are built into the evaluations of Data Stewards. A formalized method for gauging the value of improving data quality is in place and a portion of that value is attributed to the Data Stewardship effort. |
| Optimized | • *Data Stewardship integrated into the organization*: Data Stewardship is implemented at the corporate level. Formal data management programs and metrics are in place. Data Stewards are viewed as an integral and necessary part of data management.<br>• *Sponsorship*: Ongoing communication and education across the organization is occurring such that all employees understand their responsibilities in managing data and understand that the mandate for Data Stewardship comes from the very top—and is actively supported in all levels of the organization.<br>• *Development of the metrics*: The responsibility of all employees for the management of data is accepted as part of the corporate culture, and a portion of every employee's evaluation reflects the importance of data as a corporate asset. |

**Table 9.2** Roles and Structures Dimension by Maturity Level

| Level | Description |
|---|---|
| Initial | • *How well-defined Data Stewardship roles are*: Each business and IT team define their own data roles based on specific data management needs such as data definition, quality, access, protection, and retention.<br>• *How effectively Data Stewardship roles are staffed and executed*: There is little commonality or opportunity for reuse and it is unclear whether accountability for specific data is achieved from an end to end perspective. There is a lack of a corporate-wide approach or oversight in the creation of data management roles.<br>• *Completeness and integration of supporting structures*: Each business and IT team define their own supporting structures (such as steering committees and data subject matter expert groups). There is a lack of a corporate-wide approach in the establishment of supporting structures. |
| Tactical | • *How well-defined Data Stewardship roles are*: In some business areas accountabilities for data management are more formalized and described. Some delineation of business and IT roles are in place. |

*Continued*

| Level | Description |
|---|---|
| | **Table 9.2** Roles and Structures Dimension by Maturity Level *Continued* |
| | • *How effectively Data Stewardship roles are staffed and executed*: A Data Stewardship position may be established, but there is no mechanism to ensure that the accountabilities of this role are consistent with other business areas.<br>• *Completeness and integration of supporting structures*: Consistency of supporting structures is beginning to spread across business units, especially those that must work together to solve data quality issues. A group of managers from different units may be working together to solve data issues, effectively performing some of the duties of the Data Governance Council. However, they have not officially been designated with the appropriate authority. |
| Well-Defined | • *How well-defined Data Stewardship roles are*: A corporate level Data Stewardship program is being defined and communicated. A framework of standard data management roles and responsibilities at all levels is available to support implementation. Respective accountabilities of business and IT roles in data management are explicitly defined.<br>• *How effectively Data Stewardship roles are staffed and executed*: Stewardship is being implemented in some business areas or for critical data. The sponsoring executive is actively promoting the adoption of Data Stewardship across the enterprise.<br>• *Completeness and integration of supporting structures*: Supporting structures such as centers of competency, decisioning committees, or councils are defined and becoming established. |
| Strategic | • *How well-defined Data Stewardship roles are*: Roles and responsibilities for Data Stewards are clearly and consistently defined and measured. Data Stewardship is seen as a business responsibility.<br>• *How effectively Data Stewardship roles are staffed and executed*: Business Data Stewards with the necessary skills have been designated from the appropriate business functions. The Data Stewards have been trained and are performing their responsibilities.<br>• *Completeness and integration of supporting structures*: A Data Stewardship Council has been established across the organization and is operating in conjunction with the Data Governance Board and Data Governance Program Office. |
| Optimized | • *How well-defined Data Stewardship roles are*: Everybody in the organization understands their role in managing data and information. They also recognize the Business Data Stewards as the key players in managing data and resolving data issues.<br>• *How effectively Data Stewardship roles are staffed and executed*: Data Stewardship is fully integrated and rationalized with Data Governance and development processes. The Data Stewards work together as a cohesive team in full cooperation with each other. They also work to support projects.<br>• *Completeness and integration of supporting structures*: Data Stewardship is fully integrated and rationalized with enterprise structures. |

## Standards, Policies, and Processes

The Standards, Policies and Processes dimension rates how well-defined the framework for supporting policies, processes, practices, and standards is. In addition, the existence and robustness of the policies, processes, practices, and standards themselves are rated. Finally, having executive support (endorsement) of the policies is a critical success factor and the level of endorsement increases with increasing maturity. Table 9.3 shows the various levels of maturity for Standards, Policies, and Processes.

**Table 9.3** Standards, Policies, and Processes Dimension by Maturity Level

| Level | Description |
| --- | --- |
| Initial | • *How well-defined is the framework for supporting and sharing policies and processes*: There is little or no framework for supporting standards, policies, and processes.<br>• *Existence and robustness of the standards, policies, and processes*: For data, IT development and operations standards exist. There may be some business standards for data management or methods for business areas and/or Stewards to deploy. Business data standards may exist at the application or business area level, but only a few are promoted enterprise wide.<br>• *Executive support and endorsement of the policies*: There is little or no executive support or endorsement. |
| Tactical | • *How well-defined is the framework for supporting and sharing policies and processes*: Successful local practices are shared with other business areas and some best practices are emerging.<br>• *Existence and robustness of the standards, policies, and processes*: Data management principles and guidelines are emerging in business areas based on business, legal, or regulatory drivers. A complete set of standards and methods have not been developed, nor is there an understanding of all that is required.<br>• *Executive support and endorsement of the policies*: The need for enterprise-wide standards and practices has been identified. |
| Well-Defined | • *How well-defined is the framework for supporting and sharing policies and processes*: An enterprise-wide data management policies and standards program is defined.<br>• *Existence and robustness of the standards, policies, and processes*: Selected best practices are elevated to de facto standards. There is early adoption in selected business areas and projects.<br>• *Executive support and endorsement of the policies*: There is board-level endorsement to develop and implement corporate-level data management standards. Executive sponsorship and support for standards is strengthening. |
| Strategic | • *How well-defined is the framework for supporting and sharing policies and processes*: Enterprise-wide data management and Data Governance frameworks are defined for standards and policies. Processes have become more standardized across the organization as the push for the adoption of standards and practices through review and audit mechanisms increases.<br>• *Existence and robustness of the standards, policies, and processes*: Stewardship processes have been defined, and are measured and monitored.<br>• *Executive support and endorsement of the policies*: There is a focus on teaching and promoting the standards, processes, and policies across the organization. The executives endorse the policies and promote the education of employees. |
| Optimized | • *How well-defined is the framework for supporting and sharing policies and processes*: Data management and Data Stewardship standards and practices are in place and under continuous improvement.<br>• *Existence and robustness of the standards, policies, and processes*: Broad adoption of all standards has occurred across the enterprise. Exception management processes are in place.<br>• *Executive support and endorsement of the policies*: There is continued communication and education about policies to employees for compliance. Executives are publicly supporting the policies and actively promoting adherence to them as well as the creation of procedures to implement the policies. |

**Table 9.4** Value Creation Dimension by Maturity Level

| Level | Description |
|---|---|
| Initial | • *Recognition of the value of data*: Data is purely seen in context of executing operational transactions. Data issues are seen as "IT issues."<br>• *Recognition of the value of Data Stewardship*: The value of Data Stewardship and data is not explicitly known. |
| Tactical | • *Recognition of the value of data*: Data is beginning to be used to gain insight into how business areas can improve operations and cut costs.<br>• *Recognition of the value of Data Stewardship*: Stewards prove the value of good data management practices in selected projects or business areas. Improved data quality and success of projects are seen as "wins." Value is recognized and communicated across the organization. |
| Well-Defined | • *Recognition of the value of data*: Forward-thinking business functions and analytics gain competitive advantage.<br>• *Recognition of the value of Data Stewardship*: Business Data Stewards help to use information in new ways to gain additional business insights and leverage business capabilities. |
| Strategic | • *Recognition of the value of data*: Data is recognized as a key business asset to be managed in most business functions with a focus on improving the quality of the data.<br>• *Recognition of the value of Data Stewardship*: Stewardship and data management metrics are established with a clear understanding of the value of improving data quality, cost reduction through standardization and reuse, and customer satisfaction. |
| Optimized | • *Recognition of the value of data*: Treating data as a business asset is firmly embedded in the corporate culture.<br>• *Recognition of the value of Data Stewardship*: Data Stewardship has a proven track record of driving tangible business value. Stewards are change agents that enable business value through leveraging data assets. |

## Value Creation

The Value Creation dimension rates the recognition of the increasing value of data as well as the recognition within the organization of the value of Data Stewardship. Table 9.4 shows the various levels of maturity for Value Creation.

## GATHERING THE MATURITY MODEL EVALUATION DATA

To evaluate the current state of maturity, it is necessary to gather information from a wide variety of people who work with data. This is typically done via a survey that consists of carefully chosen questions which align to the dimensions. The answers to these questions provide the data from which the level of maturity in each dimension can be calculated. For example, Table 9.5 shows questions that align to the dimensions and could be included in the survey.

**Table 9.5** Sample Survey Questions by Maturity Model Dimension

| Dimension | Questions |
|---|---|
| Organizational Awareness | <ul><li>Most of our management and leadership team are aware of Data Stewardship and Data Governance.</li><li>Most managers show interest in and actively support Data Stewardship activities across the line of business.</li><li>A Data Stewardship Council exists, is adequately resourced, and is enabled to address most of the Data Stewardship needs in the enterprise.</li><li>A communication plan designed to convey Data Stewardship objectives exists and has been implemented.</li><li>All managers favor Data Stewardship activities and may have included Data Governance projects in their budget.</li><li>A formal communication plan has been implemented that the entire organization embraces and leverages.</li></ul> |
| Roles and Structures | <ul><li>Organizational roles are designated, funded, and staffed to develop and maintain standards.</li><li>You can easily describe your organization's main products and services.</li><li>IT is closely aligned to the business.</li><li>You can easily describe your structure and governance system.</li><li>Individuals are assigned to stewardship roles and are visible, respected, and influential.</li><li>Managers of functional organizations are responsible for mapping individuals to stewardship roles.</li><li>Individuals assigned to stewardship roles possess a passion for quality as well as the required skills and knowledge.</li></ul> |
| Value Creation | <ul><li>The value of Data Governance and Data Stewardship is accepted at all levels of the organization.</li><li>Are you able to put a monetary value on your data?</li><li>All managers understand the value of Data Stewardship and have formed a partnership to champion its cause.</li><li>There is a communication plan that provides a means for demonstrating the value of the Data Stewardship program throughout the entire organization.</li></ul> |

One thing you should notice right away is that the "questions" are actually statements, which the survey participants can agree with (Yes), disagree with (No), or partially agree with (Partial). Something else you need to be careful with is that the answers to the questions (Yes or No) always change the rating of the maturity in the same direction. For example, in the list of questions provided, a "Yes" answer indicates a higher maturity score, whereas a "No" answer always indicates a lower maturity score. This is important because the survey results are converted into numerical scores. Thus if a "Yes" answer sometimes means a higher maturity score and sometimes means a lower maturity score, the calculations get much more complex.

**Table 9.6** Level Setting for Organizational Awareness Maturity Dimension

| Level | Score Range |
|---|---|
| 0: None | 0–5 |
| 1: Initial | 6–13 |
| 2: Tactical | 14–20 |
| 3: Well-defined | 21–25 |
| 4: Strategic | 26–30 |
| 5: Optimized | 31–37 |

## EVALUATING THE RESULTS OF THE MATURITY SURVEY

As noted previously, a set of calculations is performed based on the answers to a survey. At its simplest level, a numerical value is assigned to each answer, and a range of values is chosen that sets which level of the dimension to pick. For example, Table 9.6 shows a possible range for the Organizational Awareness dimension. Note that the range of scores for each level will vary with the dimension since the number of questions (and, thus, the maximum score) will be different for each dimension.

## MEASURING PROGRESS IN MATURITY

The most useful way to use the designated levels and dimensions of Stewardship maturity is to lay them out in a grid, as shown in Fig. 9.1. By examining the intersection of each dimension with each level (as detailed in Tables 9.1–9.4), you can rank your Stewardship maturity for each dimension. Fig. 9.1 shows the appropriate cells (intersection of the current level in each dimension) circled.

The next step is to have the Data Stewards recommend (and the Data Governors approve) the target levels for each dimension. It is not always possible or necessary to get to *Level 5: Optimized* in each dimension, but the Data Stewards and Data Governors should set the goals that the organization will strive for, and the goals should be to show progress in increasing the level of maturity. These goals can then be documented by the arrows stretching from the current state to the target goals in the grid, as shown in Fig. 9.2.

Once you have your initial level for each dimension recorded, you should periodically revisit (perhaps every 6 months) the Stewardship

**NOTE**

In this example a value of 1 was used for each "Yes" answer, a value of 0 was used for each "No" answer, and a value of 0.5 was used for each "Partial" answer.

It is important to point out that the calculation is more complicated than previously described. You need to deal with averages and choose whether the average is taken across the entire population or only particular business functions. For example, some of the more technically focused questions are better answered by participants in IT. Further, you need to deal with questions that are skipped because a participant has no real idea of the answer.

| | Level 1 | Level 2 | Level 3 | Level 4 | Level 5 |
|---|---|---|---|---|---|
| | Initial | Tactical | Well-defined | Strategic | Optimized |
| Organizational awareness | IT manages data ; BDS defined for some business applications ; local SMEs promoting BDS for DQ. | Some business areas having success in adopting Data Stewardship ; Some executive support ; local teams or individuals championing Data Stewardship and DM. Isolated attempts to educate and raise awareness. Some recognition of needing both business and IT in effort. | Corp executive sponsor emerges. Need for Data Stewardship across org. Need for business and IT accountability in DM. Push for corp. level Data Stewardship program. | Stewardship part of enterprise-wide DM and DG. Broad executive understanding of need for stewardship across functional areas. Integrated into development process. Wide educational effort | Data Stewardship implemented at corp level. Formal DM programs and metrics in place. Ongoing communication and education so that all employees know their responsibilities to manage info. |
| Roles and structures | Each business /IT team defines data roles with little commonality. No corporate-wide approach to roles or structure. Accountability is not achieved end-to-end. | Accountability achieved in some business areas ; some business and IT roles in place. Data Stewardship position may be established but no accountability mechanism for this role. | Corp-level Data Stewardship program is being defined. Standard DM roles and resp to support implementation. Accountabilities for business and IT roles in DM defined. Stewardship being implemented in some business areas for key data. Sponsoring executive actively promoting adoption of Data Stewardship corp-wide. | Roles and resp of data stewards clear and consistently defined. Data Stewardship is business resp. Communities of practice established. | Data Stewardship fully integrated and rationalized with corp-wide DG processes. Everyone understands their role in managing data. |
| Standards, policies, and processes | IT standards exist ; no standardized DM methods in the business. Some business standards for applications or business area, few for corp-wide. | DM principles emerging based on business, legal drivers. No complete set of standards, no understanding of requirements. Need for Corp standards identified. Local and best practices emerging. | Endorsement to implement corp DM standards. Corp DM policies and standards program defined. Selected practices made into standards. Executive sponsorship for standards is strengthened. | Corp DM/DG framework defined for standards ; DM programs and methods with education and promotion across org. Stewardship processes measured and standardized, audited. | DM standards in continuous improvement, broad adoption of standards, exception management in place, communication and education for all employees. |
| Value creation | Value of data not known. Stewards are not adding value. Data for transactions and reporting. Data issues are IT's resp. | Stewards prove value in some projects or business areas. Improved quality of data and value recognized. | Corp-wide recognition of data as an asset. Stewards use data in new ways and gain insights and new capabilities. | Stewardship and DM metrics established. Clear understanding of value in improving DQ, cost reduction. | Data Stewardship has proven track record of driving tangible business value. Stewards are change agents. |

■ **FIGURE 9.1** The Stewardship Maturity Grid with the initial (current) levels for each dimension displayed (solid rounded rectangle). The text in each of the cells is a summary of the text in Tables 9.1—9.4.

Maturity Grid and ask the Business Data Stewards to ascertain the current level for each dimension. Planning tasks and setting goals that increase the maturity levels in each dimension will cause the overall level of maturity to increase over time, reaching the assigned targets and maintaining Data Stewardship at those maturity levels.

## IDENTIFYING GAPS AND REMEDIATION

Once you have figured out where you are (the current level for each dimension) and where you need to be (the target level for each dimension), the next task is to identify the gaps you have and how to close those gaps

| | Level 1 | Level 2 | Level 3 | Level 4 | Level 5 |
|---|---|---|---|---|---|
| | Initial | Tactical | Well-defined | Strategic | Optimized |
| Organizational awareness | IT manages data; BDS defined for some business applications; local SMEs promoting BDS for DQ. | Some business areas having success in adopting Data Stewardship; Some executive support; local — Isolated attempts to educate and raise awareness. Some recognition of needing both business and IT in effort. | Corp executive sponsor emerges. Need for data — Increase in maturity level — for corp. level Data Stewardship program. | Stewardship part of enterprise-wide DM and DG. Broad executive — functional areas. Int ed into development p ess. Wide educational effort | Data Stewardship implemented at corp level. Formal DM programs and metrics in place. Ongoing communication and education so that all employees know their responsibilities to manage info. |
| Roles and structures | Each business/IT team defines data roles with little commonality. No corporate-wide approach to roles or structure. Accountability is not achieved end-to-end. | Accountability achieved in some business areas; some — Increase in maturity level — but no accountability mechanism for this role. | Corp-level Data Stewardship program is being defined. Standard DM roles and resp to support impleme tation. Accountabilities for ness — business areas for k ta. Sponsoring executiv actively promoting adoption of Data Stewardship corp-wide. | Roles and resp of Data Stewards clear and consistently defined. Data Stewardship is business resp. Communities of practice established. | Data Stewardship fully integrated and rationalized with corp-wide DG processes. Everyone understands their role in managing data. |
| Standards, policies, and processes | IT standards exist; no standardized DM methods in the business. Some business standards for applications or business area, few for corp-wide. | DM principles emerging based on business, legal drivers. No complete set of standards, no understanding of requirements. Need for Corp standards identified. Local and best practices emerging. | Endorsement to implement corp DM standard. Corp DM policies and st ds — Increase in maturity level — standards. Exec sponsorship for sta rds is strengthened. | Corp DM/DG framework defined for standards; DM programs and methods with education and promotion across org. Stewardship processes measured and standardized, audited. | DM standards in continuous improvement, broad adoption of standards, exception management in place, communication and education for all employees. |
| Value creation | Value of data not known. Stewards are not adding value. Data for transactions and reporting. Data issues are IT's resp. | Stewards prove value in — Increase in maturity level — data and value recognized. | Corp-wide recogniti f — gain insights and re capabilities. | Stewardship and DM metrics established. Clear understanding of value in improving DQ, cost reduction. | Data Stewardship has proven track record of driving tangible business value. Stewards are change agents. |

■ **FIGURE 9.2** The Stewardship Maturity Grid with the target levels for each dimension displayed (dashed rounded rectangle).

(remediation). This is the *real* value of doing a maturity assessment, that is, the creation of a list of things to work on.

To work through identifying the gaps, you need to compare questions that were answered with a low score to how that question would be answered at the target level. For example, one gap in the Organizational Awareness dimension might be:

● Gap: There is a wide variance across managers regarding whether they have interest and/or actively support Data Stewardship activities across lines of business.

Once the gap has been identified, the Risk/Impact and priority of the gap also need to be identified, usually through discussions with key stakeholders, including the Business Data Stewards and Data Governors:

- Risk/Impact: A successful Data Stewardship program requires support from management, which then helps to change the culture (change management) to align the company with objectives for successful governance. Participation in Data Governance and Data Stewardship should not be "optional."
- Priority: High

The mitigation is a general approach to closing the gap, while the recommendation may include a more detailed, step by step approach to the solution:

- Mitigation: Continue to engage the teams with regards to progress and deliverables to provide current and short-term value. Work with the Data Governors and Data Stewards to ensure they understand the direct impact that they are having to the process and how it benefits all the various levels of the organization.
- Recommendations:
  - ○ Identify key managers whose support is crucial to Data Governance and Data Stewardship in each line of business.
  - ○ Create education plan to inform them on what Data Governance and Data Stewardship entail, what advantages they bring, and what is needed to make them successful.
  - ○ Communicate achievements and risks to selected group on a regular basis (part of Communication Plan).
  - ○ The Data Governance Program Office should find ways to build executive support and make sure that Data Governance and Data Stewardship are pushed down the organization as they tie to job descriptions and budgets.

The final step in the analysis of the gap is identify roles that must participate in the mitigation and recommendations:

- Roles: Executive Steering Committee, Data Governance Board, Data Governance Program Office (especially the Data Governance Manager).

## SUMMARY

The maturity of your Data Stewardship effort—measured in levels across a set of dimensions—is an important way to rate how the program is progressing and becoming more robust. The first step is to establish the levels and dimensions, most likely based on a maturity model available in the literature that is adjusted for your organization. The next step is to rate the current maturity levels and determine what the target levels should be. This exercise enables you to identify and prioritize areas of improvement so that you can get more out of the Data Stewardship program. From the gaps identified by the maturity model evaluation, identify the steps that need to be taken to close the gap, and which roles need to participate in that effort. Finally, you need to revisit the maturity on a periodic basis to determine the current maturity level and see if progress is being made.

# Big Data Stewardship and Data Lakes

## INTRODUCTION

With the advent of "big data" and the move to implement "data lakes," a natural question that comes up is how "big Data Governance" (or "big Data Stewardship") is different from "regular" Data Governance or Data Stewardship. The assumption on the part of those asking these questions seems to be that there *must* be big differences, and that the roles, procedures, and metadata captured are also quite different. And, that these differences could require a wholesale restructuring of Data Governance and Data Stewardship efforts. But nothing could be further from the truth. While there *are some* differences (as will be discussed in this chapter) most of what has been built and implemented will remain largely the same. Big data and data lakes make Data Governance and Data Stewardship even more important because much of the promise of these technologies requires *more* Data Governance and Data Stewardship in order to be valuable.

### THE FALLACY OF UNSTRUCTURED DATA

Another common misconception is that "unstructured data" somehow changes the importance or need for Data Governance and Data Stewardship. What is often meant by unstructured data is textual data that is written out by various processes and not stored in a rigid structure such as a relational database. For example, web logs often contain valuable information (which is recorded nowhere except in the web log) such as who has logged into the system, how often, and what web pages were accessed. But from the standpoint of Data Governance, this data is *not* unstructured! In fact, it has a well-defined structure, which is set by the program writing out the text. The process for changing that structure is quite different from a relational database (and some would say it is easier)—"simply" change the code that writes out the data. No need for new tables, new columns, changes in datatypes, or adjustments to foreign keys. But make no mistake—the data has structure and is largely worthless unless that structure is supplied via metadata to those who need to use the "unstructured data."

*(Continued)*

Data Stewardship. DOI: https://doi.org/10.1016/B978-0-12-822132-7.00010-3

**(CONTINUED)**

And, just like any other kind of data, if the information recorded in this type of "unstructured data" is considered valuable enough to be governed, then all the same steps need to be taken to bring it under governance.

Another example of truly unstructured data is documents (such as a Word document or a PowerPoint presentation) or "objects" that are simply stored as is with the intent that they can be found later and opened in the originating application or something similar. But here again, when it comes to governance, metadata about the documents or objects is what is governed, and that metadata has structure. For example, in order to know the business function that would steward a Word document, something about the document must be known and recorded such as the title, topic, subject, and sensitivity of the document.

## DATA STEWARDSHIP AND BIG DATA

Over the years, many companies have found it valuable to capture ever-increasing quantities of data. This is both because the infrastructure (networks, storage, and easily-changeable configurations for structures) has matured and gotten vastly less expensive, and more importantly, because companies have realized that a lot of value can be gained by analyzing and comparing the data collected. I say "more importantly" because if there was no value in collecting large quantities of data, they wouldn't do it, no matter how cheap the infrastructure becomes.

A good example that almost anyone can relate to is a chain of grocery stores. The register records every item that is purchased, how the purchases are grouped (onto a single receipt), and even (when the grocery chain has a loyalty card program) *who* purchased the items. As you can imagine, this leads to a vast quantity of highly detailed data from which the grocery chain can extract value. For example, by analyzing lists of items that are often purchased together (such as frozen waffles and syrup), the grocery chain can provide coupons that are both more useful to the customer and more profitable to the company. I (and probably you) have seen this sort of analysis *not* carried out properly. Thus I might buy a box of frozen waffles, and the store gives me a coupon for a free box. This makes no sense because I have proven that I'm willing to pay money for the waffles, so why give it to me for free? Instead, if the "big data" available shows that waffles and syrup are often bought together, and I buy waffles but *not* syrup, it would make more sense to give me a free (or discounted price) on syrup. This outcome helps to get me thinking of buying these items together (good for the store) and provides a discount to do so (good for me).

The point is that in the days when it was impractical to keep the purchase data at the level of granularity needed to perform such analysis, companies may well not have done so, settling instead on the summaries and aggregations needed only to control inventory and ordering. The business data elements and the rest of the metadata needed to govern and steward the data would not have included the granular data (such as individual retail transactions, grouping by receipt, and identification of the customer) that can add value today. But in today's world, where the value added by such granular data returns value to the company, the additional business data elements and other metadata *would* be collected, governed, and stewarded (as shown in the example in Fig. 10.1). Thus, once again, Data Governance and Data Stewardship are more important than ever before—though the processes and roles are largely the same. In addition, the rest of the processes that include Business Data Stewards (such as data quality improvement) are larger—but not really any different. As illustrated here, *more* data collected usually means more metadata collected as well.

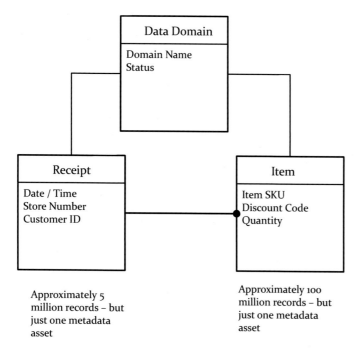

**■ FIGURE 10.1** More granular data requires a small additional amount of metadata, but possibly a *lot* of extra data.

# DATA STEWARDSHIP AND DATA LAKES

With the advent of "big data" and the need to be nimbler when working with data came an architectural construct called a "data lake." It is a system that holds data that is collected from various source systems and all stored in that one system. In some ways a data lake is like a data warehouse, in that part of the data lake stores data that has been combined from other systems. But unlike a data warehouse, a data lake stores data in various zones, including "raw" (looking like it does in the source system) and various transformed forms. These transformed forms (which often combine data from multiple source systems) are specialized for tasks such as reporting, visualization, analytics, and machine learning.

## Data Lakes and Metadata

As you might expect, metadata plays an important part in the use and governance of a data lake. A data lake is a data management platform, and as with any other data management platform, the data within it must be described, understood, owned, and inventoried. Lineage must be understood to prove integrity, and in most of the zones, the data quality must be known. In fact, in many companies, data cannot be loaded into the production data lake (a process called "ingestion") until the metadata has been collected and documented. Many data lakes even incorporate a metadata "catalog" to hold all this required information.

You may have also heard the term "data swamp," which is taken to mean a data lake in which the appropriate metadata management is not in place, and that lacks Data Governance. Much like a data warehouse, Data Stewardship and curation of the data is needed, along with metadata capture.

Sound principles of data definition, data production, and data usage are also needed. This is because the usefulness of a data lake is driven by knowing certain things about the data sets in the data lake, including:

- What is available in the data lake? Like any other data store, you have to know what is available before it can be useful. Knowing what is available includes not only what the data means, but what systems served as sources for the datasets, how those datasets were transformed and combined, and the quality of the data in the dataset. Much of this information (metadata) is contained in the "catalog".
- How can I find the data I'm looking for? The same data may be available in multiple zones of the lake. As we'll see, zones are handled differently (different levels of data cleanliness and different

levels of Data Governance). Thus you not only need to know what data is available, but which zone it is in, or, if it is in multiple zones, which zone is most useful for your purposes.

- How was the data selected? Different data is selected from different sources, combined in different ways, and ingested into the data lake. Depending what how the data was selected (and where it was selected from), you may find certain datasets more useful (or less useful) than others.

- What access is available? Getting at the data in a data lake requires sophisticated processes that make the access available. There are different publishing methods and distribution systems as well as different levels of access. For example, you may not have access to certain repositories of data because they contain sensitive or private information that you do not have permission to see and use. You may be able to get access, but you'll have to go through the appropriate procedures to do so.

From another perspective, the same questions you would ask if you were doing analytics in a data warehouse also need to be answered if you're doing analytics in a data lake. These questions highlight the need for rigorous Data Stewardship, at least in any of the zones where analytics are being performed.

These questions include:

- *Who owns the data and can answer questions about it?* This is a classic question that users ask and one of the most obvious drivers for Data Stewardship. In the presence of a robust set of tools to record metadata, this information can be found in the Business Glossary (possibly in combination with a metadata repository).

- *How do I find the right data elements that meet my needs?* Once again, robust Data Stewardship (and a good Business Glossary/ metadata repository) provides the answer to this crucial question. The business user determines the data they need to solve a particular business need, and the results of Data Stewardship provide the location of the needed data.

- *How do I clean the data to an appropriate level of quality?* In consultation with the Business Data Stewards (either by business function or by data domain—as described in Chapter 11: Governing and Stewarding Your Data Using Data Domains) a determination can be made as to the level of data quality that will be sufficient to support the business need. After that determination, the actual data quality can be ascertained by data profiling, as described in

Chapter 7, The Important Roles of Data Stewards. If the data quality is insufficient to support the business need, an issue can be raised, and a project started to mitigate the issue and bring the quality up to the level needed.

- *What is the right security for the data being used?* The compliance and privacy parameters for data should have been established when the business data elements were defined. If these parameters were *not* set, then it will be necessary to consult with the subject matter experts (who are likely situated in your Risk, Privacy, and Compliance organizations) in conjunction with the responsible Business Data Stewards to establish those parameters during ingestion. The question then becomes whether the data analysts trying to use the data are allowed to have access to the sensitive data. If they do not have the necessary access, then the appropriate processes (as described in Chapter 7: The Important Roles of Data Stewards) would have to be followed to gain access to the data.

- *Is the data being monitored for adherence to standards?* The Data Governance/Data Stewardship effort is responsible for adhering to the standards and policies related to data. Usually, a different group will be responsible for monitoring whether the adherence is adequate and reporting on any shortfalls along with designing mitigating steps. Thus although monitoring for adherence to standards is usually done outside of the Data Stewardship effort, that adherence—and the advantages that come with it—starts with Data Stewardship.

## Determining the Level of Data Governance for the Data Lake

As we've already mentioned, the metadata about the data in the data lake as well as the level of Data Governance for the zones are decisions that need to be made. Each zone may have a different amount of curation and "strictness" of Data Governance. To a certain extent, the metadata and level of Data Governance are something of a balancing act. Overdoing the amount of metadata collection (whether in the catalog or elsewhere) stifles the usefulness and flexibility of the data lake due to the overhead of collecting the metadata before bringing in a new dataset or modifying an existing dataset. Put another way, the more you know (metadata) the more useful the data is, but also the more work it is to add datasets and make changes to structures. Since ease of adding data and flexibility of structure are two of the primary advantages of using a data lake in the first place, you must balance the benefits against the cost.

What is likely to happen is that the metadata collected and level of Data Governance will be set based on the use of the data in the zone. The goal is to use the data with a level of confidence consistent with that use. Things to think about include:

- There is a need to tune the Data Governance to the priorities and context (use) of the data. For some people, a level that some would consider a "data swamp" might be perfectly acceptable for their needs.
- Certain decisions drive the data lake in one direction or another. For example, if a zone in the data lake becomes the source of data for regulatory reports, it needs extremely good metadata, cataloging, Data Governance, and lineage.
- In some zones, lightweight Data Governance on adding, naming, and curating the data protects the data lake shared resource from the "tragedy of the commons."

> **DEFINITION**
>
> The "tragedy of the commons" is a situation where individual users, acting independently according to their own self-interest, behave contrarily to the common good of all users by depleting or spoiling the shared resource through their collective action. In the case of a data lake, insisting on perfect metadata and rigorous Data Governance is inconsistent with the purpose of a data lake, and doing so would ruin the data lake for the users who don't need that and that can't support that effort.

## Metadata Created in the Data Lake

As data is combined in inventive ways in the data lake to serve the business needs, the question arises as to who is responsible for the newly created/derived business data elements. This is especially true in an organization with a strong Data Governance operation since the idea that the business data elements should remain largely undefined and that no one is accountable for the data is repugnant and may even violate data management policies. The issue extends especially into data quality since this "new" data is often created for new purposes or business drivers, and there is no guarantee that the data quality is sufficient for these new purposes and, thus, must be profiled to find out. Closely aligned to the evaluation of the quality of the data are the data quality rules against which the data will be evaluated—and there must be an accountable business function or data domain to define those rules.

So who is responsible for the metadata that must be generated as data is manipulated within the data lake? Figuring that out can be problematic because by the time the data reaches the fully integrated zone, it includes data from many source systems and, thus, integrates the knowledge/metadata expertise of many different Business Data Stewards. This integration must be done carefully and well and linked back to a common vocabulary of business data elements. This common vocabulary must be enhanced as new business data elements are defined and derived.

The data is initially brought into the raw zone of the data lake from source systems in a process called "ingestion." Where the source system(s) providing the ingested dataset do not have all the business data elements defined and governed, many companies will demand that it be done when brought into the data lake. This would include establishing the privacy and compliance parameters of the business data elements, updating the physical location as being in the raw zone of the data lake, and monitoring adherence to standards. In addition, when the data in the source system did not have data quality rules defined and used to profile that data, that may be done during ingestion as well.

When the data in various zones are combined and integrated together to form the contents of another zone, these same processes must also be carried out; though depending on the "rigor" of the required Data Governance in the zone, some steps may be skipped.

Fig. 10.2 illustrates how this might look.

## Proposed Roles for Governing in a Data Lake

Due to the complexity of data manipulation in a data lake, there are a lot of roles that get involved with deciding what data to ingest, determining what that data means, how sensitive it is, tracking the lineage, and in gauging the quality. Many of these roles are part of Data Stewardship and Data Governance or work directly with roles in Data Stewardship and Data Governance. Further, as data is moved through various zones in the data lake, and combined and integrated to meet new business needs, Business Data Stewards play increasingly important roles.

Interestingly, most of these roles are *not* new. We have discussed virtually all of them earlier in this book or will discuss them in Chapter 11, Governing and Stewarding Your Data Using Data Domains. Fig. 10.3 shows these roles being involved in common data lake—related tasks such as declaring a new zone, ingesting new data into the lake, and transferring data between zones within the lake.

## Data Stewardship in the World of Data Lakes and Fast Data

As with "big data" (discussed previously), there is not much difference between performing Data Stewardship in the new world of data lakes, with just a few exceptions:

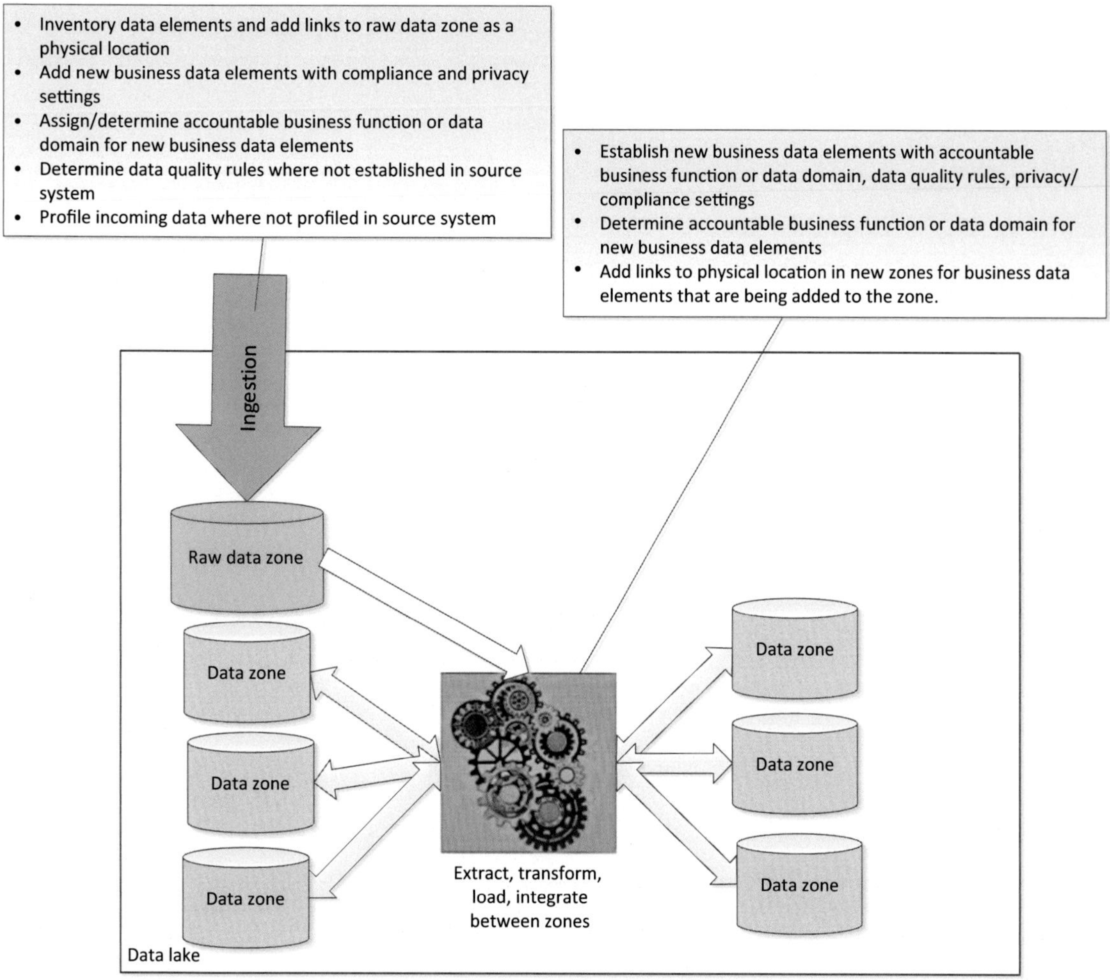

- Inventory data elements and add links to raw data zone as a physical location
- Add new business data elements with compliance and privacy settings
- Assign/determine accountable business function or data domain for new business data elements
- Determine data quality rules where not established in source system
- Profile incoming data where not profiled in source system

- Establish new business data elements with accountable business function or data domain, data quality rules, privacy/compliance settings
- Determine accountable business function or data domain for new business data elements
- Add links to physical location in new zones for business data elements that are being added to the zone.

Ingestion

Raw data zone

Data zone

Data zone

Data zone

Data lake

Extract, transform, load, integrate between zones

Data zone

Data zone

Data zone

■ **FIGURE 10.2** Generating metadata as a data lake is evolved and governed.

1. It must be *fast*. With extremely fast changes in what data is ingested, how it is manipulated, and how it is accessed; Data Stewardship cannot afford to be the bottleneck, and the response needs to be quick and efficient—and consistent with the decisions about the level of Data Governance for different zones.

2. It is even *more* important. With the perceived flexibility and ease of exploration of a data lake, the usage is probably going to escalate quickly. But bad decisions can be made if the data is misinterpreted, misunderstood, or of poor quality. Thus governing that data becomes

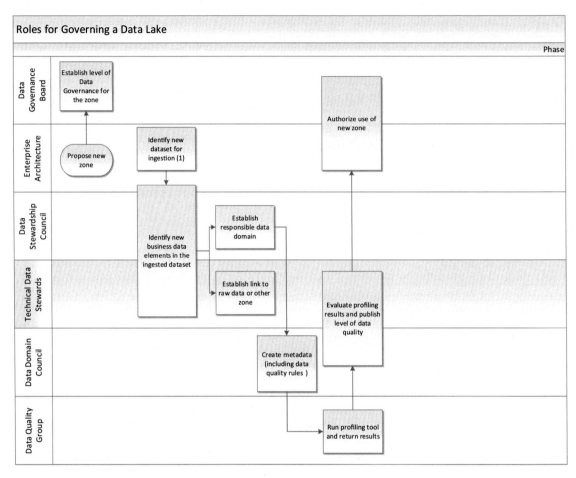

**■ FIGURE 10.3** Roles for some of the governance in a data lake when using data domain-based Data Stewardship.

more critical the more it is used. Further, with many streams of data all converging on the data lake, certain metadata—like lineage—is crucial.

With vast quantities of data and extremely high-powered computing and cheap storage, you can get into a world of "fast data." Fast data handles and uses the data as fast as it arrives, opening new vistas of discovery. Essentially, the data is ingested at millions of events per second and as fast it is ingested, data-driven decisions are made and real-time analyses carried out. But with automated decision-making comes considerable responsibility—many of the scenarios for the use of fast data (such as decisions based on the feed from security cameras) have significant consequences if done incorrectly.

## SUMMARY

While there are differences in performing Data Governance and Data Stewardship with big data, fast data, and data lakes, those differences are not large, and do not require a wholesale restructuring or discarding of tried and true procedures. There *are* differences—some decisions need to be made that were not needed before (such as the level of Data Governance for a data lake zone), but most of the differences have to do with a "need for speed" and added complexity due to the nature of a data lake. In addition, with many people needing to contribute knowledge about the data in the data lake, a good case can be made for governing your data by "data domains," as discussed in Chapter 11, Governing and Stewarding Your Data Using Data Domains.

# Governing and Stewarding Your Data Using Data Domains

## INTRODUCTION

Probably the most important concept in Data Governance is that decisions have to be made about data—and the metadata about that data needs to be defined. This is the starting point for almost everything associated with successful Data Governance. Key to making these decisions correctly and defining the metadata is that the people doing that work—the Business Data Stewards—must have a good working knowledge of the data. Furthermore the Business Data Stewards must know and take into account the needs of their stakeholders—those people who depend on the data to run their parts of the business. In the early days of Data Governance (and in some enterprises today), this was done by a relatively small group of Business Data Stewards recruited from the business functions who own the data. They are expected to know the data, know who the stakeholders are, and have the skills to achieve the knowledge required to make good decisions and define the metadata. But as the amount and complexity of the data—as well as the amount of metadata that must be understood and documented—became larger and larger, it became more and more difficult to know enough and collaborate with everyone needed. As a result, the Data Stewardship effort may turn to "data domain-driven Data Stewardship."

Data domains are logical groupings that bundle similar data together and have decisions made by a group of knowledgeable Business Data Stewards working together in a formal group. Working on data in data domains formalizes a lot of the processes that Business Data Stewards have been performing informally. By making the informal processes and relationships to stakeholders formal and documented, the processes become repeatable and of higher quality.

But make no mistake, setting up and running data domain—based Data Stewardship is neither easy nor quick. In this chapter we will explore the techniques and expected results you can achieve.

> **NOTE**
>
> Because of the need for maturity and experience in Data Governance (as explained in the "Data Domain—Based Data Stewardship Requires a Mature Organization" section) to be successful in data domain—driven Data Governance, many organizations begin with business function—driven Data Stewardship and switch to data domain—driven Data Stewardship after establishing a smoothly functioning Data Governance effort.

Data Stewardship. DOI: https://doi.org/10.1016/B978-0-12-822132-7.00011-5

## THE CASE FOR DATA DOMAIN–BASED DATA STEWARDSHIP

As noted in the introduction, basing your Data Stewardship effort on data domains can be a more rigorous way of approaching this important effort. However, for a variety of reasons that we will explore in this chapter, use of data domains require a certain maturity in the organization's approach to managing its data.

## Where did Data Domain–Based Data Governance come from?

Previously, Data Governance tended to be based on business organizations or business functions. The reason that business *function*–based Data Governance was attractive is that it tries to stay away from the organization's structure, which changes over time through reorganizations. But, realistically, business functions tend to mirror the organization closely. Over time, therefore, as the organization structure changes or people change organizations, the people in Data Stewardship roles also change, interrupting the continuity of stewardship knowledge and requiring ongoing replacement of various kinds of Data Stewards (with training).

In addition, business unit or business function–based Data Stewardship tends to lead to fragmented glossaries of business data elements. These fragmented glossaries (typically based on what that the business function does) make it difficult or impossible to gain a single integrated glossary of business data elements, leading to duplicate business data elements and conflicts between term definitions across the various glossaries.

Even when there is a realization that ownership of business data elements needs to be shared, the effort to decide who needs to be involved in decision-making and documenting those responsibilities can be fragmented and difficult to maintain as the population of decision-makers can end up being different for each business data element. Many organizations depend on the designated Business Data Steward to know who the stakeholders are, and consult with them, though there is rarely any audit trail that this has actually been done.

The ideal situation (when possible) is to have a single, enterprise-wide shared glossary of business data elements that follow the same naming standards and rigorous rules for creating definitions, derivation and usage rules, and establishing quality thresholds. This does not mean that there will be *no* business function level glossaries, but it does mean that when a term is shared across multiple lines of the business, it should be populated and governed at the enterprise-level glossary.

## The Value of Data Domain–Based Data Stewardship

Data domains are a tested way to govern business terms across functional areas of the enterprise. The data domains establish "logical" categories or groupings of data that are deemed important and necessary to a firm's normal business operation. They are managed by relatively stable "governance groups" (called Data Domain Councils in many organizations) that govern the business data elements which are associated with each data domain. Groups of Business Data Stewards are led by a Lead Data Steward under the management of the Data Domain Council Manager. The Business Data Stewards in each data domain are drawn from the line of business and represent (in general) people who are experts on the business data elements in each data domain. Of course not all Business Data Stewards in each governance group are experts on all the associated business data elements, so the decision-making mechanism must allow for Business Data Stewards who feel they are *not* experts on a particular business data element to abstain from the decision-making process. Fig. 11.1 shows a simplified structure of data domains, the Data Domain Council(s), and the associated business data elements that are governed by data domains. As shown in the figure, Data

- A Data Domain Council can govern multiple Data Domains on different levels.
- Data domains are organized so that Business Data Elements belong to one (and only one) data domain.

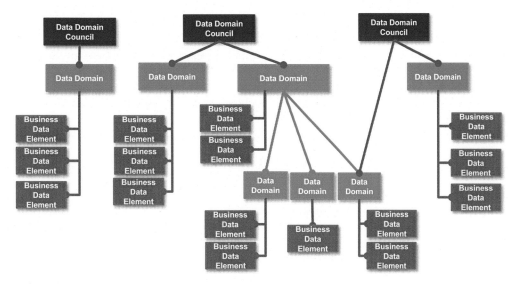

■ **FIGURE 11.1** Data Domain Governance Basic Structure.

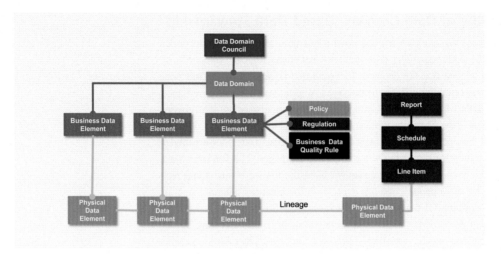

■ **FIGURE 11.2** Business Data Elements are related to many other kinds of metadata.

Domain Councils can be responsible for multiple data domains, and business data elements are linked to a single data domain.

As shown in Fig. 11.2, the governance of business data elements may cascade to other important metadata, such as physical data elements, data quality rules, and other metadata that affects the use of the governed business data element.

The advantages of using data domains (and Data Domain Councils) over individual owning Business Data Stewards who consult offline with stakeholders should be clear. All stakeholders should be represented in the Data Domain Council, and the process for reaching any decision will document who participated and what their individual decision was, thereby leaving a clear audit trail.

**PRACTICAL ADVICE**

With many Business Data Stewards having a "say" in the decisions that are made about the metadata associated with a data domain (and thus a Data Domain Council), a written and authorized procedure must be in place to determine what the overall decision is based on the individual decisions of the participants ("votes"). The procedure must lay out:

- How many votes are needed for a decision to be made? The obvious choices are a simple majority or unanimous agreement. In the case of a simple majority, a decision is fairly straightforward—just count the votes. However, this can leave many Business Data Stewards (who feel they understand the data and have a stake in the decision) feeling ignored and unwilling to follow the decision. On the other hand, a unanimous decision may be very difficult to achieve. In the real world, though, the usual process includes a full and open discussion with the entire council where any differences can be worked out and the voting results are known before the voting even begins. This is the ideal situation.
- What do you do if one or more Business Data Stewards feel unqualified to make a decision? While the ideal case is that the participants in the Data Domain Council are interested in all the council's data, in the real world this rarely happens. There are bound to be instances where one or more of the Business Data Stewards lack either the knowledge or the interest in some of the data because they don't use it. Because of this, there needs to be a mechanism for the Business Data Steward(s) who find themselves in this situation to abstain from voting, and the decision is then based on those who *do* vote. That said, abstaining should be an active choice rather than simply not participating in voting. Otherwise you may find yourself in the situation where many Business Data Stewards don't bother voting because they are "too busy" and you won't know whether that represented abstaining from voting or ignoring their role as a Business Data Steward.
- The clear definition of the division of responsibilities between the Lead Data Steward and the Data Domain Council Manager.

## DATA DOMAINS EXPLAINED

A data domain is a *logical* construct that groups together data related by subject areas. These groupings are often based on business process, business transactions, reference or master data, and products, but other groupings can be created that align to specific usage and/or business architectures. That is, according to the EDM Council, data domains are not physical repositories or databases. The categories or groupings are deemed important and necessary to the enterprise's normal business operation. Further, the categories can include internally generated data and externally acquired data. It is imperative that these strategic categories of data are identified, defined, and inventoried to ensure their proper maintenance and use throughout the organization. A sample list of data domains (and their type) is shown in Table 11.1

Data domains are important because they organize data and enable clear governance and management of data by Business Data Stewards across the organization accountable for data quality and the use of the data throughout its lifecycle.

Data domains are used in the following ways:

- Mapped to business functions to establish a common understanding on the scope of what is being governed and managed. The transactional data domains tend to be mapped to lines of business, while the derived data domains tend to be mapped to corporate functions such as Risk, Finance, and Reporting.

**Table 11.1** Sample Data Domains by Type

| Type | Description | Sample Data Domains |
|---|---|---|
| Transactional Data Domains | Data created as part of business transaction, representing the data needed to fully define the details and structure of the transactions | 1. Deposits<br>2. Credit Card<br>3. Commercial deposits<br>4. Retail deposits<br>5. Residential Loans<br>6. Consumer lending<br>7. Commercial Lending<br>8. Auto lending<br>9. Market Advisory Service<br>10. Wealth Management |
| Reference Data Domains | Data used for master and reference data, that is, data elements that describe an object and serve as the basic building blocks of any system design (e.g., customer data, product data) | 11. Party<br>12. Product<br>13. Organizational Hierarchy<br>14. Employees<br>15. Geography |
| Derived Data Domains | Data used to combine transactional data in specific and defined ways to produce results critical to necessary enterprise use cases, such as financial reporting | 16. Accounting<br>17. Audit<br>18. Finance<br>19. Credit Risk<br>20. Market risk<br>21. Operational risk<br>22. Regulatory reporting<br>23. Anti-money-laundering<br>24. Taxes |
| Discovery Data Domains | Data used for discovery analytics, that is, data that enables key insights (e.g., consumer behavior) | 25. Sales<br>26. Customer Relationship Management |

- Used to assign an accountability model for defining, sourcing, and managing critical data that is shared across the organization.

Data domains are often established by enterprise Data Governance, and aligned to support enterprise data policy and standards, including Governance, metadata, data quality, and data provisioning.

## KEY BENEFITS OF DATA DOMAINS

Although setting up and governing by data domains requires significant effort, there are notable advantages to expending that effort, as shown in Table 11.2.

## SPECIFYING AND SETTING UP DATA DOMAINS

One of the very first tasks (and arguably the most important) is to specify the set of data domains that will be governed and to which the business data elements will be associated. While there is no set way of getting to a set of data domains that satisfy the enterprise's needs, there are some important considerations, as summarized in Fig. 11.3. This requires considerable dedication to the effort by the business functions. It is often advisable to obtain "outside help" in the form of consulting with experience as well as highly developed facilitation skills. Experienced consultants can provide a sample set of data domains that can serve as a starting point and if possible, expertise in the business(es) of the

**Table 11.2** Key Benefits of Data Domains

| Business Function–Based Approach | Data Domain–Based Approach |
|---|---|
| Fragmented and incomplete architecture for Data Governance | Supports *coordinated governance* of data content and physical architecture by bringing together business and IT for similar data (such as in Approved Provisioning Points for data) |
| Limited linkage between enterprise and line of business governance and decision-making | *Connects* the Line of Business and other group activities with enterprise Data Governance |
| Organizationally based data definitions and specific usage silos | Enables the establishment of *consistent shared meaning*, usage, and business value from the data |
| No mechanism to ensure alignment of business strategies with enterprise data objectives | *Ensures alignment* of business strategies with enterprise Data Governance through shared communication and oversight |
| Governance processes are driven by shifting organizational structure and uneven line of business participation | *Shields Data Governance* activities from organizational changes, with representation based on data and not reporting hierarchy |
| One-size-fits-all Data Governance | Different data domains allow *flexibility* to support different Data Governance requirements depending on business needs |

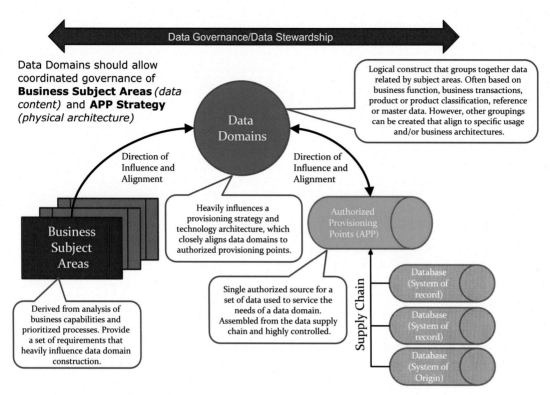

**Data Governance/Data Stewardship**

Data Domains should allow coordinated governance of **Business Subject Areas** *(data content)* and **APP Strategy** *(physical architecture)*

Data Domains

Logical construct that groups together data related by subject areas. Often based on business function, business transactions, product or product classification, reference or master data. However, other groupings can be created that align to specific usage and/or business architectures.

Direction of Influence and Alignment

Direction of Influence and Alignment

Business Subject Areas

Heavily influences a provisioning strategy and technology architecture, which closely aligns data domains to authorized provisioning points.

Authorized Provisioning Points (APP)

Derived from analysis of business capabilities and prioritized processes. Provide a set of requirements that heavily influence data domain construction.

Single authorized source for a set of data used to service the needs of a data domain. Assembled from the data supply chain and highly controlled.

Supply Chain

Database (System of record)

Database (System of record)

Database (System of Origin)

■ **FIGURE 11.3** Design considerations for Data Domains.

enterprise. In categories such as healthcare, retail, financial services, insurance, and other large industry blocs, the beginning set of data domains may prove to be very similar to the finished set.

The key thing to understand from Fig. 11.3 is that data domains should allow coordinated Data Governance and Data Stewardship of data content from Business Subject Areas and drive toward a reasonable physical architecture through Authorized Provisioning Points (APPs).

## Business Subject Areas

Gathering a list of Business Subject Areas is a good starting point. This is because you will need data domains that reflect the data in these subject areas. Further, if local business glossaries (sets of business data elements) are available, they will likely already be associated with a business function that is very similar (and in some cases identical) to business subject areas.

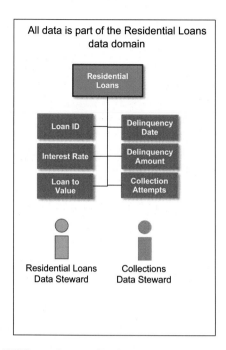
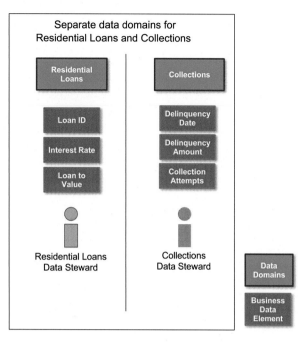

■ **FIGURE 11.4** Two ways of handling data domains for nonproducts such as "Collections".

There may well be a temptation to identify business subject areas by the products that the enterprise sells and services. For example, if a financial services organization sells residential mortgages, it may well make sense to have a "Residential Loan" data domain. However, you should not limit yourself to products. There may be many things that the enterprise does which are *not* products, and yet it is imperative to govern data for that function. In the current example, the organization will likely have a function (and its associated data) for collecting on delinquent loans (often called "Collections"). While much of the data from Residential Loans will be pertinent to Collections, that business function will have its own data that might be associated to a Collections data domain. Another way to approach this situation, however, is to simply have a Residential Loans data domain, and Collections is represented in the Data Domain Council for that data domain. These two situations are shown in Fig. 11.4.

## Business Data Elements

Understanding the enterprise's data usually focuses on the business terms that the business uses. These terms (or business data elements as referred to in this book) have a definition stated in business language, and quite often a set of business rules that define how they are derived, what logical valid values they might have, the privacy/sensitivity of the data, what business processes these terms contribute to, how to evaluate whether the physical data associated with the terms are of good quality, and much more. In fact, a Data Governance effort usually begins with collecting and defining the key or critical business data elements (as described in Chapter 4: Implementing Data Stewardship), since these serve as a gateway to many more Data Governance efforts. Additionally, the "ownership" and "stewardship" of such business data elements is recorded.

When Data Stewardship is performed in a silo defined by a business function, the ownership of the business data elements resides in business functions. Thus although a bank may sell both residential mortgages and commercial mortgages, if these products are sold by two different divisions or subsidiaries, the business data elements may exist in multiple business glossaries, usually with slightly different definitions despite the fact that the many of the terms are more or less identical. Fig. 11.5 shows a sample of what a complete set of Loan Accounts and Transactions data domains (and sub data domains) might look like.

The problem gets even more complicated when discussing "Parties" who participate in transactions of one sort or another. Some business data elements should belong to a generic "Party Master" data domain, whereas other elements exist only when the party is an individual, and some only when the party is a nonindividual such as an organization or business (see Fig. 11.6). Complicating this still further is that even when a business data element exists for an individual party and a nonindividual party, the

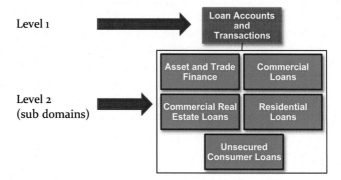

■ **FIGURE 11.5** Two levels of data domains related to Loans.

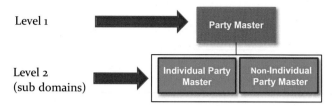

■ **FIGURE 11.6** Splitting up the Party Master data domain into two parts.

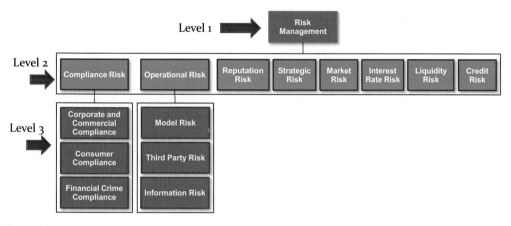

■ **FIGURE 11.7** Risk Management is a data domain that covers a lot of different data.

sensitivity of that information may be different—and it may be protected differently. For example, while the full name of an individual is considered "private and confidential," the full name of an organization is not.

All of this influences the selection of data domains in two ways:

1. The data domains must be comprehensive enough to cover all of the business data elements and provide a "home" for each one, often reflecting the business function or product that it has in the fragmented business glossaries.
2. The data domains must be granular enough so that the business data elements can be governed by membership in one and only one data domain. This drives the data domains to have a hierarchy with sufficient levels to allow for this granularity, without becoming so fragmented that the number of data domains becomes unmanageably large. An example of such a hierarchy for risk management is shown in Fig. 11.7. You'll notice that when the parent domain covers a lot of different kinds of data, the number of data domains can grow quite large.

## Authorized Provisioning Point

An "authorized provisioning point" (APP) is a highly controlled single source for a set of data used to service the needs of a data domain. These are seldom, if ever, the original source of the data. Instead, an APP represents the trusted distribution point for data assembled from the data supply chain (see Fig. 11.8). The key to having a good APP is that the data is fully governed—that is, fully defined at the business data element level, mapped to the physical instantiation (physical data element), possessing well-defined data quality rules, and profiled with a result that proves that the data is of high-enough quality to meet the business purposes. Further, the lineage of the supply chain is well-documented so that auditable proof is available of the integrity of the data in the APP.

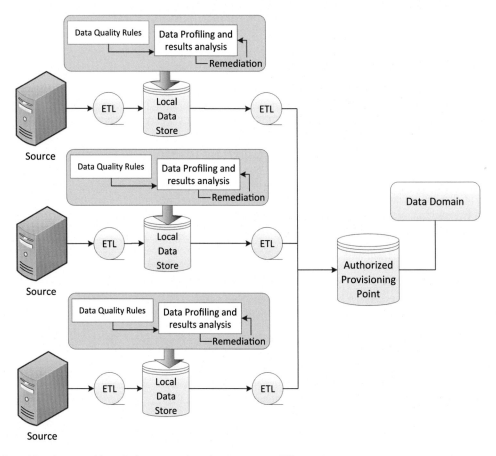

■ **FIGURE 11.8** One of many possible supply chains to an authorized provisioning point (APP).

Data domains should heavily influence the provisioning strategy, and thus architects have a role in the determination of the data domain determination. An efficient and well-constructed provisioning strategy closely aligns data domains to authorized provisioning points. To summarize, while creating an APP that services a data domain is not the primary constraint on determining data domains, when the opportunity arises, data domains should be chosen where a reasonable APP can be created to supply the data related to that data domain.

## GOVERNING DATA DOMAINS

Based on everything we've discussed so far, it is clear that data domains are important to the implementation and maintenance of Data Governance. Specifically:

- Data Governance routines will be implemented and aligned with data domains.
- Data Stewardship representation in these governance routines will come from business and functional groups across the enterprise.
- Data domains will also drive the orientation of APPs.
- Data Governance and Data Stewardship roles can be assigned directly at the data domain level, or grouped into "Data Domain Councils" that manage or govern multiple related data domains.
- The Data Domain Council has the following responsibilities:
  - Governs the business data elements attached to their data domain(s).
  - Establishes the metadata (definition, name, management of the assignment of compliance and privacy attributes, etc.).
  - May govern key relationships to other metadata assets related to the business data elements: business data quality rules, creation and usage rules, regulations that affect the business term, related polices, etc.

> **NOTE**
> An APP may be a zone in a data lake. But whether it is or not, the requirements for a robust APP remain the same.

## Data Domains and Data Domain Councils

The Data Governance roles can be done directly at the data domain level, or grouped into Data Domain Councils that make the Data Governance decisions for multiple data domains. While potentially less flexible, using Data Domain Councils usually makes the most sense for several reasons. First, companies of any reasonable size can have a large number of data domains, so managing each data domain (and all the people in the governance roles) individually can be very unwieldy. A grouping of data domains that is managed by a single Data Domain Council is easier to manage and is more easily scalable.

Second, many data domains are similar enough to each other (while being granular enough to support the cardinality of the relationship between business data elements and the owning data domain) that bundling them together under the auspices of a single governing Data Domain Council makes sense—as well as being more scalable. This is especially true when you realize that many sub-data domains are linked to a single parent data domain.

An example should help. Fig. 11.9 shows how complex the governance can become if attempted at the data domain level. Even with the relatively small number of data domains that can be shown in a simple diagram, you can see how the determination of roles and people in roles can become unwieldy, especially when each of the governing groups must meet frequently.

> **NOTE**
>
> We will discuss the various roles shown in the figure in the "Staffing the Data Domain Council" section.

By analyzing the similarities of the data domains, it is possible to create (and later assign governance roles to) Data Domain Councils that make decisions for multiple data domains. Fig. 11.10 shows how the data domains could be combined. The obvious result is not only a much more reasonable set of governance groups to manage, but also an easier time of assigning resources.

Legend: ● Data Officer ● Data Domain Council Manager ● Lead Data Steward ● Business Data Steward

**Data Officer Business Areas**

| Data Domains | | Regional Bank | Intl Bank | Global Markets | Securities | Financial Crimes | Risk Mgmt | Finance | Lending |
|---|---|---|---|---|---|---|---|---|---|
| Transaction | Deposits | ● | ● | | | ● | ● | ● | |
| | Residential Loans | ● | | | | ● | ● | ● | ● |
| | Commercial Loans | ● | ● | | | ● | ● | ● | |
| | Credit Card | | | | | ● | ● | ● | |
| | Market Advisory Svc | | ● | ● | ● | | ● | ● | |
| | Wealth Management | ● | ● | | ● | | ● | ● | ● |
| Master/ Reference Data | Party Master | ● | ● | | ● | ● | ● | ● | ● |
| | Product Master | ● | ● | | ● | | ● | ● | ● |
| | Organizational Hierarchy | ● | ● | | ● | | ● | ● | ● |
| | Geography | | | ● | | | ● | ● | |
| Derived Data | Finance & Accounting | ● | ● | ● | ● | | ● | ● | ● |
| | Risk Management | ● | ● | ● | ● | | ● | | |

■ FIGURE 11.9 Resource assignment across data domains and Lines of Business.

- Having a unique set of participants (Lead Data Steward, Business Data Stewards, Data Domain Council Manager) for each data domain becomes impractical as the number of data domains increases.
- However, many data domains have the same (or a very similar) set of participants. These can be governed by a single "Data Domain Council." This is effective especially when there are many sub domains linked to a parent data domain.

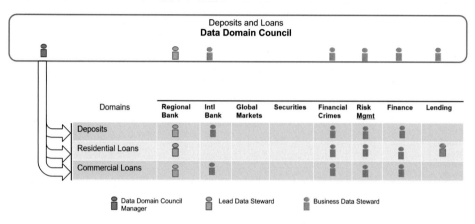

**■ FIGURE 11.10** Creating a Data Domain Council to govern similar data domains.

## Data Domain Council Structure and Governance

The overall structure of a Data Domain Council and its relationship to the local (business function) Data Governance groups is shown in Fig. 11.11.

The members (Business Data Stewards) come from the designated business functions. They are appointed by the Data Governors of their business function, who, in turn, are appointed by the local Data Officers. Within a Data Domain Council, one of the Business Data Stewards is designated as the "Lead Data Steward" and provides guidance and direction, as well as expertise about the data to the other Business Data Stewards in the Data Domain Council. The Lead Data Steward is typically chosen from the business function that has the most at stake in managing the data associated with the data domain.

There are many relationships as shown in Fig. 11.11, some of which have been previously discussed:

- The Lead Data Stewards are members of the enterprise-level Data Stewardship Council, where they coordinate their efforts, establish the data

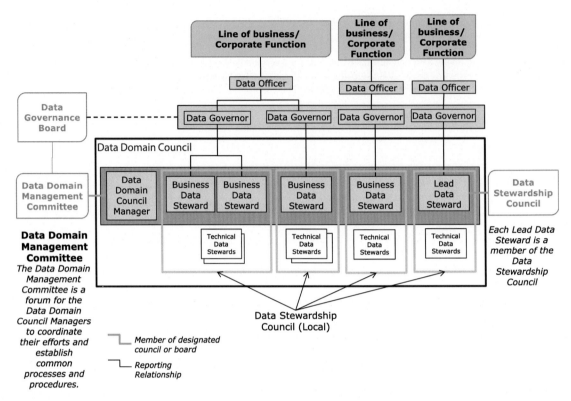

**Data Domain Management Committee**
The Data Domain Management Committee is a forum for the Data Domain Council Managers to coordinate their efforts and establish common processes and procedures.

■ **FIGURE 11.11** The overall structure of a Data Domain Council.

domain ownership of business data elements, and make other important group decisions. This council is led by the Enterprise Data Steward.

- The Data Governors are members of the enterprise-level Data Governance Board, whose duties are discussed in Chapter 1, Data Stewardship and Data Governance: How They Fit Together.
- The Data Domain Council Managers are members of the Data Domain Management Committee. This committee is a forum to coordinate the efforts, establish common processes and procedures, and work out any cross-data domain issues.
- Depending on the complexity of the work managed by a line of business or corporate function, it may have a local Data Stewardship Council, which may include the Technical Data Stewards affiliated with the line of business or corporation function due to the applications they support that then support the business function.

## Staffing the Data Domain Council

Each Data Domain Council member has a specific role with clear accountabilities, as summarized in Fig. 11.12.

The Lead data steward is nominated by the Data Governor that represents their business function. While being an "ordinary" Business Data Steward requires (usually) less than 25% of the person's time, leading the group of Business Data Stewards in a Data Domain Council as well as being a Business Data Steward representing a business function can well take 50% of the person's time. Lead Data Stewards are responsible for:

- Representing the primary business function for the data domain(s) that the Data Domain Council manages. This is often the business function that produces and depends on the data, based on the theory that the business function wouldn't produce the data if it wasn't very important to that function.

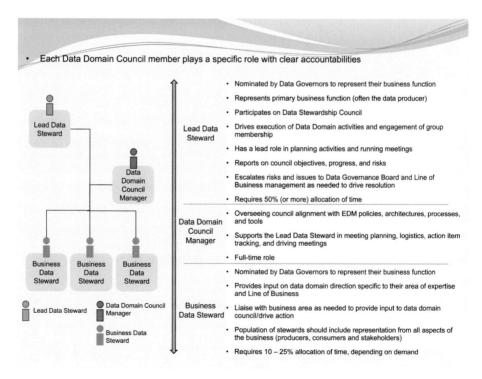

■ **FIGURE 11.12** The membership of a Data Domain Council is made up of specific roles.

- Driving execution of data domain activities and engagement of group membership.
  - Driving the execution of the activities means gaining a consensus with the participants on what needs to be done and the priorities of both the tasks and the data that is managed.
  - Participation by the member Business Data Stewards is very important, and the Lead Data Steward needs to help them stay engaged. It is all too easy for some of the Business Data Stewards to become disengaged and prioritize other activities over those of the Data Domain Council. This can lead to only a few dedicated Business Data Stewards participating on a regular basis, and the decisions made then no longer reflect the interests of all of the stakeholders.
- Reporting on council objectives, progress, and risks. As objectives are set out by management for the Data Domain Council, the Lead Data Steward needs to work with the Data Domain Council Manager to translate those objectives into specific objectives that need to be met at the Data Domain Council level, as well as report the progress on those objectives. In order for objectives to be met, tactics have to be formulated that enable meeting those objectives as well. Finally, risks that endanger the goals and objectives need to be reported. For example, if there is nonparticipation by a significant portion of the Business Data Stewards, there is a risk that decisions will not reflect the best interests of all the stakeholders, and that must be reported.
- Discussing and reaching resolution on issues and how to mitigate risks with the other Lead Data Stewards under the auspices of the Data Stewardship Council. When the risks and issues cannot be solved at the Data Stewardship Council level, the Lead Data Stewards (again, in collaboration with the Data Domain Council Manager) escalates risks and issues to the Data Governance Board and Line of Business management as needed to drive resolution.

The Data Domain Council Manager is a full-time role and may represent multiple Data Domain Councils. They should be focused on the specific tasks discussed. They are responsible for:

- Overseeing council alignment with policies, architectures, processes, and tools. Many other groups interact with the Data Domain Councils and provide requirements in all of these areas that the Data Domain Councils need to follow. For example, there may be policies dictating how metadata is determined (naming, quality of definition, whether names of all business data elements must be unique) as well as (from an architectural standpoint) that APPs must be aligned to data domains. There may also be rules around which tools (business glossary, metadata repository, data profiling) are officially sanctioned and must be used. The Data Domain Council Manager is responsible for ensuring that these requirements are followed and considered when the council makes decisions.

- Supporting the Lead Data Steward in meeting planning, logistics, action item tracking, and driving meetings. While the Lead Data Steward is responsible for all these items, many are not (at least at first) practiced at them. In addition, the Lead Data Steward has other responsibilities than being the lead for the Data Domain Council. The Data Domain Council Manager will be hired with an eye toward having experience in all these areas, and it is expected that this individual will provide the extra help that the Lead Data Steward will need.

The Business Data Stewards are nominated by the Data Governors that represent their business functions. This role requires 10% to 25% allocation of time depending on the demand. If the Business Data Steward is an expert on a group of data that is being worked on at the current time (for a project, regulatory, analytics, or other purpose), providing the input needed can take significant time, and even temporarily exceed 25%. Business Data Stewards are responsible for:

- Providing input on the direction and functioning of the data domain specific to their area of expertise. This input is normally specific to business data elements and related metadata that they are very knowledgeable about, and what other information or related business data elements should be included in the data domain's responsibilities.
- Liaising with their business function as needed to provide input. As stated earlier, one of the most important roles for the Business Data Steward is to represent their business function. Consulting with the business function (and especially the Data Governor) about anything they are not sure about is a crucial

---

**IN THE REAL WORLD**

As with business function–driven Data Stewardship, it is important not to overwhelm the Business Data Stewards. If a large block of data needs to be governed which requires the expertise of a single or small group of Business Data Stewards, this can become a bottleneck, and the time allotted for the effort must be adjusted accordingly.

---

**NOTE**

The population of Business Data Stewards for a Data Domain Council must represent the data producers, consumers, and stakeholders.

## KEY DATA GOVERNANCE ACTIVITIES THAT CAN BE DRIVEN BY DATA DOMAINS

There are five main Data Governance activities that can benefit by being driven by data domains. By focusing on these activities by data domains, decisions are made that support the correct definition, quality, and use of that data. Each Data Domain Council's agenda is driven by the data producers' and consumers' needs. These activities include:

1. Standard vocabulary and metadata. The business data elements managed across the data domains comprise the "vocabulary" of the enterprise. This vocabulary needs to include the high-priority terms that the enterprise uses, and must follow the rules that have been set up for determining which terms are considered high priority and thus need to be governed and managed. In addition, the rules for creating the metadata must be followed. These rules include naming conventions, definition standards, data quality rule standards, proper use of standardized compliance and privacy ratings, and other metadata that should be created and managed in a standardized manner.

2. Use of a Data Control Framework. A standardized data control framework can be (and should be) applied to the data in a data domain. The Data Domain Council can work to identify which data needs controls, and which controls are appropriate.

3. Identification and buildout of authorized provisioning points. A good goal is to have a single (or small number) of authorized provisioning points for the data within a domain. It is rare that such a datastore will exist for all data across the domain, but the Data Domain Council can work with the Technical Data Stewards and architects to identify the "best" sourcees of the data and whether it is feasible to combine them into an authorized provisioning point. Even when it is not feasible, at least the "golden source" (most trusted and controlled source) should be identified and documented.

4. Data quality issue management. Since the Data Domain Council deals with many aspects of the data associated with the data domain, understanding and resolving quality issues with that data is a key responsibility of the council. This not only includes participating in evaluating the results of data profiling, but helping to identify root causes, documenting the issues, and participating in the formulation of solutions to not only fix the existing data, but prevent the re-occurrence of the issues.

5. Regulatory and audit issue assessment and resolution. Most large enterprises (and many small ones) are heavily regulated. The regulatory bodies assess what the enterprise is doing, and a lot of that assessment

is around data, including weaknesses in processes that use data or prove data integrity. Issues identified by the regulators are among the most important that an enterprise has to deal with, so these issues are key to the activities of the Data Domain Council. They can include poorly defined and understood data, poor quality or nonexistent controls that must be strengthened, and data quality that is unknown or that does not support proper compliance to the regulations. All these concerns become important to the Data Domain Council when they affect the data that the council is charged with managing. Audit issues are only slightly less important. While auditors don't have the enforcement (and punishment) powers of the regulators, their job is to spot trouble before outside agencies and regulators do. It is also to uncover issues that can raise a variety of risks to the enterprise. The auditors—the "third line of defense"—are there to *protect* the business by finding these issues before they become a big problem. As a result, audit "findings" must also be among the most important items dealt with by the Data Domain Councils.

> **NOTE**
>
> When discussing risks to an enterprise, it is common to talk about "three lines of defense." The first line of defense is the business function, that must identify risks and accept responsibility for managing the risks. The second line of defense is the Risk organization (which can take many forms) that ensures that the business function is carrying out their responsibilities. As noted previously, the audit function is the third line of defense.

## DATA DOMAIN—BASED DATA STEWARDSHIP REQUIRES A MATURE ORGANIZATION

While use of data domains to manage business data elements can make it easier to create a shared enterprise glossary as well as manage data in logical categories, it is by no means easy to set up and maintain, and really does require a highly collaborative working environment and a fairly mature Data Governance organization. To be successful, it is necessary to achieve the following:

- Agreement on a common set of data domains, including the hierarchical structure. Not only do the data domains need to cover all the important business categories for the enterprise, but the subdomains need to be granular enough to enable a business data element to be managed by a single data domain (and Data Domain Council). Gathering the people together who represent the various business functions and establishing the data domain structure is a major undertaking, and the enterprise has to have the appetite to perform this task. While it is not strictly necessary to establish *all* the data domains you will ever need in that first effort, you should try to get to a structure that covers as wide a range of business functions as possible because "getting the band back together" later can be difficult if a significant number of data domains are discovered to be missing. In addition, as business data elements are populated into the data domain structure, it gets harder and harder to restructure the data domains and move the business data elements into the new structure. *A more mature organization will have a better idea of what data domains are applicable and how they should be organized.*

- Define the business data elements. The original "seeding" of the enterprise glossary can be a major effort as well. If the individual lines of business or business functions have business glossaries, this effort involves gathering up those business data elements, analyzing the definitions, deduplicating the business data elements across glossaries, and reaching agreement on the business data elements to include. If there are no well-developed business glossaries to work from, then it may be possible to use common terms in the industries that the enterprise is in, such as FIBO for the Financial Services industry or ACORD for the Insurance industry. It is often wise to consider terms from "industry standard" vocabularies even when business glossaries *do* exist, as you can then consider whether "special" business data elements in your enterprise are really different from the "standard" terms. *A more mature organization will have local business glossaries, as well as workable and tested standards for naming and defining business data elements.*

- Associate the business data elements with a single data domain. Business data elements need to be governed, and that is done by the Data Domain Council for the data domain to which the business data element is attached. To reduce complexity, a business data element should be attached to only a single data domain. The discussions about *which* data domain that should be can be quite heated, especially in the early stages when the data domains may not be defined at a granular enough level to make picking the right data domain "obvious." *A mature organization will have business processes in place to examine, discuss, and resolve differences for proposed business data elements.*

- Identify the expertise of the community of Business Data Stewards (usually available from line of business Data Governance groups) and assign them to the Data Domain Councils for data domains. *A mature organization will have identified Business Data Stewards with expertise in various business functions, from which the Data Domain Council Business Data Stewards can be selected.*

- Identify and assign Data Domain Council Managers to manage the Data Domain Councils which govern each data domain. These individuals coordinate their efforts as well as oversee the Business Data Stewards in the Data Domain Councils. They are usually fairly senior people with expertise in the data domain(s) managed by their

**NOTE**

A warning sign that the data domains may not be correctly structured is when an individual Business Data Steward (with expertise in a business function) ends up as part of the Data Domain Council for many different unrelated data domains.

councils. The Business Data Stewards in the Data Domain Councils have a "dotted line" reporting relationships to the Data Domain Council Manager, but officially report into their business lines and likely still participate in the line of business Data Stewardship Council. *A mature organization will be more willing to dedicate the time of senior managers to perform as Data Domain Council Managers, as well as enable business function Business Data Stewards to participate in the enterprise level Data Domain Councils in addition to their regular daily duties.*

## CREATING A DATA DOMAIN

Creating a new data domain requires careful thought and specification of the metadata describing the data domain. The "careful thought" comes in when considering what the new data domain will contain, and where it will be located within the existing hierarchy. Typically, creating a new data domain would require the agreement of the Data Domain Council Managers, as well as the Lead Data Stewards for any data domains affected by the change.

Besides the name of the data domain, the following items must be determined:

- Purpose: Typically, a data domain is created because:
  - A new dataset needs to be governed which does not "fit" into existing data domains.
  - A failure in the granularity of the data domains is noticed and must be dealt with. For example, an initial data domain handled "Party" information, but it became very clear that there were large differences between "individual" party (a person) and nonindividual party (an organization). In one organization, nonindividual party (called "company") was managed by a different group than individual party, necessitating a different set of Business Data Stewards in a separate Data Domain Council. In another enterprise, both types of Party were managed by the same group but there were such large differences in the business data elements, data quality controls, privacy controls, and sources that it became imperative to separate the data into different data domains.
- Hierarchy level: A determination needs to be made as to whether the new data domain has a parent data domain (Individual Party has a parent domain of Party) and which data domain is the parent. This is usually a fairly straightforward decision, based on why the data domain is being created:
  - New dataset to be governed: The data domain will be a "level 1" (top level) domain.

*(Continued)*

---

**(CONTINUED)**

- Failure of granularity: A parent data domain will be split into subdomains which are one level down from the original data domain in the hierarchy.
- Data Domain Council: A determination needs to be made as to whether the new data domain can be managed by an existing Data Domain Council or whether a new Data Domain Council (with different representation by Business Data Stewards) needs to be created. Creating a new Data Domain Council is more likely if the data domain is being created because of a new dataset. The failure of granularity will likely be governed by the same Data Domain Council as the parent data domain, though some additional representation might need to be added.
- Authorized Provisioning Point or other source(s): The ideal situation for a data domain is to have a single authorized provisioning point. If it does, that physical application, datastore, or other location should be determined and recorded. Even when there is *not* a single authorized provisioning point, there are usually a small set of sources that are considered trustworthy, and those should be documented as well.

---

## SUMMARY

As managing data by business function–based Business Data Stewards has led to fragmented results, a more holistic approach has gained popularity. This approach: grouping and managing business data elements by logical groupings called "data domains" has become more common, especially in the enterprises where a mature Data Governance effort already exists. These data domains and their associated business data elements and related metadata make data management less fragmented and enable a common approach to data management more possible. In addition, the management processes become more rigorous, better documented, and less dependent on allowing individuals to create their own processes. Managing data by data domains does, however, require more work and resources, especially in setting up the initial data domains and relating the business data elements to a single domain.

Data domains also enable key Data Governance activities to be performed in a more standardized fashion. These activities include vocabulary and metadata, adherence to the data control framework, determining authorized provisioning points, managing data quality issues, and dealing with regulatory and audit issues.

The data domains are managed by a Data Domain Council, which is comprised of a Lead Data Steward and participating Business Data

Stewards, all drawn from the business functions that produce, consume, or are stakeholders in the data domain's data. The Lead Data Steward coordinates the activities of the Council, and works alongside a full-time Data Domain Council Manager, who helps with the logistics and ensures that the Council is aligned with Policies, Processes, and tools. The Lead Data Steward works with other Lead Data Stewards and the Enterprise Data Steward in the Data Stewardship Council as described in Chapter 3, Stewardship Roles and Responsibilities.

# Appendix A:
# Example definition and derivation

## DEFINITION OF "UNIQUE QUOTE TO CLOSE RATIO"

- The ratio (expressed as a percentage) of unique and complete quotes that result in closed sales. A sale is considered closed when a policy has resulted from the quote and the quote is thus bound.
- The "unique quote to close ratio" can be used by insurance and sales as a measure of the overall competitiveness of a product. A sudden change in the ratio may indicate that competitive conditions have changed suddenly. In addition the ratio helps sales managers and sales producers understand how many quotes actually close from month to month, and thus how much of the work done to provide quotes actually results in new business.
- This business data element does not assign agent ownership to the quotes as that is handled by "agent unique quote to close ratio."

## DERIVATION OF "UNIQUE QUOTE TO CLOSE RATIO"

- The "unique quote to close ratio" is determined by dividing the number of quotes that actually closed (resulted in bound policies) in a given time period by the number of unique and complete quotes for that time period. All accounts (including House Accounts) are counted.
- The quotes that actually closed are determined by finding those quotes that were bound and have a policy number attached to it.
- Complete quotes are those quotes that have a certain minimum of information provided and from which a premium is generated. For automobile, motorcycle, and watercraft quotes, this means that at least a BI premium was generated. For HO, CEA, and renter quotes,

this means that a coverage (C) premium was generated. For personal liability, this means that a premium was generated for umbrella liability coverage. Note that since this is the only coverage offered on an umbrella, any premium would indicate that completeness.

- Unique quotes are counted as a quote for a particular type of insurance business for a customer (identified by name and address).

# Appendix B: Sample training plan outlines

## TRAINING TECHNICAL DATA STEWARDS

- Data Governance:
  - Represents the enterprise in all things data and metadata:
    - Metadata: definitions, derivations, and creation and usage business rules.
    - Data quality: issues, fixes, data quality rules, and appropriate usage.
    - Data-related policies and procedures.
    - Champions data quality improvement and projects.
    - Instigates methodology changes to ensure the capture of metadata and protect data quality.
  - Participants in Data Governance and Data Stewardship are accountable for the data quality and metadata.
  - Data Governance Board members are high-ranking individuals with decision-making capabilities.
  - Data Stewardship Council members are subject-matter experts who know the data well and can make recommendations on how data issues should be remediated.
- Business ownership and IT ownership:
  - Business owns the data:
    - Business is responsible for data definitions and derivations, data quality, funding of data cleanup, and quality improvement.
    - Business ownership is through the Data Governance and Data Stewardship effort. All business functions that own data (including IT) are represented.
    - Strategy is to expose differences in data definitions and usage.

- Business ownership:
    - The business function or data domain that owns the business data element also owns the metadata (definitions, derivations, data quality rules, and creation and usage business rules). These cannot be changed without the permission of the owning business function or data domain.
    - Owner is determined by "who would care" if a change was made to the metadata. There is usually one business function or data domain which would be significantly impacted if the meaning, allowed values or format, or quality of the business data element changed.
- IT owns the systems and applications:
    - Implements information policies around metadata and data quality.
    - Ensures that systems operate in ways that meet business requirements.
    - Ensures that systems protect the data and the data quality to the extent they are able.
    - Ensures that systems protect data integrity.
- Business Data Stewardship:
    - Business Data Stewards:
        - Are designated by the Data Governance Board member for their business function.
        - Have a role that is already in place and being designated a steward formalizes the role. That is, the Business Data Steward is usually someone recognized by their peers as having expert knowledge about the data.
        - Are the authorities to whom questions about meaning and rules can be brought.
        - Have access to data analysts who can help get questions answered.
        - Can enforce their decisions.
        - Approve proposed changes to the stewarded business data elements. Data elements and metadata cannot be changed without the approval of the Business Data Steward.
        - Get input from data analysts who work with the data every day and are directly impacted by the decisions. These analysts often know where there are data quality issues, or where a decision may negatively impact the business data element's quality.
    - Business Data Stewards are part of the Data Stewardship Council. This council:
        - Makes general Data Stewardship decisions and coordinates the overall efforts of the Business Data Stewards.

- – Makes decisions about which business function or data domain owns the business data elements.
  - – Works together to identify whether a "new" term is actually new or a duplicate.
  - – Supports project analysts.
  - – Reviews and proposes data-related process changes.
- Technical Data Stewardship:
  - Technical Data Stewards:
    - – Are responsible to the IT Data Governance Sponsor.
    - – Are a group of system-knowledgeable IT support personnel.
    - – Provide insight and expertise into how systems, ETL, storage (e.g., operational data store), data warehouses and data marts, business intelligence, and code work.
    - – Answer technical questions about how the data "got the way it is."
    - – Are responsible for the production of data through information systems to support business processes.
    - – Support impact analysis to understand the scope of proposed changes. This includes ongoing projects as well as ad-hoc inquiries.
    - – Work together to provide an understanding of the information chain.
    - – Are responsible for warning the business if proposed changes would cause bad things to happen to the application, system, or process.
  - There is a Technical Data Steward for each major system, application, and technical process (ETL).
  - More than one Technical Data Steward may exist for a business data element if it passes through multiple systems or applications.
  - Technical Data Stewardship often formalizes and documents a role that is already in place.
  - IT owns the systems, applications, and processes that implement the business processes. These cannot be changed without the approval of the Technical Data Steward.
- Data quality, reporting, and business processes:
  - Impact on systems and applications when there is no Technical Data Stewardship.
  - Impact on data quality when there is no Technical Data Stewardship:
    - – Data quality deteriorates due to errors in system design.
    - – Data quality deteriorates when fields are overloaded.
    - – Difficult or impossible to determine root causes for data quality issues or to estimate the fix for these issues.

- Impact on reporting when there is no Technical Data Stewardship:
  - Systems produce data in ways that reporting systems cannot handle.
  - Changes in source systems or ETL are not reviewed for reporting impacts.
- Impact on business processes when there is no Technical Data Stewardship:
  - New processes are proposed and even implemented that cannot be supported by existing systems and applications. This may cause data corruption and misuse of data fields.
  - Business process owners must work with Technical Data Stewards to understand:
    - What processes and data are being proposed to be changed.
    - What business issues are being addressed and how important they are.
    - What is the proposed technical solution and what is the impact to downstream systems and processes?
- IT's role in Data Governance and Data Stewardship:
  - Supporting Data Governance tools and applications (e.g., business glossary, metadata repository, data profiling, automated data cleansing, web portal).
  - Data custodians (i.e., backups, optimization, access permissions, physical implementation, data cleanup execution, data security implementation).
  - Change management:
    - Notification of Business Data Stewards.
    - Involvement of Technical Data Stewards.
    - Impact analysis performed and communicated.
    - Sign-off by Data Stewards on changes that negatively impact data quality.
  - IT support and sponsorship:
    - IT sponsor represents and champions Data Governance and Data Stewardship within IT, as well as provides resources (i.e., Technical Data Stewards, tool support, and data custodians).
    - The IT sponsor is a leader who is respected and listened to. The sponsor also has an organization that works closely with the data and data structures.
    - The IT sponsor is directly responsible for delivering solutions to the business.

# TRAINING PROJECT MANAGERS

- Data Governance:
  - Represents the enterprise in all things data and metadata:
    - Metadata: definitions, derivations, and creation and usage business rules.
    - Data quality: issues, fixes, data quality rules, and appropriate usage.
    - Data-related policies and procedures.
    - Champions data quality improvement and projects.
    - Instigates methodology changes to ensure the capture of metadata and protect data quality.
  - Participants in Data Governance and Data Stewardship are accountable for the data quality and metadata.
  - Data Governance Board members are high-ranking individuals with decision-making capabilities.
  - Data Stewardship Council members are subject-matter experts who know the data well and can make recommendations on how data issues should be remediated.
- Business ownership:
  - Business owns the data:
    - Business is responsible for data definitions and derivations, data quality, funding of data cleanup, and quality improvement.
    - Business ownership is through the Data Governance and Data Stewardship effort. All business functions that own data (including IT) are represented.
    - Strategy is to expose differences in data definitions and usage.
- Business ownership:
  - The business function that owns the business data element also owns the metadata (definitions, derivations, data quality rules, and creation and usage business rules). These cannot be changed without the permission of the owner.
  - Owner is determined by "who would care" if a change was made to the metadata. There is usually one business function of which the business would be significantly impacted if the meaning, allowed values or format, or quality of the business data element changed.
- Business Data Stewardship:
  - Business Data Stewards:
    - Are designated by the Data Governance Board member for their business function.

- Have a role that is already in place and being designated a steward formalizes the role. That is, the Business Data Steward is usually someone recognized by their peers as having expert knowledge about the data.
- Are the authority to whom questions about meaning and rules can be brought.
- Have access to data analysts who can help get questions answered.
- Can enforce their decisions.
- Approves proposed changes to the stewarded business data elements. Data elements and metadata cannot be changed without the approval of the Business Data Steward.
- Gets input from data analysts who work with the data every day and are directly impacted by the decisions. These analysts often know where there are data quality issues, or where a decision may negatively impact the business data element's quality.

- Business Data Stewards are part of the Data Stewardship Council. This council:
  - Reviews definitions, derivations, data quality rules, and creation and usage business rules, and determines the official version of each piece of metadata.
  - Makes decisions about which business function owns the business data elements.
  - Works together to identify whether a "new" term is actually new or a duplicate.
  - Supports project analysts.
  - Reviews and proposes data-related process changes.

- Project Data Stewardship:
  - Project Data Stewards represent Data Stewardship on a project.
  - Responsible for:
    - All Data Governance deliverables (e.g., definitions, derivations, data quality rules, profiling analysis).
    - Documenting results in enterprise-wide business glossary and metadata repository.
    - Validating the deliverables with the responsible Business Data Stewards.
  - Project Data Stewards are supplied and trained by Data Governance but must be funded by the project.

- Value of having Data Governance and Data Stewardship on a project:
  - Collection of data definitions. Building a body of stewarded and understood data definitions benefits all who use the data. This is critical with conversions and migrations. The Project Data

Steward can deliver the official definition to the project without involving project personnel in long discussions.

- Collection of data derivations. This leads to a common way of calculating numbers. The project can deliver results that match the official calculation method. The Project Data Steward can deliver the appropriate derivation to the project without involving project personnel in long discussions.
- Identification and resolution of data quality issues. Poor data quality can keep a project from going into production. The risk to a project is lessened by early identification and resolution of data quality issues.
- Detection of poor-quality data. Data quality rules (which define what is meant by high-quality data) are identified and documented. The data is then inspected and compared against the data quality rules (a process called profiling) so that poor-quality data can be found early.
- Adjusting project methodology to allow for Data Governance deliverables:
  - Aligning Data Stewardship activity to the project life cycle.
  - Working with the Project Management Office funding function to budget for Data Stewardship support.
  - Initial evaluation of project for Data Governance deliverables:
    - Project goals.
    - Add, change, or delete data, and extent of that data.
    - Potential for the project to reduce or corrupt data quality.
    - How many systems will be impacted by the project?
    - Evaluation results in an estimate of Data Governance effort required.
  - Initial tasks for project manager with Enterprise Data Steward:
    - Add Data Governance tasks to project timeline (including data profiling).
    - Establish timing for Data Governance resources (i.e., Project Data Steward, Enterprise Data Steward).
    - Help project manager understand benefits of Data Governance.
    - Determine project tasks that must involve Data Governance resources (e.g., model reviews, interface reviews, conversion mapping, data quality issue review, etc.).
    - Get appropriate meeting invites.
    - Plan for data profiling where needed (and it almost always is).
  - Data Governance tasks during requirements:
    - Collection and documentation of data definitions and derivations.

- Gap analysis of data against business glossary.
- Definitions and derivations from business glossary provided to project.
- New data definitions and derivations provided by Business Data Stewards.
- Data and metadata approved by Business Data Stewards and recorded in business glossary.
- Data Governance tasks during analysis and design:
  - Collection and documentation of data quality rules.
  - Measuring the extent of data quality issues (analysis of results of data profiling).
  - Planning remediation and the impact of poor-quality data.
- Data Governance tasks during quality assurance:
  - Quality assurance test cases written and executed using data quality rules.
  - Quality assurance test cases written and executed using definitions, including whether screens show data expected based on definitions, proper valid value sets, and multiple fields that display the same data.
- Data Governance tasks during design:
  - Evaluate proposed solution for potential to corrupt data quality. Issues can include repurposing existing fields, overloading fields, repurposing existing code values, lack of data integrity check fields, field contents changed to violate existing data quality rules, and field contents changed to a different granularity.

# Appendix C:
# Class words for naming Business Data Elements

## A LIST OF CLASS WORDS

Business Data Elements must be carefully named, following the standards of the enterprise, a sample of which was provided in Chapter 6, Practical Data Stewardship. In addition to the nouns and modifiers described there, the names should end in "class words" that help you understand what sort of data the business data element describes. There are many sets of class words that have been used over the years but Table C.1 provides a sample list that could be a good place to start.

**Table C.1** Class Words for Naming Business Data Elements.

| Class word | Definition |
|---|---|
| Amount | A numeric expression of quantity with fractional precision which represents a base quantity, for example, Total Loan Amount. |
| Balance | An amount that is the result of an aggregate of base amounts, for example, Loan Fee Accrual Balance. |
| Code | A system of letters and/or numbers (classification scheme) used to represent an assigned meaning, sometimes understood within the business, for example, State Code: CA. |
| Count | The total number of items in a given unit or sample obtained by counting all, or a subsample, of the items. |
| Date | A point of time that only includes the calendar date (i.e., not a timestamp and does not include the time of day). |
| Description | Free form text used to describe or define something, for example, Party Role Description. |
| Identifier | A unique set of numbers and/or letters that identifies something. Mostly manufactured identifiers internal to computer systems, in some cases these are naturally occurring. |
| Indicator | A Boolean value (Y or N, 0 or 1) which may also be used to represent a flag or switch. |
| Name | The proper name of a person, place, or thing which may be semistructured. |
| Number | A numeral or combination of numerals and/or other symbols used to identify something. These identifiers occur naturally and are regularly understood within the business, for example, Branch Number, Account Number. |
| Percent | A numeric value shown as a rate or proportion per hundred. |
| Rank | A numeric representation of the relative standing or position of a thing based on a certain criterion. |
| Rate | A numeric rate (exchange, interest, etc.) which is represented by a number that has a fractional portion and may hold many digits of precision. |
| Ratio | Specifically denotes the relationship between two amounts showing the number of times one value contains, or is contained within, the other. |
| Semi-Structured | Represents data which is semistructured, for example, XML or JSON data |
| Sequence | A numeric expression of counting order specifically intended to indicate sequence across a set of data. |
| Term | A period of time that denotes how long an agreement is intended to be in force. |
| Text | Free-form text that has no particular format or structure, is not specifically about a thing, but generally provides information about a specific occurrence of a type of thing, for example, Address Text |
| Time | A point of time that only includes the time of day and excludes the date. |
| Timestamp | A point of time that includes the calendar date and the time of day. |
| Unstructured | Represents data with no structure, raw, or binary data. |

# Index

Printed in the United States
By Bookmasters